BIRMINGHAM NEW STREET

THE STORY OF A GREAT STATION

INCLUDING CURZON STREET

BY

RICHARD FOSTER

3

LMS DAYS

1923–1947

WILD SWAN PUBLICATIONS LTD.

NAMES AND ABBREVIATIONS

In order to make the book readable and easy to follow, commonly known or distinctive names have been used in the text even where these are strictly out of historical context. Names which are now commonplace were not always used originally. Thus, the station at Curzon Street is referred to as Curzon Street throughout the book, even though it was not until some years after it opened that the name was used. Originally it was simply Birmingham station. Similarly, New Street station is referred to as such even though it was known originally as Navigation Street or the Grand Central station. The Birmingham Canal is referred to by its commonly known abbreviation of BCN. Strictly speaking, it had three different names, starting life as the Birmingham Canal Navigation, later becoming the Birmingham and Birmingham & Fazeley Canal Navigations and finally the Birmingham Canal Navigations. The Birmingham, Wolverhampton and Stour Valley Railway soon had its name shortened for everyday use to the Stour Valley. This name has become the line's official title despite its early absorption into the LNW and the fact that it has never gone anywhere near the River Stour (the Stourbridge branch having been dropped even before it obtained its Act of Incorporation). Where necessary, the true names and the dates of changes are referred to in the text. The following abbreviations are used:

B & DJ Birmingham & Derby Junction Railway
B & G Birmingham & Gloucester Railway
B & OJ Birmingham & Oxford Junction Railway
B & WJ Birmingham & Warwick Junction Canal
BCN Birmingham Canal Navigations
BR British Railways
BW & SV Birmingham, Wolverhampton & Stour Valley Railway
BWD Birmingham, Wolverhampton & Dudley Railway
BWS Birmingham West Suburban Railway
GJ Grand Junction Railway
GU Grand Union Canal
GW Great Western Railway
L & B London & Birmingham Railway
LMS London Midland & Scottish Railway
LNW London & North Western Railway
MR Midland Railway
NCL National Carriers Ltd
OWW Oxford Worcester & Wolverhampton Railway
S & B Shrewsbury & Birmingham Railway
S & C Shrewsbury & Chester
S & D Somerset & Dorset
S & W Staffordshire & Worcester Canal
W & B Worcester & Birmingham Canal
W & BJ Warwick & Birmingham Junction Canal

ACKNOWLEDGEMENTS

My special thanks to M.R.L. Instone, T.J. Edgington, R.J. Essery, M. Christensen and E. Talbot for taking the time and trouble to read the text (in some cases several times) and for their helpful suggestions and advice. M.R.L. Instone kindly made available the results of his researches into, and analysis of, the train services to and from Curzon Street Station. Special thanks are also due to the staff of the Local Studies Department of the Birmingham Central Reference Library for their help over a large number of visits. The following people and organisations also provided assistance, which is gratefully acknowledged: Aerofilms, Birmingham Central Library, *Birmingham Post & Mail, Daily News, LMS Magazine*, LNWR Society, Millbrook House Ltd, National Railway Museum, Public Record Office, Kew, *Railway Magazine*, Signalling Record Society, *Sutton News, Sutton Observer*, S. Arthurs, E.H. Bailey, A. H. Baker, G. Barlow, S. Benton, Mrs D. Bibby, G. Biddle, P.W.J. Bishop, M.N. Bland, R. Bonser, T.W. Bourne, R. Brotherton, Mrs W. Brunton, S. Budd, R.F. Burrows, R.S. Carpenter, R.M. Casserley, D. Chapman, G. Coltas, W. Cook, J. Cooper, W. Dale, J. Davis, M.J. Denholm, M. Eaton, Mrs M. Edge, A.D. Ellis, Mrs M. Fenton, W.V. Gale, L. Gibbs, W. Gossage, C.C. Green, J. Green, G. Gribble, D.L. Hanson, D. Harris, L. Harris, H. Hickin, S.A. Holland, L. Hollins, J. Horton, D. Ibbotson, D.A. Ives, H. Jack, B.J. Jelf, E.H. Jones, P. Jordan, P. Lee, E.P. Livingstone, R.G. Lord, B. Matthews, M. Mensing, P.A. Millard, Mrs M. Moody, E. McLoughlin, Mrs Nash, H. Norton, A. Parks, Mrs E. Pettigrew, R. Pinner, D.P. Rowland, E.S. Russell, B. Sabell, H.W. Saddler, P. Shoesmith, R. Shill, F.W. Shuttleworth, G. Slater, L. Slater, B.P. Stead, J. Stanton, T. Stenson, J. Strange, J. Tatchell, G.H. Tilt, Mrs P.M. Westwood, S.M. Wood,

FURTHER READING

New Street Remembered, D.J. Smith (Barbryn Press)
A Regional History of the Railways of Great Britain:
Volume 7: The West Midlands, Rex Christiansen (David & Charles)
Volume 13: Thames and Severn, Rex Christiansen (David & Charles)
The Canals of the West Midlands, Charles Hadfield (David & Charles)
The Birmingham Canal Navigations, Volume 1 (David & Charles)
LNWR Liveries (Historical Model Railway Society)
LNWR Miscellany, Volumes 1 & 2, E. Talbot (OPC)
LNWR Signalling, R.D. Foster (OPC)
Midland Style (Historical Model Railway Society)
Great Railway Stations of Britain, G. Biddle (David & Charles)
The London and Birmingham, A Railway of Consequence, D. Jenkinson (Capital Transport)
British Railway Journal: London and Birmingham Special Issue (Wild Swan Publications)
The Birmingham & Gloucester Railway, P.J. Long and Rev. W.V. Awdry (Alan Sutton)
The LMS in the West Midlands, P.B. Whitehouse (OPC)
LNWR West Midlands Album, R. Carpenter (Wild Swan Publications)
The Making of Victorian Birmingham, V. Skipp (Author)
Solid Citizens, Statues in Birmingham, B. Pugh (Westwood Press)

ISBN 1 984103 37 2

Designed by Paul Karau
Printed by Amadeus Press Ltd., Huddersfield

Published by
WILD SWAN PUBLICATIONS LTD.
1-3 Hagbourne Road, Didcot, Oxon, OX11 8DP.

INTRODUCTION

This book looks at the history of New Street passenger station and Curzon Street goods station between the years 1923 and 1948, when they were owned and operated by the London, Midland & Scottish Railway Company.

The years up to the Great War were a period of great prosperity, growth and confidence for Britain. As an indication of this national growth, the railways of Great Britain as a whole were carrying 27% more passengers in 1913 compared to 1900, and freight traffic had increased by a remarkable 34% over the same period. In world markets, Britain occupied a position somewhat akin to that which Japan does today. All the major railway companies had improvement schemes in hand, and long-term plans were in preparation for progressive developments to enable them to handle the ever-increasing traffic, and to compete effectively. Not that it was a universally golden age; whilst the upper and middle classes could live very comfortably, for many, life was unremitting toil, with excessive working hours in exchange for pitifully small reward.

The Great War changed most things. Inflation set in during the war years, and effectively doubled prices. Britain lost its dominance of world markets, economic activity declined, and industry found it difficult to re-establish itself after the war. The world markets were more competitive and less stable than previously, and there were long periods of severe depression in world trade. As a result, unemployment reached unprecedented levels in the late 1920s and early 1930s, and real prosperity declined. Not all changes were negative: the war accelerated the process of social reform, and a number of overdue improvements were made.

Government control of the railways during and after the war illustrated clearly the benefits to be obtained from larger working units, whilst in the difficult trading conditions afterwards, it became apparent that some of the smaller companies (and those predominantly serving rural or depressed areas) would have some difficulty in surviving. After considering nationalisation and other ideas, the Government eventually decided to amalgamate the majority of the railways into four large groups. It was expected that this arrangement would give the new companies the economic power to reinvest and modernise, as well as allowing 'cross-subsidisation' of the unprofitable sections. It was also hoped that the changes would lead to some reductions in charges. However, in the very different circumstances which existed after 1923, these aspirations were only partially realised.

The London & North Western and Midland Railways, along with other companies, were therefore amalgamated to form a new company, the London, Midland & Scottish Railway. Henceforth, New Street station would have one owner and one user. In contrast, the Great Western retained its identity, and was enlarged by effectively absorbing a number of smaller companies. Thus, from 1st January 1923, Birmingham was served by two companies: the LMS at New Street, and the GWR at Snow Hill and Moor Street.

As already mentioned, the 1920s and 1930s were difficult times, and much of the railway's efforts were devoted to coping with (in real terms) greatly reduced revenues and increased costs, and the steadily increasing competition from other forms of transport. The process of restoring train services to prewar levels, let alone making real improvements, turned out to be a painfully slow exercise, and there was precious little money available for anything but essentials.

The Great War and its aftermath did much to reduce national confidence, and the resultant backlash fuelled an increasing tendency to despise Victorian values and the grand tradition of Victorian architecture. Many buildings in the cities had turned black from years of exposure to grime and sulphur-laden atmospheres; with the lack of funds to renovate them, many of the same buildings began to look more and more shabby and neglected as the years progressed. It was easy and fashionable to criticise, but required imagination to see what lay behind the dirt.

In Birmingham, there was a stark contrast between its passenger stations. Snow Hill had been completely rebuilt just prior to the Great War, whilst Moor Street had only opened in 1909; consequently, both Great Western stations still looked clean and new. By contrast, even the most recent sections of New Street (other than parts of the hotel) were, by 1925, over 40 years old, whilst the original parts were over 70 years old. Few people appeared to be able to see what an engineering achievement the great roof on the western side of the station was, or how the roofs could be used to create a magnificent and memorable entrance to Birmingham. It was easier to criticise, and to hanker for something new; indeed, criticism of New Street became a regular part of Birmingham life.

Those people who considered themselves to be spokesmen for the people of the city demanded that the station be rebuilt. One source of complaint was that the station disrupted the street pattern, causing traffic congestion in the city's inadequate streets; few remembered that the station had not in fact displaced any significant streets, and that their predecessors on the Council had, for so many years, solidly resisted expenditure on street improvements. It was decided that a new road across the station was required, to link Corporation Street to John Bright Street (or even the Bristol Road), an idea which would have funnelled a large proportion of the city's road traffic through its two principal shopping streets. Some went even further, and suggested either roofing over the station so that shops could be built above it, or the removal of the station to a less central site, on the grounds that it both cut the city in two, and that land in the city was too valuable to be used for a station! One suspects that these opinions were largely expressed by those who had forsaken the railways for the motor car, and were more concerned for their personal mobility than that of the general public, who could not afford a car.

It was certainly true that the city centre area in Birmingham was rather smaller than those of many other cities. But if the station did indeed restrict its growth southwards, no-one seemed to ask the question why the shopping area did not grow in those directions where there was no such impediment. Few seemed to appreciate that the growth and development of the city was in no small part due to the convenient and central site of its principal station.

Hardly had the British economy begun to get back onto its feet after the great depression than there was another war, this one longer and more severe in economic terms than the first. Considerable damage was inflicted on the city by bombing, and inevitably New Street station suffered its share. Very soon after the war, it was concluded that the degree of damage to the great roof over the western side of the station, combined with its age, made repair difficult, and in the circumstances it was decided to remove it. Few seemed to have mourned its passing; rather, it was seen as hastening the day when the rebuilding, which people had convinced themselves would solve all problems, would begin.

As was the case after the Great War, Government control of the railways during the Second World War led to a belief that there would be some benefit in reorganising the railways. This time the method chosen was nationalisation, an option which had been rejected on the previous occasion. Thus, from 1st January 1948, Birmingham's railways (and its two great stations) came under the control of a single organisation, British Railways.

The 25-year period during which the LMS was in control at New Street can be summarised as a time when the company did its best to provide a comprehensive railway service both to the general public and the business community, mostly in rather difficult circumstances. The company saw itself as providing a public service, and to some extent this consideration took precedence over that of maximising profit. Although there was a lack of sparkle and innovation, the country generally obtained very good value from its railway system during this period.

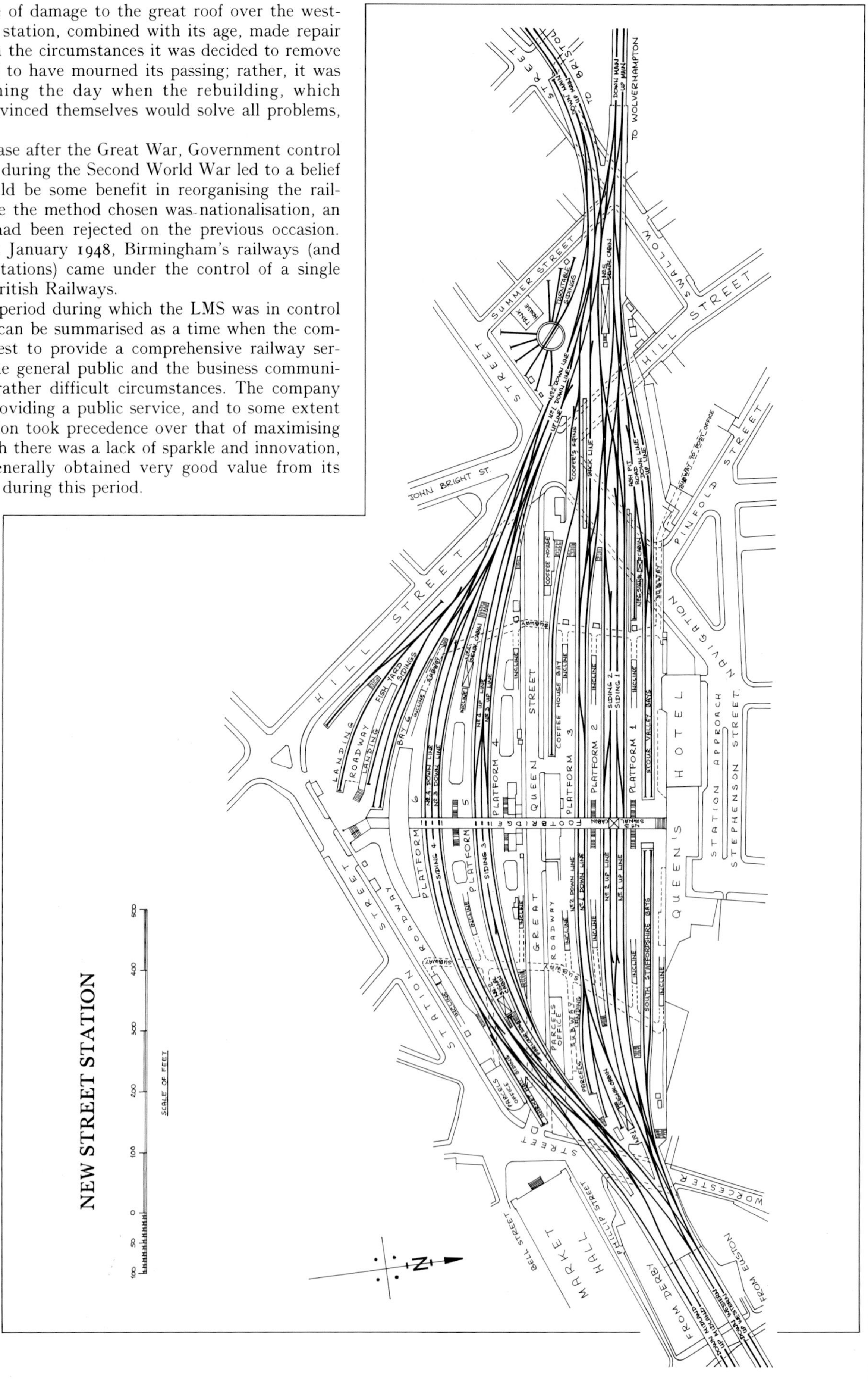

NEW STREET STATION

SCALE OF FEET

CHAPTER ONE
CHANGING TIMES

THE railway network in Birmingham became established in practically its final form at a very early date, as had the relative positions of the three railway companies which owned the lines. At the top, in terms of significance and origins, was the London & North Western, with its key passenger station at New Street and its important network of routes. Below, and more or less equal in their regional importance, were the Great Western and Midland Companies. The Great Western had its Northern main line from Oxford to Birmingham and on to Wolverhampton, Shrewsbury and ultimately Birkenhead, together with other important lines in the Black Country and around Wolverhampton. The Midland's main route ran effectively north-east and south-west, and the company shared the use of New Street. Its network largely complemented that of the LNW, and the latter had, by a series of provisions in Acts and agreements, ensured that the Midland could not build any competing lines or start any competing services without its agreement. This, coupled with the geography of the region, ensured that each of the companies effectively had clearly defined territories, with the result that competition was relatively limited.

Between the GW and LNW, competition was largely restricted to traffic for particular destinations, such as Liverpool (Birkenhead) and London; prior to 1900, the LNW had the upper hand in most cases due to the superiority of its routes. Once the relative positions of the three companies had been established, the LNW was content (other than for essential improvements, such as enlarging New Street station and the new link lines it built in the 1880s), to leave things as they were. Its primary interests lay in the great industrial areas and cities in the north, notably Liverpool, Manchester and Leeds, and the areas between. The northern districts generated more traffic, though competition was very intense. The LNW therefore had to work harder for its share of the traffic. More railway companies were involved, and operated largely without protectionist agreements, such as those between the LNW and the Midland in Birmingham.

While Birmingham came well down the list of priorities for the LNW, the position was rather different for the GW. Birmingham and the Black Country was by far the largest population centre it served outside London, and the area was also one of its largest sources of goods and mineral traffic. However, the GW's ability to exploit Birmingham area traffic was limited by the indirect nature of its main line to the south. Traffic to both London and the West Country had to go via Didcot, and total mileages were significantly in excess of those via the rival LNW and Midland routes to London and Bristol respectively.

Provided the GW was prepared to offer price structures which offset the longer distances, the disadvantage was probably not too great as far as the majority of the goods traffic was concerned. However, the greater distances were a bigger handicap when it came to passenger traffic, and did not further the image of the company's routes as acceptable alternatives. For most of the nineteenth century, the GW seemed prepared to accept these disadvantages, and be content with what traffic it could get.

In the late 1890s, the Great Western finally emerged from its long period of complacency, and embarked on an ambitious investment policy designed to improve and strengthen its competitive position. In addition to building new locomotives and rolling stock, and carrying out station improvements, the GW decided to build a number of completely new sections of line to shorten point-to-point distances, and hence enable radical improvements in services and journey times to be made. With the importance of Birmingham and the line to the north, it was not surprising that improvements to the route between London and the Midlands were high on the list of priorities.

The new works put in hand consisted of three parts:

1. Construction of a new cut-off line between London and Banbury which would permit high-speed running, and reduce the route distance from Paddington to Birmingham to about the same as that from Euston.
2. The construction of a new route via Stratford to Cheltenham giving the company:
   - (a) by using running powers south of Cheltenham, its own route from Birmingham to Bristol, enabling it to compete directly with the Midland for passenger traffic, and
   - (b) a route for freight to South Wales and the West which avoided the difficult route via Worcester and the Malverns.
3. Improvements to the lines through Birmingham to increase capacity and ease congestion, and accommodate extra traffic. Included in this was a complete rebuilding of Snow Hill station.

At this time, Birmingham was expanding. With increased population and greater prosperity, there was a growing demand from people to live in 'nice areas', further from the city centre and their work. Prior to 1900, the built-up area to the south of the city centre quickly gave way to the fields of rural Warwickshire; inevitably, residential development therefore began to take place southwards, towards Solihull. As

GREAT WESTERN RAILWAY — NEW WORKS AFFECTING BIRMINGHAM, 1906–1919

New Route to London

Aynho Junction to Ashendon Junction (on the Great Western & Great Central Joint Line) opened to passengers on 1st July 1910, on which date through, direct passenger services to and from Paddington commenced.

New Route to Cheltenham and the West

Honeybourne & Stratford line doubling completed:	9th February 1908.
North Warwickshire line opened to passengers:	1st July 1908.
Cheltenham & Honeybourne new line, final section opened to passengers:	1st August 1908.

Improvements to Main Line Through Birmingham

Snow Hill station rebuilding completed:	1913
Moor Street station opened to passengers:	1st July 1909
Moor Street station opened to goods:	7th January 1914
Tyseley, new station opened:	1st October 1906
Tyseley to Olton widening completed:	21st January 1907
Hockley to Snow Hill widening completed:	13th October 1909
Handsworth Junction to Soho widening completed:	19th December 1909
Soho to Hockley widening completed:	21st July 1912
Moor Street to Bordesley widening completed:	16th November 1913
Bordesley to Small Heath widening completed:	1919

part of its improvement plan, the GW was able to exploit this trend by developing a useful range of suburban services and stations.

As major stages of the improvement works were completed, the GW's presence in Birmingham was transformed. It now had a large, clean, well laid-out and efficient station at Snow Hill, whilst line capacity and operating efficiency had been much enhanced by the provision of quadruple track between Olton and Moor Street, and between Snow Hill and Handsworth Junction. There were only two shortcomings: the site at Snow Hill was not large enough to allow all of the increased passenger traffic to be accommodated there, and the difficult, steeply-graded section of line through the covered way between Moor Street and Snow Hill could not be widened at an affordable cost. Thus, it was necessary to build a new suburban station for local trains to and from the south at Moor Street, and the two-track section under the city centre remained an awkward bottleneck. These points apart, the GW was now able to compete on equal terms with the LNW and Midland for traffic to the south and west. The Great War began before all the intended works were completed, and some, such as the widening between Olton and Rowington Junction (Lapworth), were deferred.

The LNW was quick to react to the impending threat to its near-dominance of the lucrative and prestigious London passenger traffic. In 1905, well before the GW's new line to London was opened, a much accelerated service of express trains was introduced, and journey times by the best trains were cut to two hours; this was considered to be the best that the GW was likely to be able to achieve when its new route was completed. The LNW had therefore scooped the pool as far as publicity was concerned, and when their new line was finally complete, the GW would only be able to offer to match journey times that the LNW trains had been running to for some years.

The GW could have adopted an aggressive attitude, and attempted to provide a fractionally faster service, but the company was realistic enough to know that the LNW would then simply reduce its times by a minute or two, and so it would go on. Both companies were only too well aware of what had happened in the past, when unrestrained competition had led to companies trying to beat each other in providing the shortest journey times. Quietly, the two companies got together, and agreed what service each was to offer. In January 1910, nearly six months before the GW direct passenger service started, the LNW and GW General Managers signed an agreement that the minimum time between Birmingham and London (Euston, Paddington and Marylebone) should be two hours. The agreement was to last for five years, subject to six months' notice on either side. Eventually the Great War intervened, and in recognition of the circumstances (and the need for economy), the minimum time was increased to 2 hours 10 minutes, in December 1915. It is of interest to note that such was the general progress on the railways over the next 40 years that two hours was still the standard London–Birmingham time in the 1950s.

So far, the LNW's only concrete reaction to the GW improvements had been the acceleration of its own London service. There had been no attempt at any commensurate infrastructure improvements, although there were problems which needed solutions. When the extension to New Street was planned back in the 1870s, travel by train to work in Birmingham was practically unknown, and there was thus no need to plan facilities to accommodate a 'rush hour'. Even when the enlargement work was completed in the mid-1880s, no such traffic was evident and, as Chapter 3 shows, it was not until the 1890s that any real amount of such traffic was apparent. Once established, however, the traffic increased rapidly, and between 1890 and 1910 the number of trains departing from New Street between 4.30 and 6.30 p.m. increased by well over 50%. This growth at the peak time was accompanied by continual (but lesser) expansion in traffic throughout the day; the number of trains that had to be accommodated at New Street was increasing steadily. The day was fast approaching when the station would reach its capacity, and something would have to be done if the increases in traffic were to be effectively accommodated. The problem was clearly worse at the morning and evening (home to work, and vice-versa) peaks — this was a traffic that New Street had never been designed for.

The difficulty was obvious; any enlargement would be extremely expensive and difficult, and there were likely to be considerable battles with the owners of properties affected, the local authorities, and vested interests, something with which the LNW was only too familiar. It is perhaps not surprising that, although the problem was considered, finding and implementing a solution was put off (as the company also did in respect of the rebuilding of Euston station). Consideration was also no doubt given to the associated question of widening the lines on either side of New Street, southwards towards Coventry, and along the more difficult Stour Valley line towards Wolverhampton. The LNW had a large programme of line widenings and other improvements in mind, however, and the Birmingham routes were clearly some way down the list. By 1914 the company had, for instance, obtained Parliamentary powers to complete the quadruple tracking of its main line all the way from Rugby to Preston, and the work was being undertaken in small stages.

In order to stave off the day when the real problem — New Street — had to be tackled, in October 1910 the company authorised about the only improvement that could be effected at a low cost: the joining together of the Stour Valley and South Staffordshire bay platforms to make two through platforms. While this did not increase the station accommodation, the operational improvements that would be gained (greater flexibility, and a reduced need for shunting) would have given a small but welcome increase in station capacity. Subsequently, the scheme was extended to include construction of an additional footbridge, which would have overcome the problems of overcrowding which had always afflicted the old one. However, the outbreak of war in 1914 occurred before any work had begun, and the scheme was postponed.

The Great War put an end to any significant developments on the LNW section of Birmingham's railways. Had there been a few more years of peace and economic growth, not only would the relatively minor works already approved have been carried out, but other works designed to increase line and station capacity would have eventually been put in hand, too.

Although the British economy suffered from peaks and troughs, just as it does today, the general trend from the beginning of the Victorian period up to 1914 was one of significant growth. Britain dominated many (though not all) sectors of world markets, occupying a position in world trade somewhat similar to that of Japan today. General levels of trade and prosperity steadily increased and between 1880 and 1913, national income rose in real terms by over 30% per head of population. This situation was reflected in the continual increase and improvement in railway goods and passenger services. Although it was not recognised at the time, nor indeed until some time after the end of hostilities, the Great War was to change almost everything; events were set in motion which were to lead inexorably to Britain becoming a very different place.

The first priority was clearly to win the war, and everything else was sacrificed to

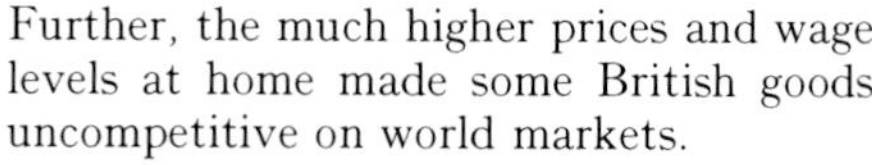

this goal. At home the Government, quite correctly, took overall control and direction of the railways. It was clearly essential that the resources of the railways should firstly be directed to ensure that troops and wartime materials were in the right positions at the right times, and that transport should be deployed as efficiently as possible to this end. This could only be achieved by centralized control, and by suppressing the narrow and sometimes conflicting interests of individual companies and their shareholders. The politicians promised that, in return for the loss of control, and for the essential services which they would be called upon to give, the railway companies would be fairly treated once the war was won. The need for large numbers of men to join the armed forces, and for those who stayed at home to maximise their efforts in producing the essential arms, ammunition and other essentials of war, brought about publicity campaigns designed to increase patriotic fervour. In return for fighting for King and Country, the men were promised that, once the war had been won, Britain would become a far better place than ever before in which to live; indeed, it would be a 'land fit for heroes'.

War brought with it a new phenomenon to Britain: inflation. From the beginning of Victorian times up to 1914, prices and wage levels had generally remained relatively constant. Within a short period, all this had changed; prices of most goods rose dramatically, including those of many essentials. Wages had to be increased regularly to compensate, and in an attempt to avoid civil unrest in these trying circumstances, many employers, such as the railways, introduced systems of 'Cost of Living' increases. By 1918, general levels of prices and wages were double those of 1914; and it did not end there, for both continued to rise until the end of 1920. The increase in wholesale prices, which reflected industry's costs, was even greater.

After four years of hardship, the first promise was fulfilled: the war was won. There was great optimism and enthusiasm; people wanted to get on with their lives and return to where they had left off in 1914. Beyond that, there was the 'land fit for heroes' to look forward to. However, there was much to be done first — the railways were worn out, and there was a backlog of maintenance, renewals and re-equipment to attend to.

Behind the scenes, things were not all they seemed, and it was to be a long time before the full significance of what was happening began to sink in. During the war, Britain had unavoidably neglected its world markets, and the need for the manufacture of war materials meant that many customers had been deprived of the products they needed. Other countries, notably America, had taken advantage of this preoccupation, and had moved into many of the markets which Britain had previously dominated. In other cases, customer countries, unable to get what they wanted from Britain, had set up factories to make the goods themselves. Against this, British factories took time to re-adjust to peacetime production; in addition, machinery was worn out, and equipment and methods were outdated. Further, the much higher prices and wage levels at home made some British goods uncompetitive on world markets.

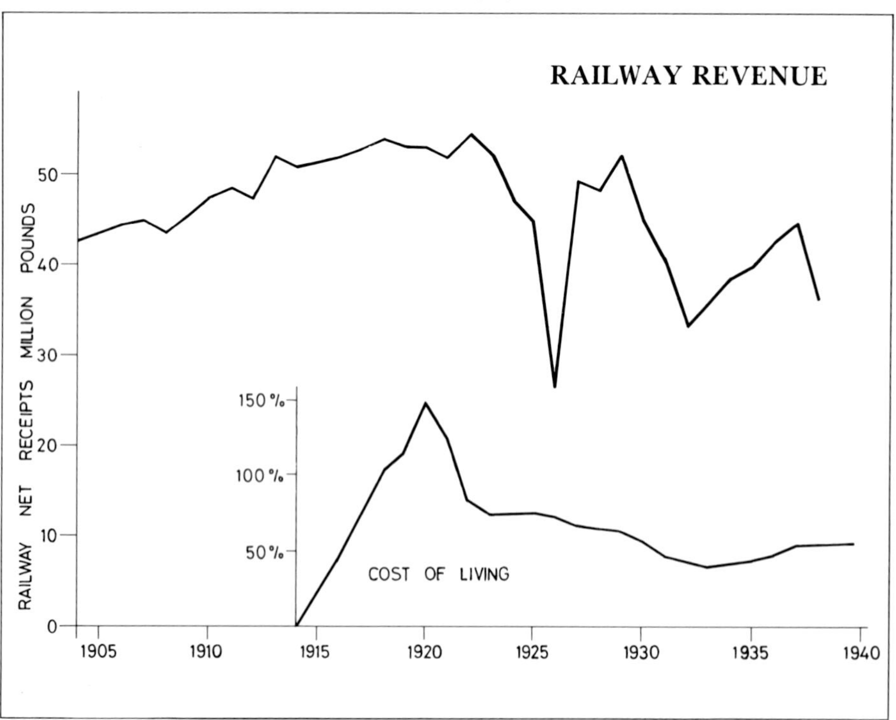

On the surface, the figures looked good. In 1924, Britain's national income was 90% higher than it had been in 1911, but this was only in terms of money earned. In real terms, after allowing for inflation, the new figures represented a drop in national income per head of population of about 5%. Railway net receipts, which stood at a figure just slightly higher than in 1914, were in reality worth half of what they had been. This meant that dividends, and the amount of money available for capital expenditure, were also worth half of their prewar values.

While under Government control, railway receipts had been pooled for simplicity, which enabled labour to be released for the forces by reducing accountancy work. Payments were made to the companies out of the income (which went to the Government) on terms equal to prewar receipts. Most obviously, this failed to allow for the fact that some companies (such as the LNW and Midland) bore a much higher proportion of the burden of special wartime traffic than others. When the accounts were eventually done, it was found that total earnings and traffic had in fact been much greater than before the war. With the war over, however, the politicians soon forgot their promises, and the Government kept the extra money. This was money which should have been directed to getting the railways (and hence, industry) back to peak efficiency as quickly as possible.

By 1921/2, with postwar optimism still firmly in the ascendancy, the railways had virtually completed the exercise of recovering from the effects of the war, and began to look to the future, which still appeared to offer so much. For the railways, there was a special cause for hope: the Railways Act of 1921 was to weld the railways of Britain into four huge companies. The financial and economic strength and earning power of these large units was thought to be such that many things which had not been possible before would be brought within reach. There were ample grounds for expansionist thoughts.

The Midland Railway came forward in 1922 with ambitious plans for improving its system, including, within the Birmingham area, a scheme to remove the bottleneck at Kings Norton station, and that between Halesowen Junction and Barnt Green, on its line to the west. The proposal was to open up Cofton tunnel, and provide four running lines between King's Norton and Barnt Green. Work began in 1924 but was undertaken at a somewhat leisurely pace, which was

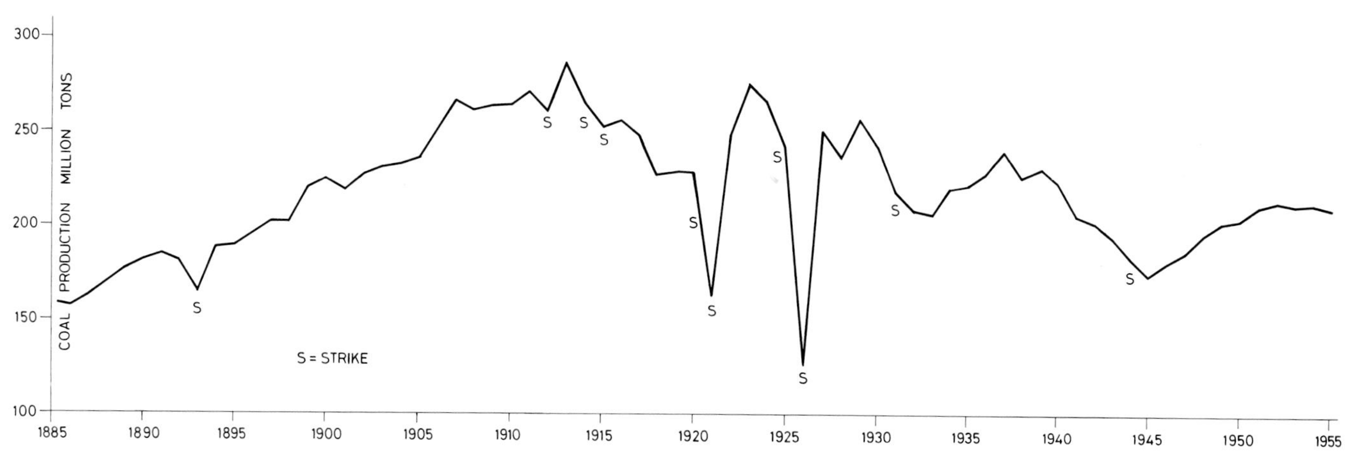

exacerbated by geological problems in the ground around the tunnel; as a result, the scheme was not completed until 1930.

From the middle 1920s, Britain's economy began to descend inexorably into deep recession. Levels of unemployment, which were already large, rose to unprecedented heights. The crash of the Wall Street (New York) stock market in October 1929 reduced levels of business confidence even further than they had been, and the British economy plunged to rock bottom. Between 1929 and 1932, railway net receipts fell by over 35% to just over £33 million, a figure which, even before allowing for inflation, was lower than that of 1900.

The railways' financial position was almost entirely dependent upon industrial output — and especially of industries such as coal and iron, which had been particularly hard hit. This, coupled with the fact that, even in the best postwar years, the companies had been unable to achieve prewar levels of receipts, changed the nature of railway finance.

If the earning power of railway shares was considerably diminished, then the prospects were limited too. The Railways Act of 1921 limited the profits that the railways could make to a 'standard revenue', based on prewar earnings; anything earned above this figure had to be ploughed back in reduced charges. Thus, there was no prospect of share dividends reaching prewar levels in real terms. In fact, railway revenues in the interwar period never even reached the 'standard revenue', let alone any higher. With the gloomy economic situation and the increased competition from road transport, the prospects were none too bright. Railway shares therefore ceased to be the 'blue chip' investments they had been since the beginning of the railway era. This meant that it was effectively no longer possible to finance large-scale capital investment in railway improvements and modernisation at commercial rates of return. Almost all railway investment from this time forward would have to be assisted to some degree by the State.

An easy way in which industry could cut back its costs was by the reduction of manpower, either as a result of lower output, or through increased mechanisation. To offset the huge increases in prices and wages brought about by the war, there was considerable pressure on industry to reduce manpower; this, coupled with the general reduction in activity, led to significant unemployment after 1918. When it became clear that this situation was not going to change, the Government began to make money available to public bodies and others, to enable them to undertake works which would have a public benefit. These were intended to create jobs in themselves, and to stimulate industry (and hence jobs in those industries) by creating orders for manufactured goods.

Large sums of money were expended by local authorities on public works (most notably on road improvements) under these unemployment relief schemes throughout the 1920s and 30s. A surprising amount of Britain's main road network was improved by this means, and in Birmingham, a sizeable proportion of today's total length of dual carriageway dates from this period. Birmingham City Council expended some of the money on a programme of widening roads where they passed under or over railways by building new bridges, and widening others. As most of the bridges had been built when the area around them was largely fields, the growth of the city and the new phenomenon of road traffic had made many of the structures completely inadequate, or even dangerous. Examples of bridge replacement at this period include Aston Lane, under the GJ line near Aston Station, and Avenue Road, Kings Heath, both in 1931/2.

Eventually, in 1932/3, the economy turned the corner, and at last things began to improve. It was a slow process, however, and there was a long way to go just to get back to the 1914 situation; consequently, unemployment remained high. The Government continued its policy of encouraging public works, now aimed at stimulating demand and hastening the recovery.

The railways were seen as an essential part of the country's infrastructure, and, during the summer of 1935, extensive negotiations took place between the Treasury and the four railway companies regarding the advancement of railway investment. This led to an agreement over a package of new works and the associated financing arrangements. The agreement was ratified by Parliament under the Railways (Agreement) Act 1935, which received the Royal Assent on 20th December 1935. The Act outlined the objective thus:

'The Government is desirous that facilities for the transport of passengers and merchandise may be increased by electrification, provision of new equipment and improvement of railway works . . . the work to be commenced as speedily as possible.'

The Act provided for the Government to raise money on the railways' behalf for use on a specified set of projects. Repayment would be guaranteed by the Government, thus allowing the money to be made available on advantageous terms. The estimated cost of the schemes put forward by the four companies amounted to £29 million, of which the largest single share, at just over 10 million, was to go to the LMS. This was to cover the following:

1. Electrification of railways on the Wirral.
2. Modernisation of Stonebridge Park power station.
3. Construction of 369 steam engines and 270 carriages.
4. Rebuilding Euston station.
5. Resignalling at a number of places on the Western Division main line.
6. Improvements at various passenger and goods stations.

The proposals offered advantages for Birmingham. Orders for carriages went to Birmingham firms, and one of the centres to be resignalled was New Street station. The new engines and carriages promised better and more comfortable train services. Works to be undertaken by the Great Western included the enlargement of Hockley goods station.

Just when the economy seemed at last to be firmly on an upward path, and there was a general feeling of optimism for future prosperity, war broke out again. For the railways, the events of the Second World War mirrored, to some extent, those of the First. They were again placed under Government control, and passenger services were fairly heavily curtailed to allow resources to be concentrated on essential war transport. As before, it was found possible to restore a few services once the initial panic was over. As the war reached its height in 1941, drastic reductions in passenger services had to be made, reflecting the situation in 1917.

Most remarkably, in view of what had happened regarding railway revenues in the Great War, the railway companies allowed themselves in 1941 to be persuaded to sign an agreement with the Government, whereby they would accept a fixed rental for the use of the railways during the period of Government control. The arrangements were very similar to those of the first war; the Government would take the receipts in consideration of its control, out of which it would pay the rental, which was set on the basis of the prewar receipts. Once again, wartime traffic and revenues proved to be considerably higher than prewar, and the agreement allowed the Government to pocket the difference. Thus, over the four years 1941 to 1944, the railways' earnings amounted to £350 million, of which the companies only received £174 million. Once again, the railways were deprived of money which should have gone towards railway improvements, and to the shareholders.

In most respects the Second World War had a much greater impact on both the people at home and on the railways. The war was longer, and the development of aircraft made it possible to bomb targets all over Britain without undue difficulty. This made the conditions under which the railways had to operate very difficult, and the blackout made work in marshalling and goods yards both hazardous and slow. Work frequently had to be stopped for long periods while air-raid warnings were in force, which often caused the completion of work to be delayed until the following afternoon. Traffic was delayed while bomb damage was repaired, whilst the loss of facilities and rolling stock made things even more difficult. Although the railways were classed as a 'reserved occupation', many experienced men left the railway service to join the armed forces.

For the industry and the economy, the impact was also more extensive than during the Great War; the conflict was now highly mechanised, and a considerable proportion of manufacturing capacity had to be given over to the production of the machinery, weapons and ammunition required. German submarines inflicted heavy losses on the merchant fleet, and the remaining maritime resources had to be concentrated on bringing in vital supplies — food, and raw materials for war production. The results were the same as before — loss of markets and increases in competition. Technology moved on by leaps and bounds, rendering much production capacity obsolete.

After the cessation of hostilities in 1945, there was a lot of war damage to be repaired. As before, the railway had received minimal maintenance and much was worn out; the task of catching up with the arrears therefore began. The Government decided that the restoration of industry was the top priority, and the railways were therefore unable to obtain all the materials (particularly building supplies, and steel) they needed for reconstruction, slowing down progress. All in all, recovery was a slow and sometimes painful process. Rationing of food, for instance, did not end until 1954, and it was around that time before many passenger services returned to anything like prewar levels; indeed, some never did.

New Street station emerged from the war looking even more rundown and dishevelled than it was when it had been the subject of much complaint in the 1920s and 30s. Parts had been damaged by bombing, while the remainder had been neglected, and there was much glass missing from the station roofs. It was decided that the large roof on the LNW side was beyond repair; it was therefore taken down, and replaced by some extremely ugly 'temporary' canopies. The 'temporary' nature of the canopies was explained by promises of a reconstruction scheme when circumstances improved, but like so many temporary arrangements, these canopies achieved some degree of permanence, and remained in use for over 15 years.

As had been the case after the Great War, the unified operations and organisation brought about by Government control was seen to have brought significant benefits in terms of traffic working, general efficiency, and particularly in handling inter-company traffic. The virtual elimination of directly competing services had brought useful savings in costs, and also in the provision of locomotives, rolling stock and other facilities. On the other side of the coin, the financial position of the railway companies was relatively weak; the system was run down, and needed very significant investment just to restore things to their 1939 condition, let alone modernize. Costs had risen significantly, and, as before, revenues had not kept pace. The London & North Eastern Railway had not paid a dividend on its ordinary shares for some time, and there was no real prospect of the position changing. It was expected that the GW would be unable to pay ordinary share dividends after 1948 or 1949, and the dividends of the two other companies were tiny. Something had to be done. A new Government, which had definite ideas on how nationally-important industries should be controlled, came into office in 1945; the scene was set for change.

CHAPTER TWO

NEW STREET AND BIRMINGHAM'S RAILWAYS UP TO 1948

RAILWAY traffic grew considerably in the first decade of the twentieth century, as the passenger train service details in Chapter 3 illustrate. The facilities at New Street station had hardly changed since completion of station enlargement work in 1885, and pressure on the accommodation both for passengers and trains was increasing, with problems of congestion beginning to manifest themselves. A new traffic had developed which had hardly been anticipated when the station was enlarged: travel from the suburbs to the city each morning to work and travel back each evening. This traffic was a particular problem, since it was concentrated within two quite short periods of time.

The problems were not confined to finding space for the trains. The footbridge, which acted as both a footpath between those parts of the city north and south of the station, and as the main access for passengers to and from the platforms, had been a problem almost since the station opened. Now it was becoming increasingly congested as a result of growth in population, and the increase in railway passenger traffic. The problem was exacerbated by two other factors. The development of tram and bus routes had led to a situation where some terminated in the area around one side of the station, whilst others terminated around the opposite side. Passengers between routes regularly used the footbridge to get from one service to another. Being a busy thoroughfare, and under cover, the bridge attracted loiterers and undesirables, who contributed to the general crowding on the narrow bridge and stairways. At times, passengers had quite a struggle to get through the crowds to reach their platforms, and could, on occasions, miss their trains altogether. The hotel, too, was in need of modernisation, while the increase in the numbers of people travelling and requiring accommodation meant it regularly had to turn customers away.

The real solution was fairly obvious: the station needed to be enlarged to make room for the additional traffic. Given the city centre location of the site and the crowding-in of buildings all around it, the difficulties and costs of an enlargement were likely to be considerable. In 1910, the LNW made an attempt to grasp the nettle, and put forward about the only scheme that could address two of the problem areas at a reasonable cost. The £100,000 proposal was to enlarge and refurbish the hotel, using the small area of spare land between Navigation Street and Stephenson Street (see Volume 2). At the same time, the Stour Valley and South Staffordshire bay lines, part of platform 1 and adjoining the hotel, were to be connected together to form two through platforms. This would improve station working and flexibility, and reduce the need for conflicting movements and for shunting, giving a modest but nonetheless useful increase in station capacity.

As design work on the bays scheme and associated hotel enlargement progressed, proposals to overcome the third problem area — the footbridge — were developed. In 1912, the LNW put the results of its work to Birmingham City Council, proposing that a second footbridge, parallel to the existing one, should be constructed. This would extend from a point adjacent to the existing steps up from Station Street, right across the station to the hotel. It would then connect with a subway leading under the booking office and hotel building to steps up into Stephenson Street. The proposal would involve demolishing the excursion booking office, which stood where the steps were to be.

The new bridge would mainly be used by pedestrians wanting to get from one side of the station to the other, leaving the old one for the use of railway passengers; thus, the crowding and inconvenience would largely be overcome. Looking beyond the basic proposal, the separation would help to make possible, if required, the conversion of the station to 'closed' status, with access to the platforms only by ticket through barriers. This was becoming common practice at large stations, and such an arrangement had the advantages of easier ticket checking, and the reduction of journey times as trains would no longer have to stop at places like Stechford and Vauxhall for tickets to be collected. Opportunities for theft of parcels and luggage from the platforms would also be reduced.

The LNW indicated that the new footbridge would cost £12,000, and stated that it was prepared to build and maintain the structure if the council would contribute half the capital cost, and cover the cost of lighting. After the usual rounds of discussion, the council agreed to the proposals in the spring of 1913; unfortunately, the Great War began before any work was undertaken, and the scheme was postponed. Officially, the proposal for the bays was not heard of again, although the idea was suggested by others from time to time; it was to be 50 years before the bays were converted into through lines. The incredibly small amount of use made of the bays by 1948 is an indication of their operating limitations. Work on the hotel had started, and fortunately this portion of the scheme was brought to completion.

The outbreak of war in 1914 brought proper maintenance of the station to an end, and out of necessity it was allowed to deteriorate. By the end of hostilities, the station was showing its age, and looking distinctly careworn and neglected. The oldest parts of the station dated back well over 60 years, and the new parts (the Midland side) over 30 years. The roof and buildings were blackened by long exposure to the city atmosphere and smoke from the engines. The atmosphere in the station and the problem of dirt were made worse by the overall roofs, which contained the engine smoke, making it slow to disperse. Much of the glass in the roof had not been cleaned for a considerable time, and had become blackened by smoke; this reduced the amount of natural daylight entering the station, making it seem even more dingy. Wartime neglect meant that some glass was missing from the roof, and quite large areas leaked appreciably in wet weather, adding to the general unpleasantness of waiting for trains. However, the missing glass and leaks in the roof were eventually attended to.

There were other things to complain about, too. The gas lighting system was now quite old, and reflected the lighting levels customary in the 1880s. With much of the population now familiar with electric lighting and the much better illumination given by modern incandescent mantles, the lighting over the large spaces of the platforms and within the high roofs now appeared unacceptably dim. The low level of light made the place seem even gloomier. Complaints were persistent after the war, encompassing the general dowdiness and neglect, the dirt, poor lighting, the overcrowding on the footbridge, and the almost total lack of seats on the platforms for passengers.

In 1919, attempts were made to revive the new footbridge scheme, but the city council decided that the idea was out of date — it now wanted something much more grandiose. The amount of motorized road traffic was now increasing, and the roads in the city were rapidly becoming busier, so it was decided that a road across the station connecting Stephenson Street with Station Street was required. By January 1923, this idea had grown to a road from Stephenson Place to John Bright Street, thereby making a new route from Corporation Street to the Bristol Road. The City Engineer conceded that the road would be expensive as it would involve alteration of existing buildings, including the station roof, and demolition of property, including a fair portion of the Queen's Hotel. During the same month, it was suggested that the bridge scheme might be a suitable undertaking to be adopted as a means of providing work for the unemployed.

By October, when the proposal was submitted to the LMS for approval, it had grown into a scheme for a road linking Corporation Street (which formed the main route into the city from Derby, Lichfield and Aston — later the A38) with the Bristol Road (which formed the main route to the south-west, also later the A38). The road was to be 80ft wide (compared with Corporation Street's 75ft), and was to be lined with shops on both sides. The council claimed it still had in reserve the powers to construct a road bridge across the station to line up with Ethel Street and John Bright Street, which it had obtained under the LNW Act of 1876. It was stated that this road would not meet current traffic requirements, but perhaps the need for an excuse was not surprising in view of the fact that the council had already allowed 47 years to elapse without doing anything about it. The new bridge would effectively replace the original scheme.

At a lecture in January 1925, the City Engineer stated that the bridge was to be constructed in reinforced concrete, and explained the reasons why it was needed. He said that the station acted as a barrier, and cut the city centre in two. The bridge was designed to overcome this, and would unify the areas on each side of the station. Quite why the city was so concerned to improve links with the area to the south of the station is not entirely clear. If there really was pressure for

A gang of platelayers standing clear for an ex-LNW tank drifting back into Platform 2, at the south end of the LNW side of the station. The light area in the distance beyond the engine was the open section between Worcester Street bridge and the South tunnel. No. 1 signal cabin features behind the signal. The bell hanging from the corner of the cabin was used to attract the attention of the shunters or station staff when the signalman needed assistance or had information for them. ***Birmingham Post & Mail***

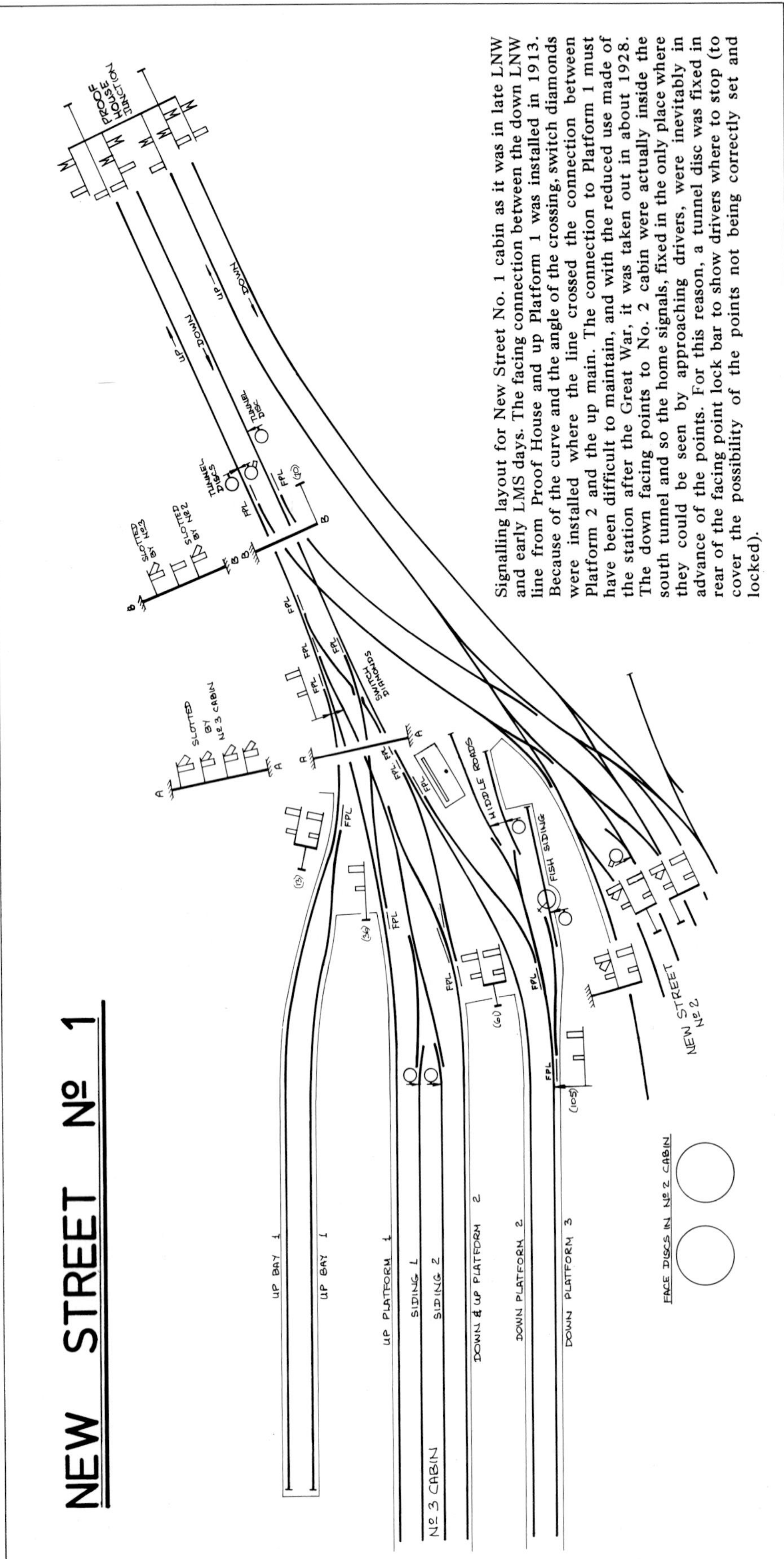

Signalling layout for New Street No. 1 cabin as it was in late LNW and early LMS days. The facing connection between the down LNW line from Proof House and up Platform 1 was installed in 1913. Because of the curve and the angle of the crossing, switch diamonds were installed where the line crossed the connection between Platform 2 and the up main. The connection to Platform 1 must have been difficult to maintain, and with the reduced use made of the station after the Great War, it was taken out in about 1928. The down facing points to No. 2 cabin were actually inside the south tunnel and so the home signals, fixed in the only place where they could be seen by approaching drivers, were inevitably in advance of the points. For this reason, a tunnel disc was fixed in rear of the facing point lock bar to show drivers where to stop (to cover the possibility of the points not being correctly set and locked).

more shops, as some people claimed, one wonders why the shopping area had not spread further in areas that were not restricted, such as further along Corporation Street, and deeper into the streets off New Street and Corporation Street. In many ways, the station was simply an easy target on which to place the blame for other deficiencies. A significant factor was that the city had begun its long obsession with the motor car, and the station was seen by those who advocated more extensive use of motor transport as a hindrance to developing the city to meet the increasing demands of road traffic. It was true that the city's road system was woefully inadequate, but then it always had been. The Street Commissioners had been well aware of this fact in the 1840s, and wanted to do something about it. The town council had resented the expense of the proposals, however, and had managed to get rid of the Street Commissioners in 1854. Since then, other than for Corporation Street and Colmore Row, precious little had been done.

It is a pity that Mr. (later Sir) Herbert Manzoni, a later City Engineer and instigator of the city's new post-Second World War look, did not read the lecture before designing the inner ring road. This road was effectively the replacement of the station bridge scheme, joining as it did the A38 north and south of the city centre. The ring road cut the city centre off from the whole of the rest of the city, not just the small area on the south side, around John Bright Street and Station Street, which New Street station had allegedly severed. While the New Street footbridge, which joined the two areas, may not have been perfect, it was certainly more attractive and safer than the subways that the city foisted on its inhabitants as part of Manzoni's concrete straitjacket ring road scheme.

At the same lecture in 1925, the City Engineer spoke of the council's plans for a proper civic area in the city; the site chosen was the lower end of Broad Street. A start had been made with the construction of the Hall of Memory, and the area was eventually to link up with other municipal buildings — presumably the library, council house and town hall. This was yet another scheme which was hardly rushed to completion; Centenary Square, as it became, was completed in 1991.

Once the New Street bridge scheme moved from bold ideas to the reality of having to pay for it, resolve diminished, and progress became slow; through to 1929, it was always expected that the council would consider details 'shortly'.

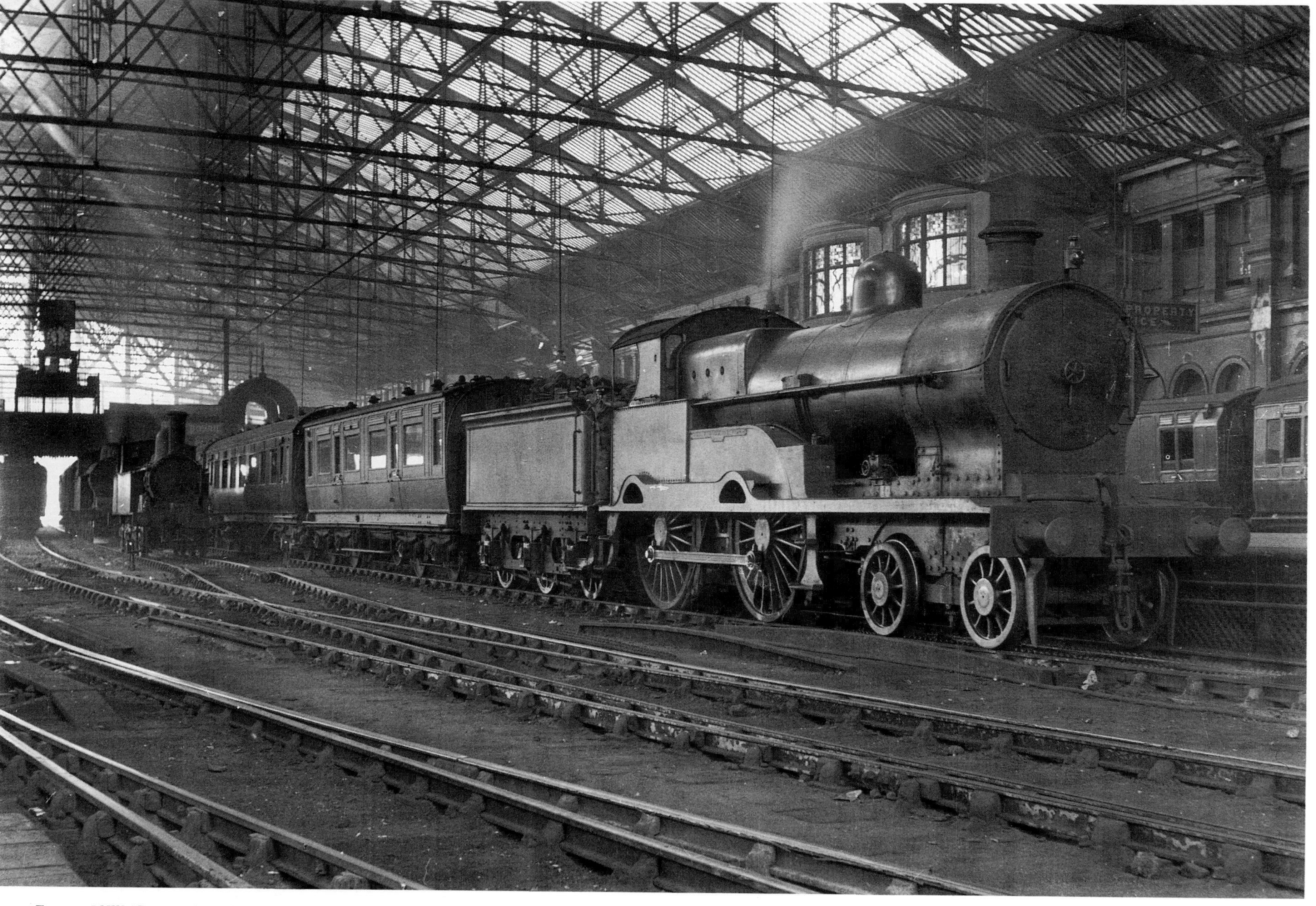

Former LNW 'George the Fifth' class locomotive *J. P. Bickersteth* bearing LMS number 5331, alongside Platform 1 in 1930 with a train for Coventry and Rugby. The girders by the engine's bogie wheels supported the east end subway roof. The windows above belonged to the hotel. The two LNW engines on the centre siding were awaiting their next turn of duty. The coal tank was doing duty as the western side south end station pilot or south end shunt, whilst the 4–4–2 'Precursor' class tank behind was waiting with the stock of a later train to Sutton Coldfield and Four Oaks. The large and very prominent four-faced clock on the far left was added to the roof of the tiny No. 3 signal cabin in 1926. It dominated this side of the station until both the roof and signal cabin were taken down in 1946/47.

A. W. Flowers

LNW 2–4–2 tank No. 6636 of Nuneaton shed (2D) standing under the footbridge in Platform 1 in 1938. This engine was still at Nuneaton in 1945. No. 3 signal cabin can be seen above it. The LNW pattern 'bridge arm' just visible above the carriage was the up home signal for No. 2 up line. The loudspeaker on the arch of the footbridge over the far entrance to Platform 2 was part of the public address and train announcement system which was installed throughout the station in 1935. The idea had been developed by Mr. J. Harrison, who was appointed station master in 1934. It was he who made the first announcement; by 1940 there was a team of six regular announcers. The hands on the two clock faces of the train departure indicator on the left, were pushed round manually by the station staff to point to the time of the next departure. The first finger board in the rack covered trains to Bescot and Walsall via Monument Lane and Soho Road.

J. A. G. Coltas

By this time, various people had pointed out that it was perhaps not a good idea to funnel all the traffic through the city centre, and that a viaduct across Station Street and John Bright Street would cut that area off even more than it was already. Others suggested that if Suffolk Street and Smallbrook Street were widened, they could form part of a ring road to take most of the road traffic. The station bridge scheme, like the Ethel Street proposal before it, was quietly dropped, leaving the people of Birmingham without the benefit of either road or footbridge.

While the council played with its ideas for a bridge across New Street, the LNW (and later, the LMS) remained silent over what plans, if any, they now had for the station. To some extent they were trapped; no work of any significance could be undertaken without involving the bridge scheme, and nothing could be decided there until the council had determined what it actually wanted to do. In any event, the pressure to do something had been diminished by the downturn in rail traffic. The LMS was content to do the minimum.

To counter some of the complaints about the gloominess of the station, it was decided, in September 1924, to replace the old gas lights with new ones of the latest type. The new low-pressure inverted incandescent gas lamps were first installed experimentally on Platform

A quiet interlude on Platform 1 with 'Prince of Wales' class 4–6–0 No. 25818 standing on a train of empty stock c.1937. The engine was based at Stafford shed and had probably worked a terminating service into New Street from the north. The picture clearly shows the clock on the top of No. 3 signal cabin with cycle advert above. *L. Hanson*

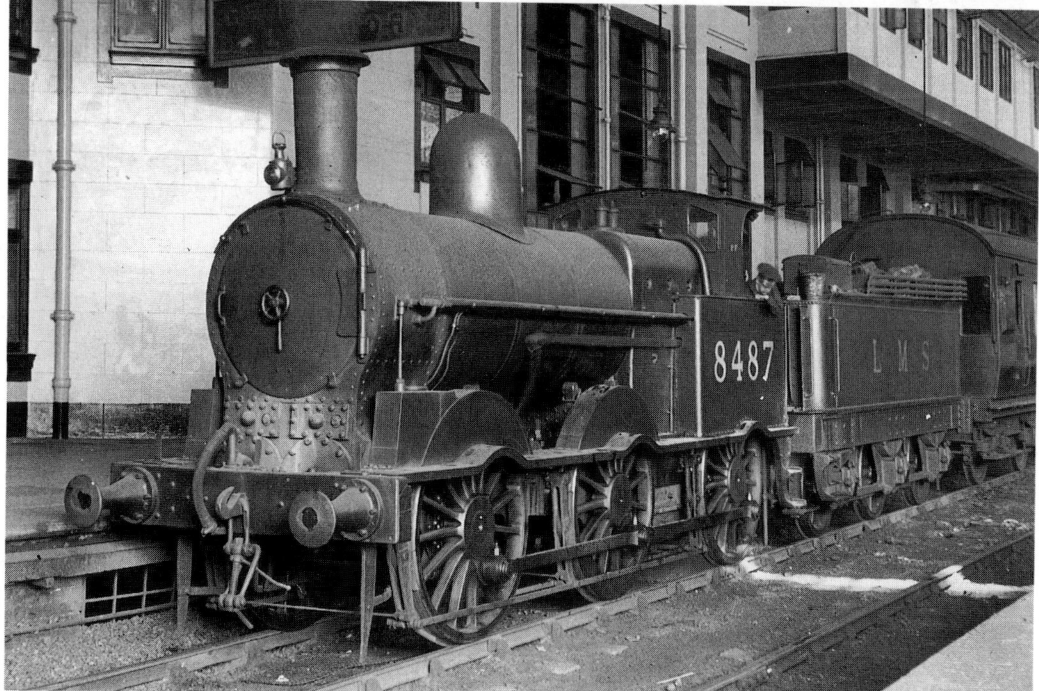

Ex-LNW 'Cauliflower' (so called because of the shape of the LNW crest they used to carry on the centre wheel splashers) 0–6–0 No. 8487, in rebuilt condition with a Belpaire boiler, is seen here in the Stour Valley Bay A in 1931 with a train to Harborne. This platform was for many years the favourite platform for Harborne trains, although they often departed from Platform 2, and had to depart from there during the periods when No. 6 signal cabin was closed. The modern looking buildings behind the engine with their metal-framed windows formed part of the back of the west wing of the Queen's Hotel, which was completed in 1917. Note how they projected onto the platform, a perpetuation of the old buildings in Little Queen Street which noticeably projected into the station when it was built (see the plan on page 13 of Volume 2). At first-floor level, even more space had been won for the hotel by cantilevering part of the buildings over the platform. *A. W. Flowers*

A study of LNW 'Precursor' 4–4–2 tank No. 6789 standing in siding No. 2, adjacent to the north face of Platform 2, in 1934. The enamel LNW shed code plate on the smokebox door was LMS practice. They were formerly carried on the back of the cab roof. The LMS system of shed coding was not introduced until 1935. Shed 10 was Aston. The 'Claughton' behind at Platform 1 was on a southbound train. This was No. 5964 *Patriot*, the LNW War Memorial engine which had been built in 1920 as No. 2097 and was fittingly renumbered 1914 when it was named. The name was transferred to No. 5500 in 1936 and hence became the name for the class of engines which replaced the 'Claughtons'. Note how dirty the glass in the station roof had become by this time, significantly reducing the light within the station. The hose-pipe between the tracks was used for filling the lavatory tanks on carriages.

'Precursor' class 4–4–0 *Amphion*, LMS No. 5248, on middle siding No. 1 near the centre of the station. Platform 1 and the South Staffordshire bays can be seen in the background. Judging from the load of coal on the tender, the engine had not long left the shed. The LNW enamel shed plate on the smokebox door shows its home shed was No. 8 Rugby. The headlamp code denoted an ordinary passenger train. *A. W. Flowers*

3. Gas lighting technology had improved considerably over the previous 20 years, and the new lighting was much brighter than that it replaced; it was therefore decided to replace all the platform lighting in time for the winter. At the same time, the lighting inside the station buildings and in the hotel was improved. Some parts of the station buildings were still gas lit, and these were changed to electric lighting.

By this time, the Paxton ridge and furrow roofing, which filled in the space between the large roof on the LNW (old) side of the station and Navigation Street, was in need of extensive repair. In the circumstances, the easy way out was taken, and during 1925 the roofing was simply taken down and not replaced; this area of the station was then left open to the sky. On the credit side, this no doubt helped with the smoke problems, but otherwise it just contributed to the air of neglect.

After the Great War, the Midland was quite certain about what it wanted to do in Birmingham. In 1922, it brought forward plans to widen the two miles of line between Halesowen Junction and Barnt Green to four tracks, and to rebuild King's Norton station with four platforms (there were already four tracks for the 2¾ miles from King's Norton to Halesowen Junction). Two other schemes were proposed at the same time; widening between Broadholme and Ambergate, and between Chevet and Snydale (near Oakenshaw), both on the Derby & Leeds section of the Midland main line. As well as offering the opportunity to eliminate bottlenecks, all three schemes had another factor in common: all, because of the geography, were extremely expensive in relation to the extra length of trackwork created.

Two of the schemes involved opening-out tunnels, and the third required deep cuttings and a viaduct; no doubt this is why the work had not been done earlier. It is a matter of conjecture as to whether these were the next schemes the Midland would have tackled, had it remained independent, or whether these proposals were advanced because it was thought that the great new company, with its supposed greater resources, would be in a better position to pay for them.

The necessary plans and Parliamentary papers for the King's Norton and Barnt Green widening were deposited in November 1922, and formal approval for the three schemes was given by the Midland Board at its last meeting in December 1922. The timing of the decision could be construed as an act carried out safe in the knowledge that the cost would not fall on the company's shareholders alone.

Good reasons could, however, be advanced for undertaking the Birmingham widening. At the heart of the scheme was the removal of Cofton Tunnel, which was said to be the narrowest tunnel on the main lines of the Midland system, with a maximum width of 23ft. This meant that, in places, the 'six foot way' was as little as 5ft 1in, restricting the use of modern, wider, rolling stock and engines.

The amalgamation brought forward the possibility of increased traffic on the line. The LNW had always preferred to send its North to West of England traffic via Shrewsbury and the GW route via the Severn Tunnel to Bristol; it had avoided sending all but the absolute minimum via Birmingham and the Midland route to Bristol. The amalgamation would bring the whole route via Birmingham under the new company's ownership, and it was

No. 3 signal cabin on 31st March 1927 shortly after the four-faced clock was installed on the roof of the signalman's hut. The two lever frames, the one on the right controlling the up lines and the other the down lines, can be clearly seen. The frame on the right was of the older SK446 type with foot treadles instead of hand-worked catch handles. The frame on the left was of the more modern type with loop handles. Note the LNW lever collar hanging on a hook near the top of the left-hand corner of the hut. *British Railways*

reasonable to expect that the LMS would then prefer to keep the traffic on its own metals, and use the route via Birmingham and Gloucester. This would bring more traffic to the Midland line, and the improvements between King's Norton and Barnt Green would be essential if the traffic was to be worked expeditiously. In practice, most of the ex-LNW traffic continued to travel via Shrewsbury.

Intense negotiations with objectors and Birmingham City Council followed the deposit of the King's Norton and Barnt Green plans. On 2nd May 1923, agreement in principle was reached between the LMS and the City Council on the proposals, which involved some changes to the accommodation works. The original plans had included a new road bridge to replace the level crossing in Station Road, King's Norton. It was agreed that this was not necessary, and that Station Road should be stopped up, and a footbridge provided for pedestrians. Instead, the LMS agreed to build a wider bridge to carry Pershore Road South over the railway, with the company contributing £2,500 toward the roadworks.

To the west of King's Norton, the railway company would allow a new road to be constructed across the railway as a southwards continuation of Selly Oak Road. The LMS would give the necessary land and easements free of charge, and contribute £12,000 towards the council's costs of constructing the new 65ft-wide bridge. Powers for the widening, in accordance with the revised plans, were incorporated in the London, Midland & Scottish Railway Act 1923. Once again, the council never quite got round to building its new road.

Widening schemes generally take a long time to execute. It takes time to purchase the land and undertake the accommodation works, whilst working alongside an existing railway is difficult, and slows down progress. This scheme was made even more demanding because of the need to open out Cofton tunnel. In the event, the timescale was further extended by the decision to undertake the work in two stages. The widening at King's Norton station was started first, and only when that was well advanced was the removal of Cofton tunnel and the widening to Barnt Green put in hand.

The new footbridge at Station Road, King's Norton, was erected in April 1925, and was immediately branded as unnecessarily ugly by the local press. In October, Pershore Road South was closed to allow rebuilding of the bridge (the old bridge and the junction signal box being in the way), leading to complaints that the level crossing at Station Road had been closed a short time before, thus preventing its use by diverted traffic (the diversions being very circuitous as a result).

Work began on the Cofton and Barnt Green widening in the autumn of 1925. It was estimated that the excavation necessary to remove the 440 yard-long tunnel and widen that section of line would involve the removal of half-a-million cubic yards of spoil, and that the whole works would take two or three years. In the event, geological faults in the ground around the tunnel seriously hindered and delayed the works, and a large concrete retaining wall had to be built to support part of the new cutting. The problems did not end there; after the ground had been removed from above most of the tunnel and preparations were being made to demolish the arch, a section collapsed without warning on 11th May 1928, unfortunately killing four men and injuring several others. Rail traffic had to be suspended for several days while the debris was removed and the remainder of the tunnel was made safe. The work was finally completed in 1930.

Meanwhile, other railway works, largely financed by money made available by the Government to relieve a little of the chronic unemployment (which characterised most of the 1920s and 30s), were put in hand in the Birmingham area. In November 1926, the LMS completed a new 390ft-long warehouse at Camp Hill for the accommodation of fruit and vegetable traffic in connection with the nearby Smithfield Markets.

In 1930, the GW started work on widening its Northern main line between Olton and Lapworth. This had been part of an ambitious prewar improvement project, but this part of the work had been cancelled due to the onset of the war. The

A detail view of the west side of the signal cabin in 1938. By this time, the lever frame had been replaced by a new one with loop catch handles instead of foot treadles (see opposite). The frames worked some points and signals in the centre of the station and a set of face discs in the cabins at the two ends of the station. The operating rods from the levers passed down the outside of the footbridge girders and disappeared beneath it. From there they passed sideways to a point near the platform staircases from where they could be dropped to ground level. From the platform, rods or wires were run to the points and signals or to Nos. 1 or 5 signal cabins as appropriate. Note the bell on the left-hand corner of the cabin. Advertising signs had spread onto the cabin since the 1927 picture was taken.

J. A. G. Coltas

Reboilered 'Claughton' 4–6–0 No. 5962, rebuilt with Caprotti valve gear, and resplendent in lined LMS red livery about to depart from Platform 3 with a northbound express. With the signal off for the train to depart, the train crew can be seen looking back intently for the guard's signal. It was quite common for trains to have to stand with the engine, and sometimes the first coach, forward of the signal when a long train had to be accommodated or when it was necessary to draw a train forward as far as possible so that another train could be brought in behind. Although the engine was fitted with lamp irons, the two headlamps were of the LNW 'socket' type. The first coach was an ex-LNW family saloon. *A. W. Flowers*

'Prince of Wales' 4–6–0 *Lusitania* standing at the west end of Platform 2. This engine, originally LNW No. 1100, became 5673 under the LMS. Later, when it was decided to give the new range of standard engines numbers in the 5000 series, the former LNW engines in the same series were renumbered by the simple expedient of adding 20,000 to the original LMS number. Note the pile of platform barrows.

Author's collection

widening was completed in May 1933. The GW announced further works in 1931: a new goods shed was to be built at Small Heath to relieve the depot at Moor Street, which was already overcrowded (it had only opened in 1914), and improvements were to be carried out at Hockley and Soho goods depots (the latter had been opened in 1910).

The LMS put in hand construction of new warehouses at Curzon Street goods depot in 1930 (Chapter 5). This was followed in 1933 by the announcement of plans to construct new mechanised coaling plants at Aston and Monument Lane engine sheds. The plant at Monument Lane was brought into use in the summer of 1934, the coal bunker having the capacity to store 800 tons. Improvements at Lawley Street Goods were put in hand late in 1934.

The 1930s saw some small improvements at New Street which were of great benefit to passengers. In December 1932, Mr. J. Hall was appointed to the new post of 'Passenger Enquiry Inspector' (similar inspectors were appointed at other important stations on the LMS at the same time). His job was to assist passengers by answering enquiries and directing them to their trains, and, to make him stand out, he was given a maroon uniform and hat, both liberally embellished with gold braid. With such a task, Mr. Hall soon acquired an encyclopaedic knowledge of the workings of the station, enabling him to answer most questions without reference to notes. Evidently, Mr. Hall was something of a martyr, for he remained in what must at times have been a rather thankless job for 18 years, until his retirement in December 1950, with 48 years of railway service behind him. He was replaced by Joseph Watson, a former guard.

In October 1935, work began on the installation of a system of 25 loudspeakers around the platforms, to permit train announcements to be made to passengers. The loudspeakers were linked together in groups, to allow the train announcer to confine his announcements to specific areas (and to reduce the echoes which made announcements so hard to hear in stations with overall roofs); up to 13 speakers could be used at once by the announcer, who was given a tiny office on platform 1. This was the first public address system at a station in Birmingham, and was brought into use at the end of November 1935. Generally, no announcements were made at night, in deference to the hotel guests. Wartime shortages of staff brought the first lady to the microphone in May 1941: Miss Olive Dew was 21 years old, and had started as a shopgirl, moving to New Street as a parcels porter after the outbreak of the war.

By 1935, the economic position of the country was at last showing steady improvement. The Government took steps to stimulate activity by encouraging expenditure on works which were of public benefit, and the Railways (Agreement) Act 1935 made further money available to the railways. The LMS was quickly off the mark with the simplest of its proposals — the construction of 369 locomotives and 270 carriages, and orders for these were soon placed with outside firms. A substantial proportion of the orders for carriages went to Birmingham firms: The Metropolitan Carriage & Wagon Company, and The Birmingham Railway Carriage & Wagon Company.

The other proposal to affect Birmingham was resignalling. The company proposed the installation of colour light signals between Euston and

Continued on page 31

Final adjustments being made to one of the train announcement loudspeakers which were installed at New Street in 1935.
LMS Magazine

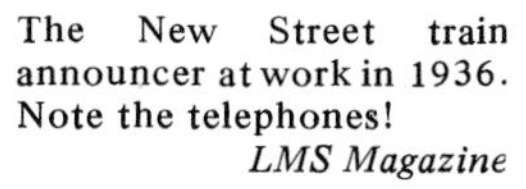

The New Street train announcer at work in 1936. Note the telephones!
LMS Magazine

'Cauliflower' No. 8529 of Coventry shed shunting empty stock out of Platform 3 on 7th May 1938. Note that the movement had been made under the direction of the shunt signal arm on the left-hand doll of the bracket signal, the main arm remaining at 'danger'. *L. Hanson*

LNW 0–6–2 tank No. 6876 of Monument Lane shed leaving the south face of Platform 2 with a local train for the Stour Valley line on Saturday, 20th August 1938. The first coach was an ex-LNW cove-roof brake third. Comparing this picture with that on page 50 of Volume 2 shows that the smoke deflector plate fitted to the bracket signal above the engine to protect the right-hand arm from smoke had since then been removed. As a result, the two arms above the platform line had turned completely black! *L. Hanson*

LNW 4–4–2 tank No. 6797 at the head of a local train at the south face of Platform 2 on 23rd April 1935 with the engine crew deep in conversation in the cab. Note the LMS crest on the bunker side and the mesh screens to protect the cab rear windows from breakage by coal in the bunker. The engine was in LMS 'Crewe black' livery. *L. Hanson*

'Patriot' class 4–6–0 No. 5521 *Rhyl* in beautifully turned-out condition at the head of the afternoon express for Manchester, London Road, on Saturday, 7th May 1938. At this date the engine was allocated to Bushbury shed. The train had been drawn well past the signal in order to accommodate it in the platform. Because the first coach was not adjacent to the platform, the van was having to be loaded across a large gap. Having to load vans beyond the ends of platforms was not an uncommon problem at large stations when trains were

On the same day, Fowler 2–6–4 tank No. 2403 departing from Platform 3 with a semi-fast train (express headlamps) to Stafford. This engine was allocated to Stafford at the time.
L. Hanson

This photograph was taken on Wednesday, 4th May 1938, from the upper windows of the Central Technical College in Summer Street, which features in the background of some of the pictures taken at the north end of the station. The centre of the photograph is dominated by the massive bridge carrying Hill Street over the station throat. This joins Navigation Street (also carried on a huge bridge over the platforms) at ninety degrees, near the right-hand edge of the picture. The somewhat faded timber advertising hoarding in the angle between the bridges was for the Birmingham Garages Ltd. who, until the 1970s, had premises just off the picture to the right (presently a car park). Just visible at the very bottom of the picture is the edge of the turntable pit. From the turntable, eight short locomotive sidings led off, each with its own ash pit. One of these can be seen in the picture, as can one of the two water columns. The tracks disappearing under the brick arch just above the LMS standard class 2P 4–4–0 gave access to Platform 3 and the Coffee House Bay (left) and a short locomotive siding (right). The two-arm bracket signal in front of this bridge was the home signal for No. 4 cabin and controlled entry for up trains into Platforms 4 and 5. The miniature arm below the bracket controlled entry to the centre siding No. 3. This signal was removed when the gantry signal on the left was replaced by colour lights. The down Back Line signal (to the right of the tank engine) had been placed to the right of that line for sighting purposes. Since the skyline of Birmingham has changed so much, it is of interest to look at the buildings which can be seen in the background of the picture. The white building on the left, in the middle distance, was the back of the Forum cinema (latterly the ABC and closed in the 1980s). The rather pretentious building to its right and behind, with arched and dormer windows, fronting onto Ethel Street and Stephenson Street, has since been replaced by a 1960s nondescript brick and concrete affair called Winston Churchill House. The roof of the Theatre Royal (which fronted on to New Street) is visible above the building. The theatre was damaged in an air raid in April 1941 but continued in use until closure on 15th December 1956. The Guild Hall building, in a pleasing glazed brick, can be seen further to the right, in the triangle formed by Stephenson Street, Navigation Street and Pinfold Street. It survives in good condition. The top two floors of the 5-storey brick building just visible down Navigation Street, and fronting onto Stephenson Street, formed part of the Midland Hotel with offices on the intermediate floors. Today the ground floor is used for shops and was, until the early 1990s, the home of that rabbit-warren of a book shop, Hudsons (later Dillons). The Queen's Hotel also features on the right-hand side of Navigation Street (also fronting onto Stephenson Street) and to its right the huge bulk of the station roof. The Central Technical College disappeared in the 1960s and car parks now occupy its site.

L. E. Copeland

Willesden, and at Birmingham, Crewe, Preston, Rugby, Stafford, Warrington and Wigan, plus small-scale signalling improvements elsewhere. Much of the signalling equipment at these places was quite old, and there was a lack of modern aids to working, such as track circuits and electrical controls. Colour light signals aided working because they were so much easier for drivers to see, and were a particular boon in fog and bad visibility. Resignalling also offered opportunities to increase line capacity and reduce manpower.

At New Street, the mechanical signalling largely dated from the 1880s. In view of the difficult arrangements of the station and the approaches through the tunnels, the almost total lack of track circuits (which had not been available when the signalling was installed) was a particular disadvantage. The confined approaches to the station, with all the tunnels, bridges and curves, made the semaphore signals difficult to sight, whilst the presence of smoke, which tended to linger in the tunnels and under the station roofs, made the driver's task even more difficult. Considering the difficulties under which the men had to work, and the (by now) rather outdated equipment, the station's safety record was a tribute to all those involved in its working. Under the resignalling scheme, it was therefore proposed to install multiple aspect colour light signalling throughout the station area, together with track circuiting.

The company did not have the resources to undertake all the resignalling work at once, and that at New Street was fairly well down the list. Unfortunately, war broke out in 1939 before the resignalling programme was complete. The work at Rugby had just been finished, while that at Crewe and Wigan, and between Euston (excluding the station) and Willesden, were nearing completion, and work continued to complete these schemes. In the cases of Preston, where work had just started, and New Street and others, where the schemes were still at the design stage, the work was postponed in view of the wartime emergency.

This is not to say that nothing was done. In 1938, the signalling at Proof House Junction was improved, with fairly extensive track circuiting being installed. This allowed control of the signals on the Walsall or Overhead lines, formerly worked by Curzon Street No. 2 cabin, to be transferred to Proof House Junction, although all the signals remained as semaphores. At the same time, some new track circuits were installed at Grand Junction, and on the tunnel approaches (Midland and Western) to New Street No. 5.

As the 1930s progressed and the economy slowly improved, housing development began to take place near the London & Birmingham line around Coventry, and between there and Birmingham. Most notable was a Government-assisted scheme by Birmingham Corporation for extensive council housing estates to be built on the green fields beyond Stechford, around Lea·Hall, Kitt's Green and Garrett's Green. The LMS had already seen the problems that housing development alongside its railways could bring, notably in London. The developments brought an increasing demand for passenger train services, and eventually a situation could be reached where, to meet that demand, additional tracks were necessary. These could not be provided because the houses had been built up to the railway fence, making widening prohibitively expensive.

Although the double-track line from Rugby to Birmingham was quite adequate to accommodate the existing traffic (apart perhaps from New Street, and the outdated and inadequate Coventry station), the LMS Board decided that it would be prudent to make provision for the construction of extra tracks, should they be needed in the future. Proposals were therefore brought forward in 1936 to purchase strips of land on one or both sides of the line between Adderley Park and Tile Hill, in order to ensure the company would have enough land in its ownership to enable four tracks to be provided, even if houses were to be built all the way along the railway. Parliamentary

Continued on page 36

On Saturday, 7th May 1938, 'Cauliflower' No. 8597 standing in Siding 1 just beyond the west end of the main face of Platform 1, which was occupied by a train. Navigation Street bridge features on the far left. The wall behind the engine used to support the Paxton roof. It was reduced in height when the roof was removed in 1925. The brickwork of the new top courses is still noticeable in this photograph taken 13 years later.

L. Hanson

This was the largest of the Birmingham cabins, being constructed in connection with the station enlargement work and having 144 levers when opened in 1884. It was of the LNW Type 4 design and of size T: 80ft 4½in long. It retained its LNW name and had not been fitted with LMS nameboards. The LNW name can be seen in the centre of the cabin and was made of 4in high cast-iron letters screwed direct to the fascia board. Of interest are the main windows. These were of the LNW standard design, mounted as usual, in sets of two or three sashes. However, as was common at large and busy boxes where the best possible view for the signalmen was essential for safety, the sashes were fitted with large sheets of plate glass and the centre vertical glazing bars omitted. The signal gantry to the right spanned all the foreground tracks. With the limited space available, it is interesting to see how the signal engineers got over the problem of accommodating the signal, resting one end on the cabin roof! A supporting leg was in fact provided inside the cab structure and this can be seen through the windows. This gantry was of wood construction and spanned the equivalent of about five tracks. In later years, wood construction was limited to spans of up to two tracks. The truss structure mounted under the timber gantry beams is also of interest. This was necessary to provide strength and rigidity to the gantry, which was in use by 1890 and probably dated from the 1884 resignalling. The small windows seen in the cabin front above the main windows, just to the right of the third doll from the left, were provided to enable the signalmen to see all the arms and lights clearly. The signal cabin was extensively damaged in an air raid in 1940, but, surprisingly, the gantry survived into BR days. The tracks behind the cabin were the LNW Stour Valley (or Wolverhampton) lines into the LNW side of the station (Platforms 1-3). The track immediately in front of the cabin was an up line common to the LNW and Midland routes known as the up 'Back Line' and giving access to Platforms 1 and 2. The three signal arms facing the camera controlled movements on this line and read as follows (left to right): To Platform 1, To Siding 1, To Up side of Platform 2. The two tracks curving round to the right were the Up and Down Midland lines from Gloucester entering the Midland side of the station, whilst the one immediately in front of them, occupied by the locomotive in the right foreground, was the Down Main No. 2 line. The next two dolls on the gantry (with backs to the camera) controlled movements to either the LNW or Midland lines from the Down Main No. 1. The remaining three dolls controlled movements on the Down Main No. 2 to: LNW, Midland, or Down Neck. The substantial water tower behind the cabin served the locomotive water columns, whilst the two huts on the left were LNW Webb standard all-wood portable huts of the type introduced in 1885.

L. E. Copeland

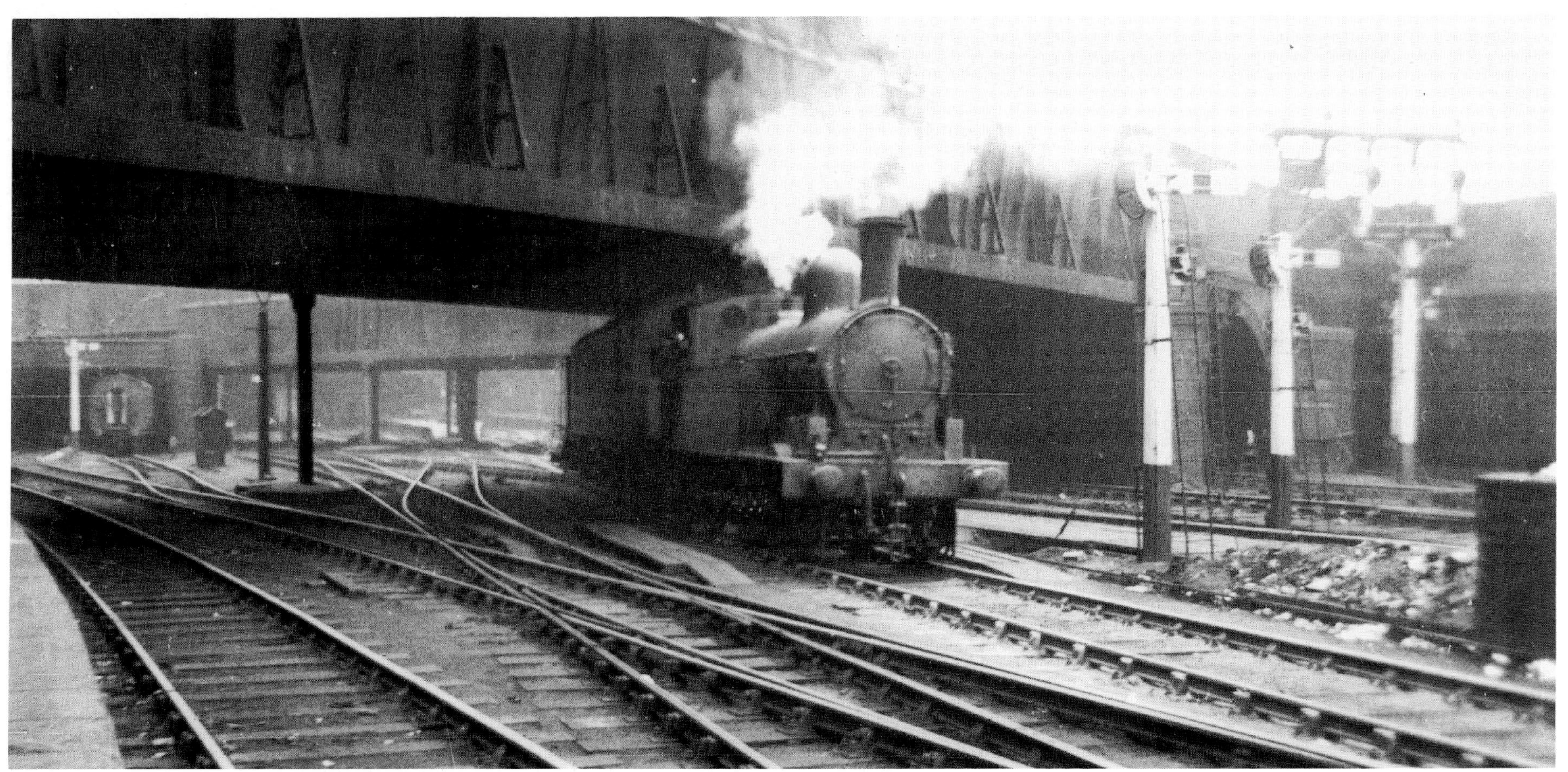

The long Stour Valley up bay platform was an excellent vantage point from which to observe and photograph the comings and goings of the trains and shunting movements at the west end of the station. This picture was taken in 1937 from just behind No. 5 signal cabin and shows LNW 0–6–2 tank No. 6929 on north shunt or pilot duties, shunting vehicles under Hill Street bridge. On the left, the end of a carriage can be seen standing in the Pit Siding alongside the Stour Valley Down Bay. Note that all the signals were still of LNW pattern.

P. B. Whitehouse

This aerial photograph was taken from a point above the west end of the station on 30th July 1938. Part of the yard at Central Goods is visible at the bottom centre of the picture, whilst Suffolk Street can be seen in front of the depot and running along the bottom of the picture. The scene in this area has now changed out of all recognition, as is the case with the area between New Street and Moor Street stations. In the 1960s a huge swathe was cut through the buildings and streets in the area in order to construct the city's inner ring road. This cut the city centre off from the remainder of the city in a much more effective manner than the station ever did, and succeeded in isolating the John Bright Street area far more effectively than it was already. This view shows how the left-hand end of New Street station was dominated by Navigation Street, in which several trams can be seen. They look positively tiny against the width of the street. The Central Technical College, from which the pictures on pages 30 and 32 were taken, features near the corner of Navigation Street and Suffolk Street, whilst Station Street can be seen bordering the right-hand side of the station, with the Market Hall beyond, and above that the Great Western's Moor Street station. The tracks leading away from the New Street south tunnels towards Proof House Junction can be seen in the far distance, the kink in the line showing the area in which the 1896 widening changed from the south side (through the tunnels) to the north side (across Fazeley Street and New Canal Street) of the original line. A little to the left, at the very top of the picture, the sheds and office buildings of Curzon Street goods station can just be made out. The roofs of the wholesale meat and vegetable markets feature on the extreme right of the picture, straight across from the Market Hall, whilst the new office block and cinema buildings which replaced the old Grammar School after it closed in 1936, can be seen near the centre of the picture. The white of the office block contrasted sharply with the smoke-blackened form of the Exchange Buildings next door. The large light-coloured building near the top left of the picture was Lewis's department store which closed in July 1991 following a short period in receivership.

Aerofilms Ltd.

A view looking across Hill Street and Navigation Street towards the LNW side of the station. Queen's Drive, to the right of the main roof, can be seen lined with taxis, whilst the tall narrow structure to the left was the Queen's Hotel. The church spire of St. Martin's, Bull Ring/Digbeth, can be seen in the distance to the right of the Market Hall. The picture was taken on 4th May 1938. *L. E. Copeland*

plans for the purchase of the necessary land were deposited in November of that year. Sufficient land was included to allow for the enlargement of the goods yards at Hampton-in-Arden and Marston Green, and for a new goods yard, to serve the Coventry area, to be constructed between Tile Hill and Coventry. The latter was the revival of a scheme that the LNW had proposed, but which had lapsed after the onset of the Great War. In due course, powers to purchase the land were embodied in the London, Midland & Scottish Railway Act 1937, which received the Royal Assent on 1st July.

At the same time, proposals for a similar land purchase exercise between Coventry and Rugby were prepared, and these were deposited with Parliament in November 1937; the necessary powers were embodied in the LMS Act of 1938.

As a result of discussions with Birmingham Corporation over the impact of the land purchase proposals on its housing scheme, it was decided to build a new passenger station at Lea Hall to serve the development. The LMS Board approved the proposed station, at an estimated cost of £14,501, in December 1936. The provisions of the 1937 Act were sufficient to allow for its construction without separate sanction, and the new station, in the classic LMS 'modern concrete' style, opened on 1st May 1939, only a short time before war broke out. Space was left behind the up platform for the extra tracks, which were never to be laid.

Once the 1937 Act had become law, the task of purchasing the strips of land was put in hand. Housing development was most likely to occur on the outskirts of Birmingham and Coventry, and initial efforts naturally concentrated on those areas. Little progress had been made on the central country section between Birmingham and Coventry, or on any of the Coventry & Rugby section, when war broke out. From a railway operating point of view, the most pressing problem was Coventry station, and a small amount of preliminary excavation work was undertaken there just prior to the war in preparation for a rebuilding scheme.

All work stopped on the outbreak of war in 1939, and the powers subsequently lapsed. With the changed attitudes to railways which marked the postwar years, they were never revived, although Coventry station was eventually rebuilt in conjunction with the electrification of the line.

For the observant, traces can still be seen of how much this far-sighted land purchase scheme had progressed before war intervened. Over some sections of the Stechford to Coventry line, the railway fence (mainly on the up side) can be seen to be set back, ready to accommodate the formation for the extra tracks. Near Canley, Fletchamstead Bridge (which carries the present A45 over the railway) was built with a span sufficient for four tracks, and is still so to this day. In terms of line occupation (rather than numbers of trains — because of the mix of fast and stopping trains), the Birmingham & Coventry line is today probably one of the busiest in the West Midlands, perhaps only surpassed by New Street station, and the Stour Valley line from New Street to Galton Junction.

As the 1930s progressed it seemed that, at last, the long years of depression were over, and that Britain was returning to the prosperity it had known before the

Great War. In a quite natural reaction to an improvement after a period of adversity, grandiose plans started to surface. Following the announcement by the LMS that it intended to undertake a comprehensive rebuilding of Euston station (something that had been overdue since the turn of the century), proposals began to appear for the rebuilding of New Street.

The more ambitious of the proposals were more concerned with what else could be crammed onto the site rather than how the much-needed improvements to the railway facilities might be effected. The proposals therefore largely concentrated on building rafts over the whole or part of the station site to allow something to be constructed above, while the railway continued to operate in the space below. One ambitious scheme, for which models were produced, envisaged a raft over the whole site. Above the railway would be a huge indoor sports arena of national importance, the roof of which — another raft — was to be an airport, and the model showed aeroplanes standing on it. Details of what sort of services were expected and what types of plane would be able to safely take off and land on the very short runways, and in the middle of a city, were somewhat sketchy!

The idea of a major sports arena is of interest in that 1991 saw the opening of the National Indoor Sports Arena in Birmingham. Following the original idea, this has been built above the railway — not at New Street, but a little further west, above the Stour Valley line and on the site of Monument Lane engine shed. Many things in Birmingham, it seems, take a long time to come to fruition! Needless to say, war intervened before any action had been taken over rebuild-

Continued on page 50

New LMS poster boards erected above the station wall at the west end of Queen's Drive, photographed on 28th May 1925. Navigation Street ran off to the left and Hill Street to the right and behind the camera. The centre poster illustrates clearly the advertiser's art. There could be no quicker way to London because the LMS had an agreement with its competitors that there should be no quicker way. Of course, if one went to Snow Hill, one would find the railway company there also offering a journey time to London of two hours! Today New Street can manage rather better than one train a day to Bournemouth and one train a week to Brighton. Ramsgate Harbour station closed in May 1926. By 1938 these LMS poster boards had gone, replaced by a large commercial advertising hoarding. In the later picture on the opposite page this was being used to advertise Maclean's toothpaste. Note the ornate gateposts and gates at the entrance to Queen's Drive. The removal of the ornate lamp posts is a sad loss to the modern streetscape.
National Railway Museum

LMS advertising hoardings at New Street on 3rd July 1929 (above) and 3rd May 1926 (right). The left-hand boards were at the corner of Pinfold Street and Navigation Street. On the extreme left a policeman in white coat and helmet can just be seen on point duty at the junction of Navigation Street and Hill Street. The right-hand picture shows the poster board in Hill Street, which was sited just to the left of the entrance to the fish and milk and carriage loading yard and near to the Station Street station entrance. Rambling tours became an increasingly popular pastime in the 1920s and 1930s and the railway companies made strenuous efforts to obtain useful off-peak income by offering cheap fares to suitable country stations. *National Railway Museum*

TWO HOUR EXPRESS SERVICE BETWEEN BIRMINGHAM NEW STREET AND LONDON

From Birmingham to London

Year	*Departure Times*					
	a.m.	*a.m.*	*p.m.*	*p.m.*	*p.m.*	*p.m.*
1922	8.40	11.15	1.0	2.30*	4.50	6.20
1930	8.40	11.45	1.0	2.35	4.50	6.20
1934	8.40	11.45	1.0	2.35	4.50	6.20
1938	8.40	11.45†	1.0†	2.35†	4.50	6.20

From London to Birmingham

Year	*Departure Times*								
	a.m.	*a.m.*	*a.m.*	*a.m.*	*p.m.*	*p.m.*	*p.m.*	*p.m.*	*p.m.*
1922				11.30*	1.15	2.20	4.35	6.0	6.55
1930	2.30*		9.10	11.30		2.20	4.35	5.50	6.55
1934	2.30*		9.10	11.30		2.20	4.35	5.50	6.55
1938	2.30*	8.10	9.15†	11.30*		2.25†	4.35	5.50†	6.55

* Scheduled for up to 5 minutes longer than 2 hours
† Scheduled time 1 hour 55 minutes

BIRMINGHAM NEW STREET STATION MASTERS

(LNW 1860 to 1897, LNW & Midland Joint 1897 to 1923, and LMS 1923 to 1948)

William Robinson	1860-1863
Robert G. Wyatt	1864-1867
Thomas Hyatt	1868-1871
William Stokes	1872-1876
John Roberts	1877-1883
Thomas W. Wood	1884-1885
John Wynne	1886-1891
John Squires	1892-1908
William Creswell*	1909-1917
George Hadfield	1918-1933
J. Harrison	1934-1937
F. G. Hewitt	1938-1942
T. Finch	1943-1948

* Appointed by Midland Railway under terms of Joint Station Agreement.

MIDLAND RAILWAY AGENT IN CHARGE

William Pearson	1865-1899
Richard Goldsborough	1900-1909
H. D. Verrinder	1910-1923

QUEEN'S HOTEL
Managers and Name Changes

Officially named Queen's & North Western Hotel from c.1876

1921-25	T. Harris
1926-36	Paul Vacher
1928	Name changed to Queen's Hotel
1936-40	H. A. Gross
1941-44	C. Cirillo Chesletta
1945-50	Reginald Langford Turnbull
1951	Denis Arthur Vernan Aldridge
1952-53	G. A. Addey-Jibb
1954-55	Donald George Carter
1956	Arthur Hatfield

LNW & LMS SUPERINTENDENTS OF CENTRAL DISTRICT

Samuel Grew	1860-1863
Walter Knox	1864
John Henry Roberts	1865-1870
William Sutton	1871-1893
Ffolliott V. Denning	1894-1896
A. Entwistle	1897-1903
C. Lowndes	1904-1908
Lancelot W. Horne	1909
Robert T. Morcom	1910-1920
James F. Bradford	1921-1932
J. F. Brook	1933-1939
G. R. Bradbury	1940-1942
J. B. Dunkerley	1943-1948

(Post retitled District Passenger Manager 1932)

PRINCIPAL MAIN LINE SERVICES
TRAIN DEPARTURES
LOCAL SERVICES
WEEKDAYS
NORTHBOUND
SOUTHBOUND
THE FOOD FOR HEALTH AND VIGOUR
COOKED IN FIVE MINUTES
Scott's Porage Oats
NOTICE
THE TRAIN SERVICES SHEWN ON THIS INDICATOR MAY BE ALTERED OR AMENDED FOR BANK HOLIDAY
SEE SPECIAL ANNOUNCEMENT
LMS
WHITE STAR LINE
SOUTHAMPTON
NEW YORK
All Clear!
NORMAL TRAIN SERVICE

LAVATORY
TRAIN DEPARTURES
PRINCIPAL MAIN LINE SERVICES
NORTHBOUND
WEEKDAYS
SOUTHBOUND
MIDLAND AND SCOTTISH Ry
ESHMENT ROOM
SOUTH AFRICA
For Glorious Sunshine and Magnificent Scenery
Christmas and New Year
TOURS TO SOUTH AFRICA
UNION-CASTLE LINE
FOR LOCAL SERVICES SEE THE OTHER SIDE OF THIS INDICATOR
NOTICE
STOUT
ALE
OOKING OFFICE
LMS
LONDON MIDLAND AND SCOTTISH Ry
REFRESHMENT ROOMS
HENRY BUTCHER & Co
ENGINEERING AUCTIONEERS
FACTORY SPECIALISTS
CHELSEA
STONE-WORKING

The LMS made determined attempts to improve passenger information at New Street. These three photographs show the most impressive and expensive of the new provisions. The new train indicator shown in the top left photograph was erected in September 1926 at the Station Street entrance to Platform 6. It was 25ft wide and contained 4,136 slots in which the times of trains could be displayed. The indicator was laid out to list the departures by destination. From left to right across the top of the 'Main Line Northbound' section, the destinations were: Smethwick, Dudley Port, Dudley, Wolverhampton; Four Ashes, Gailey, Penkridge; Walsall; Bloxwich, Wyrley, Cannock, Hednesford, Rugeley; Liverpool via Crewe; Manchester London Road via Crewe; Lichfield City; Pelsall, Brownhills, Hammerwich; Burton & Derby; Nottingham; Chesterfield, Sheffield; Matlock, Buxton; Glasgow, Edinburgh; Stamford, Peterborough. The thick horizontal lines within the table indicated the positions of tables for other destinations. These included Stafford & Stone; Crewe; Blackpool; Chester & Holyhead; Tamworth; Alrewas; Leeds, Bradford & Harrogate. By today's standards quite a few of these destinations would hardly be thought of as 'Main Line'. Their inclusion in the Main Line section masks how poorly Birmingham was served in terms of express and long-distance trains (the equivalents of today's 'Intercity' trains). Departures under each heading were set out in two columns, one for 'A.M.' departures and one for 'P.M.'. In 1928 a second indicator was provided at the Queen's Drive entrance to Platform 4 (bottom left). This was brought into use at the height of the holiday season on Friday, 17th August, and the photograph was taken a few days later. It was double-sided with Main Line departures shown on the Queen's Drive side and local departures on the left-hand portion of the platform side. It was 40ft 8in long including the platform entrance space. A collapsible gate was provided for the space to enable this entrance to the platform to be closed off if required. The two indicators were followed, at the beginning of 1930, by a new passenger enquiry office constructed at the Stephenson Place entrance of the station. This utilised the space formerly occupied by one of the entrance ways. Note the Edmondson card tickets in the racks on the back wall. The progress of rail services was such that the LMS was still proudly advertising a 2-hour journey time to London, a timing which had been introduced back in 1905. Within a few minutes it was to remain the standard time (except in wartime and for some years afterwards when trains were slower) until 1967. The enquiry office photograph was taken on 16th January 1930.
National Railway Museum

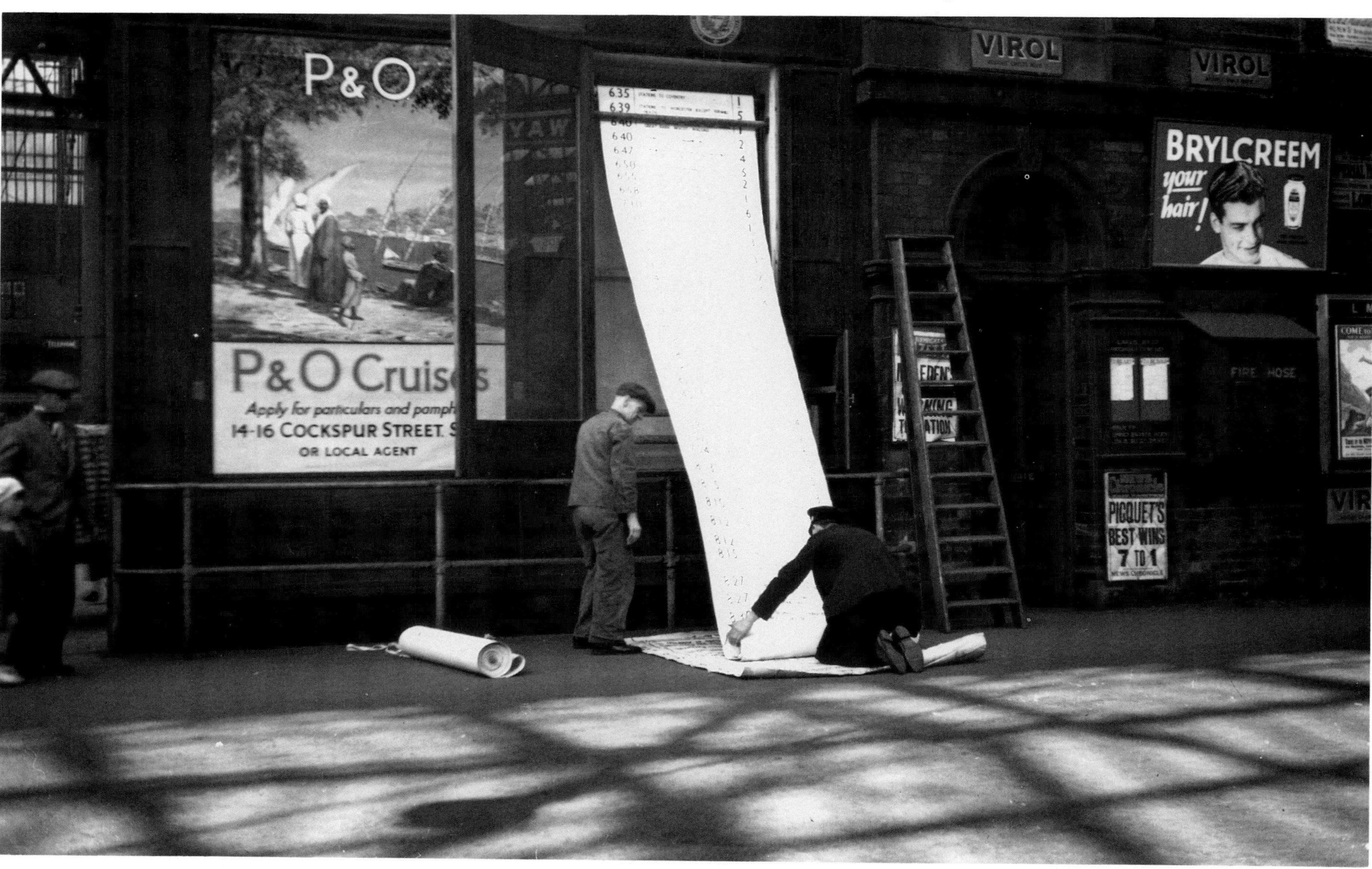

Timetable change time around 1936 or 1937 with two porters in the process of removing the old destination indicator roll from one of the roller departure indicators. This one was on Platform 4 and was set in the back of the large train departure indicator shown at the bottom of page 40. The new roll can be seen on the platform to the left. Most large LMS stations were provided with indicators of this type on the main platforms, and many of them remained in use until the 1970s. As the display could only show about 15-20 departures at one time, it was the duty of one of the platform staff to wind the display on at suitable intervals. Note the LMS crest above the indicator. The framed display cabinet to the right of the doorway advertised details of property the LMS had available for letting.

NEW STREET'S BOOKING HALL AND BOOKING OFFICES

The station entrance from Stephenson Street was reached through the arches under the old central portion of the hotel. After the hotel was extended, its entrance was repositioned from the east to the west side of the station entrance.

A few feet beyond the frontage columns and arches was a second row of columns and arches, forming an entrance colonnade. At the right-hand end of the colonnade, and with its entrance from that colonnade, was the enquiry office, installed by the LMS at the beginning of 1930. The centre four arches led directly to the main station booking hall, an incredibly small area for such a major station, especially since it also functioned as part of the public footpath across the footbridge and the main entrance way to the station.

There were two booking offices inside the booking hall (see page 60, Volume 2), that on the left being known as the 'south office' and the one on the right as the 'Stour Valley office'. The south office was the old Midland (Stephenson Street) booking office, but in LMS and BR days it sold tickets for destinations served by trains on the Western Division (or LNW) side of the station, while the Stour Valley office (the old LNW office) dealt with advance bookings, bookings for excursions, and the sale of other specials tickets (and hence was also known as the 'advance booking office').

Straight ahead, beyond the booking hall, were the steps down onto the station footbridge. To the left, a short passage led to a further small entrance-cum-waiting area, and beyond that was a separate set of stairs down on to the South Staffordshire bay section of platform 1. Part of the left-hand entrance area was closed off to form a telephone enquiry bureau, which backed onto the south booking office; this left just a narrow passage through from the left-hand arch of the colonnade. The stairs to the platform were little used in later years, partly because many people probably did not know they were there. There had been a similar arrangement to the right of the booking hall, with stairs to the Stour Valley bays, but this area was closed off when the enquiry office was built.

Moving across the station, the north booking office was adjacent to the footbridge at platform level, by the Queen's Drive entrance to platform 3 (see page 17, Volume 2); this again sold tickets for ex-LNW destinations.

On the other side of Queen's Drive, at footbridge level, were the former LNW and Midland 'bridge' booking offices. The LNW office had closed shortly after the grouping, but the Midland bridge office (on the right) continued in use, but still only sold tickets for ex-Midland destinations. Below it (and connected to it by internal stairs) was the No. 4 platform booking office, which catered for passengers going to platform 4 from Queen's Drive. Again, it sold tickets for Midland destinations, and was also known as the 'west booking office'; in LMS and BR days, it was generally only open at busy times.

At the far(south) side of the station, at the entrance from Station Street (and beneath the footbridge) was the 'Station Street' booking office, serving people entering the station from the south side (see page 14, Volume 2).

Only one of the booking offices was open continuously; this was the 'Midland bridge' office, and during the periods when it was the only office open, it would sell tickets for all destinations. The other offices closed during the night, and also in some of the quiet periods (they were normally open between about 6 a.m. and 10 p.m.).

The southbound 'Devonian' standing at Platform 6 in the summer of 1936 while the kitchen car water tanks were replenished from a hand-pumped bowser. A similar bowser (or possibly the same one) appears on Platform 2 in the photograph on page 50 of Volume 2, which was taken in 1924. The train was due to stand at New Street from 1.33 to 1.39 and ran from Leeds and Bradford to Torquay and Paignton. It carried restaurant cars from Bradford to Bristol and a through carriage from Newcastle to Bristol. ***LMS Magazine***

Midland double-framed 2–4–0 No. 20002 standing at the east end of up Platform 5 adjacent to No. 2 signal cabin on 18th June 1935. The bracket signal controlled departure from the up Platform 5 (No. 4 up line), the left-hand doll applying to movements to the LNW south tunnel and the right-hand doll to movements to the Midland south tunnel. The Midland parcels office buildings and parcels dock (Parcels Office or Market Hall Siding) can be seen behind the signal. Note the rolled-up cab storm or weather sheet on this engine and the one in the lower picture opposite.

M. F. Yarwood

Former London Tilbury & Southend Railway 4–4–2 tank No. 2109 alongside Platform 6 with a local train, probably destined for Redditch, on Thursday, 20th June 1935. These engines were displaced from their parent system by newly-built 2–6–4 tanks. The first coach appears to have been an ex-Glasgow & South Western Railway all third, while the next two coaches were LMS types. The underside of the overhanging top structure of No. 4 signal cabin features in the top left corner. Note the clock on the buildings above the footbridge and the gas lighting to the platform.
M. F. Yarwood

Midland 2–4–0, LMS No. 195, at the east end of up Platform 5 adjacent to No. 2 signal cabin. Note the letter 'S' for 'shunt ahead' on the subsidiary signal arm on the signal bracket. The two miniature (disc) signals by the footboarding controlled exit from the short 'Parlour Siding' between the platforms. The picture was taken on Friday, 25th August 1933.
M. F. Yarwood

A year and a half after nationalisation, very little had changed from LMS days. This picture shows LMS 4P Compound 4–4–0 No. 935 of Bristol shed standing in the old Platform 5 (renumbered 9 in 1946) with the 2.0 p.m. stopping train to Worcester (due there at 3.8 p.m.) on Monday, 27th June 1949. The engine's LMS number had been prefixed by a letter 'M' on the cab side sheet, indicating it belonged to the London Midland Region. The tender had been repainted to incorporate the title of its new owner, but the carriages and the engine (2P 4–4–0 No. 511, probably acting as west pilot) in the adjacent platform, still displayed 'LMS'. The effects of wartime neglect and bomb damage are very evident in the station roof.

Former London Tilbury & Southend Railway 4–4–2T No. 2106 of Bournville shed, in Bay 6 at the west end of New Street, with the 5.20 p.m. train to Redditch on Tuesday, 20th October 1936. With the reductions of passenger services after the commencement of the Great War, use of the bay platforms at New Street declined and their use for passenger services was largely limited to busy periods. *L. E. Copeland*

An interloper on the Midland side of New Street, this view shows LNW 'Cauliflower' 0–6–0 No. 28619, from Monument Lane shed, in the Fish Dock sidings at the west end of the Midland side of the station on LNW side north shunt duties on 21st May 1948. No doubt it had crossed over to transfer some vehicles from one side of the station to the other. *H. C. Casserley*

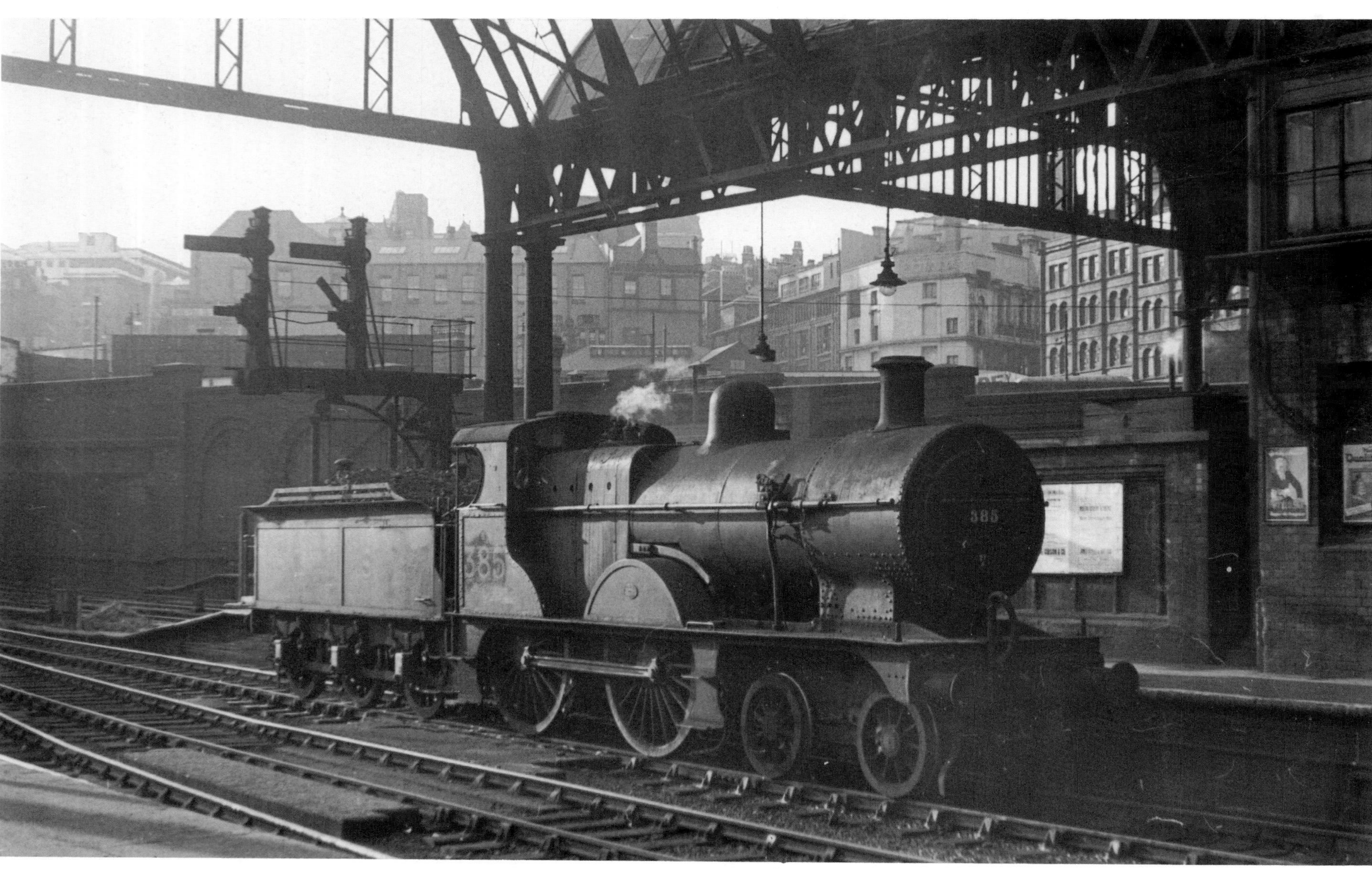

Midland 2P 4–4–0 No. 385 at the west end of Platform 9 (No. 3 down line and formerly No. 5 down platform) on 21st May 1948. The shunt ahead signal was off for the engine to proceed towards No. 5 signal cabin on the No. 1 down line. The original LNW lower quadrant arms on this bracket signal had been renewed by upper quadrant arms. The corner of No. 4 signal cabin is visible on the right.

H. C. Casserley

Midland 2P No. 512 pulling out of the west end of the centre road (No. 4 siding) between the old Platforms 5 and 6 (Nos. 9 and 10 from 1946) with sunlight shafting down through the damaged station roof on 15th August 1949. The engine was probably on west pilot duties. *E. S. Russell*

Ex-LMS 4P Compound 4–4–0s 41035 and M935 (again) double-heading a westbound Midland train at the west end of Platform 9 (formerly No. 5) on Wednesday, 4th May 1949. The first two compartments of the coach were labelled for 'Smoking', the opposite of present day practice when no-smoking areas are labelled. Behind the engines, Queen's Drive can be seen rising to join Hill Street and, in front, Hill Street bridge. Note the advertising hoarding above. No. 5 signal cabin beyond the bridge was reconstructed, as seen here, in all-timber form following extensive bomb damage in 1940. At the time this photograph was taken, a fair amount of the lower timber facing was missing from the front of the cabin. This was no doubt to facilitate work on preparing for the renewal of the lever frame. The new frame was brought into use the following month.
H. C. Casserley

ing New Street, and all the proposals fell by the wayside. New Street entered a second period of war, older, but otherwise hardly changed.

The Second World War brought with it a new problem — bombing. Birmingham was the target for extensive raids, and the local papers reported that it was (along with Liverpool and Birkenhead) one of the most heavily-bombed city areas in Britain, outside London. The first bombs fell in Erdington on 9th August 1940, and during the following two years there was a total of 367 air raid alerts, with 2,241 people killed and 140,336 houses damaged; the last raid took place on 31st July 1942. New Street station suffered, too, and the overall roofs on both sides were hit on a number of occasions, as was the hotel, but the worst damage occurred in the autumn of 1940 when there were regular raids on the city.

The first damage — and from the point of view of traffic working, probably the most serious — occurred on the night of 16th/17th October 1940, when No. 5 signal cabin was almost completely destroyed, the blast also shattering many of the windows in Victoria Square post office. The LNW side of the station was closed for 24 hours on Saturday, 26th October 1940 while debris was cleared, after high-explosive bombs fell on that part of the station. The Western District Control Office, then housed on the top floor of the buildings on the Midland side, alongside platform 6, was almost destroyed on 28th October 1940; the control staff had to spend the next year in the cramped emergency control office. No. 4 cabin suffered serious damage on 19th November, along with the roof above it. In the same raid, the Queens Hotel lost most of its windows, and the Malt Shovel public house (near the end of Queens Drive), which was a favourite haunt of a number of the station staff, was destroyed. The whole station had to be closed on the following day, Wednesday, 20th November, when a delayed-action bomb fell near No. 3 gate on Queens Drive. After a long wait, it was decided that all was safe, and the station was reopened at 4 p.m. Sixteen months later, on 13th March 1942, the bomb was dug up and found to be intact and complete with fuse! This time it was defused properly.

After the end of November 1940, there was something of a respite in the bomb-

This picture shows LMS Compound No. 1155 after it had just passed under Hill Street bridge on the connection from Platform 2 and 3 to the down Wolverhampton (Stour) line. The 4F 0–6–0 behind and under Navigation Street was shunting carriages from the up Back Line into Platform 2, whilst the LNW coal tank on the right was standing on the down Back Line. The big sign on the right advertised the Birmingham Garages. *P. B. Whitehouse*

Midland Johnson rebuild of Kirtley double-framed 2–4–0 No. 20002 rolling into the Midland side of the station in June 1935. The train had just come through the West Suburban line tunnels and probably originated from Redditch or Worcester. The ex-LNW tank on the down Back Line near No. 2 platform was on north shunt duty.
M. F. Yarwood

ing until the spring of 1941. The area around New Street was heavily bombed on Thursday, 10th April 1941, and the South and West Suburban tunnels had to be closed while debris was cleared, with the necessary checks made to ensure that the structures were safe. The South tunnels were closed for four days, while it was eight days before the West Suburban tunnels could be reopened. This was the last of the serious bombing which affected New Street station, and the only other incident of note occurred on Tuesday, 28th July 1942, when large numbers of incendiaries were dropped on both New Street and Curzon Street. Much property around the station was destroyed in the various raids, too — most particularly the Market Hall, which was left as a roofless shell.

The destruction of New Street No. 5 signal cabin on the night of 16th October 1940 illustrates both the difficulties which beset railway working in wartime, and the swiftness with which problems could be overcome when resolve and resources were directed to the task. The cabin, which was 80ft 4½in long and 12 feet wide, with a brick base 8ft high surmounted by a timber superstructure, was almost completely destroyed by a direct hit from a high-explosive bomb at about 8 p.m. The cabin also had a basement 7ft 3in below ground level to accommodate part of the interlocking (see Volume 4), and was equipped with a 152-lever (144 levers when built) LNW Webb Tumbler frame. The blast destroyed most of the brickwork of the cabin base, and damaged the timber superstructure beyond repair. About 40 levers in the frame, the instrument shelf, block instruments, telephones, batteries, relays and other equipment were totally destroyed.

The first priority was to get the running lines cleared, and institute some means of traffic control while the cabin was repaired. The following day, complete possession of the running lines was arranged, and a total of 40 wagon loads of debris were cleared up and removed. At the same time, the signal lineman's room, near the cabin, was fitted up as a temporary block post by the provision of block instruments and field telephones. For the next few days, trains were controlled from this temporary block post with the signalman directing handsignalmen and pointsmen, who set and locked the points for the appropriate route, and flagged the trains in and out of the station.

It was obviously important to reinstate the cabin as quickly as possible and, in view of the extent of the damage, it was decided to demolish the remaining portion of the brick lower storey, and replace the whole structure in one operation. For just such an eventuality, the LMS had

In 1945 it was decided to take down Cowper's great roof over the LNW side of the station. This view shows the station in 1945 just after work had commenced on taking out the centre lantern light and ventilating section. The resignalling and installation of track circuits that would enable No. 3 signal cabin to be closed had not yet been undertaken. All this time the semaphore signals remained and a makeshift roof had been erected over the cabin's lever frames to protect the signalman from the weather. At the beginning of the war, the glass in the roof was covered with a layer of hessian and tar with the twin objects of avoiding injury from flying glass during air raids and of preventing light from the station being seen by enemy aircraft. This inevitably made the platform area rather dark. The covering was still in place when this photograph was taken. Note the piles of parcels and mail bags stacked along the platforms and all the bicycles in the foreground. ***British Railways***

built a number of 'emergency' standard LMS design wooden signal cabins, which were kept in kit form at various stores, strategically located around the system. It was decided that two of the 43ft 3in-long emergency cabins would best suit the requirements; one was sent from St. Helens, and the other from Stafford. They were loaded up on the 17th (while the debris was being cleared at New Street), and one arrived on site later in the day, the second by special train during the following morning. Some alterations had to be made to the standard LMS components (which came in 10ft long panels) to suit the actual height and length of the box, while the floor was adapted to suit the LNW frame. At the same time, 40 new LNW levers were obtained (also from emergency stores) to replace those which had been destroyed.

The signal cabin construction gang was drafted in from Crewe, and commenced by repairing and altering the brickwork of the cellar (or locking pit) ready to accommodate the cabin superstructure. A start was made on 20th October with the task of erecting the first half of the cabin, which was completed two days later. The roof was temporarily sheeted to keep out the weather. Work on the second half began on 23rd October, the superstructure being progressively extended until, on the 26th, the last section was put in place. The following day saw completion of the floor, installation of the window sashes and gas lighting, and temporary weather sheeting of the roof.

Meanwhile, the fitters had stripped down the locking on the lever frame, inserted the new levers, and repaired the damage to the frame. With the cabin structure in a usable condition, work began on connecting the levers up to the points and signals, initially without locking. At the same time, the telegraph staff refixed the block instruments and telephones. By 27th October, work was sufficiently far advanced for the signalman to return to the cabin, which reopened at 6 p.m. that day, the temporary block post then being dispensed with. Although the cabin was operational again, just 11 days after the bombing, it took a little longer to complete full restoration of normality. The reinstatement of the interlocking was completed at 1 p.m. on 7th November, while the permanent slating of the roof was finished on 10th November.

Wartime traffic brought new pressures on the railway system. While the Derby & Birmingham line was already an important freight route, the Midland line to the south of Birmingham (towards Gloucester and Bristol) had been relatively lightly used. The establishment by the Government of various depots and factories in the West and South West of England, coupled with the greater use made of South Wales and Bristol Channel ports, resulted in a considerable increase in freight traffic (particularly coal) passing over the Midland route. The capacity of the heavily-graded section of line between Saltley and King's Norton was clearly important in determining the ability of the route as a whole to accommodate the increased traffic. The need to create additional capacity to handle the extra freight traffic was therefore the principal reason behind the withdrawal of the passenger services on the Camp Hill line in January 1941.

The connecting line between Bordesley Junction, on the Camp Hill line, and Bordesley GW was one of the few places where direct exchange of goods traffic between the former Midland Railway and the Great Western was possible. It had therefore long been an important traffic exchange point, and in 1922 there were twenty scheduled trip workings daily each way between Washwood Heath and Bordesley. If anything, the quantity of traffic being exchanged increased during LMS days. Something of the volume of traffic involved can be judged from the fact that, in a typical week during June 1938, just over 3,500 wagons were handed over by the LMS to the GW, and a similar number received. This volume of traffic was already straining the capacity of the connecting line, which was only single track.

Wartime traffic needs increased the importance of the connecting link still further, with a significant volume of military traffic to and from service installations and the south coast. In addition, Bordesley offered an emergency alternative route for exchange traffic between the Midland Division and the Southern Railway, avoiding the London area. Authority was therefore obtained to double the branch, and build a new signalbox at Bordesley Junction. The signalbox, which was of the LMS 'ARP' blast-proof design, opened on 6th April 1941, and the double-track curve on 13th July, the work costing £22,000. By this time, traffic had increased by some 60% compared with 1938; in the last week of June 1941, just before the double line opened, over 5,900 wagons each way were exchanged at Bordesley.

Bordesley continued to be an important interchange point for freight traffic until the end of traditional goods working in the 1960s. The importance of this postwar transfer can be judged from the fact that, in 1954, trips between Washwood Heath and Bordesley ran at approximately hourly intervals in each direction throughout the 24 hours.

During the war, to achieve the twin objects of preventing passengers from being injured by flying glass during air raids, and preventing light from the station being seen by enemy aircraft, the glazed areas of the station roof had been covered by hessian matting. This made the station even darker and gloomier than it had been before the war, and a start was made in January 1946 on the task of removing the hessian from those parts of the station roof that were to remain, thus allowing more light into the station. However, it was not until March 1951 that work began on repairing and restoring the station roofs on the Midland side.

The following photographs show progress on the work of removing the overall roof over the LNW side of the station and its replacement by steel and asbestos canopies. The above view, taken across Platforms 4 and 5 (new platform numbers) from Platform 6, shows the steelwork of the travelling gantry which was used in the demolition work. The top of the gantry was decked out in timber and on top of that a scaffold staging was erected to allow access and support the girders while they were cut up and removed. The extent of the scaffold staging is very evident in the photograph overleaf. This photograph indicates very clearly just how narrow the Platforms 4 and 5 island was. The staircase to the footbridge occupied nearly half the width of the platform. The clocks above the poster boards were part of the finger board train departure indicator. *L & GRP*

In 1945, the large roof over the LNW side of the station, now just over 90 years old, was examined. The neglect of the past 30 years, compounded by the damage from the bombs, had all taken their toll; something needed to be done urgently. Unfortunately, much other work needed to be done too, as the railways (and much of industry) were worn out after the years of wartime effort and strain. There were chronic shortages of steel and suitable labour, and in these circumstances the repair of a station roof, albeit an historic one, came low on the list of priorities. Hence, the decision was taken to demolish rather than repair it, and work began on erecting the first section of scaffold staging needed for demolition in October 1945. All the LMS would say about the future was that temporary covers would be put over the platforms pending construction of a new permanent roof.

The work, which cost £100,000, was done in stages, mainly at weekends to minimise disruption to traffic, and took about 2½ years to complete. In place of the awesome roof, low canopies of a relatively cheap, simple and functional design were erected over each platform, with no attempt at embellishment — just crude steelwork. Utility was the order of the day, and the steelwork was obtained from surplus wartime emergency stocks, kept to cover emergencies, and allow bomb damage to be repaired quickly. No. 3 signal cabin was removed, and a corrugated asbestos roof was provided as a covering to the now-exposed portion of the central footbridge and staircases. The only thing on the credit side was the provision of electric lighting throughout on the LNW platforms. Fortunately, the smaller, (and much more recent) spans of roof on the Midland side were thought capable of repair, and survived.

For many years, there had been suggestions that a more sensible system of platform numbering should be adopted at New Street. The old system was certainly confusing to strangers, if not to regular passengers: a train described as departing from platform 1 might refer to something in the main through platform, or in any one of four bays, two at the south end and two at the north end, whilst trains from platforms 2 and 5 could start from either side and/or either end of those long island platforms. The difficulty lay in the fact that each platform, regardless of the number of faces, had one number. At

Looking west from the parcels dock at the end of Platform 6, with part of the steelwork for the new platform canopies in place. Because Platforms 4 and 5 were so narrow, only single columns could be provided to support the canopy. In order to overcome this problem, the roof girders were continued across the tracks to Platform 6 to join the canopy there. Similarly, the girders for the canopies to Platforms 1, 2 and 3 spanned across the bay lines. One of the LNW platform starter bracket signals on the right had been cut down and fitted with short upper quadrant arms at a lower level so that they would be visible under the new canopy. *L & GRP*

last, as part of the initial postwar tidying-up, it was decided to do something about the problem. From Monday, 7th October 1946, a new numbering system was brought into use. Starting on the New Street side of the station, the South Staffordshire bays became platforms 1A and 2A, while the Stour Valley bays became 1B and 2B. The main through face of platform 1 became platform 3, the two faces of island platform 2 became platforms 4 and 5, and the old platform 3 was renumbered platform 6. On the Midland side, platform 4 became No. 7 and the two faces of island platform 5 became platforms 8 and 9. Down platform 6 was renumbered platform 10, and the old No. 6 bay became platform 11. Whilst it no doubt took regular travellers a little time to get used to the new system, the occasional user must have found the new arrangement very much easier to understand.

These were not the only immediate postwar activities to affect New Street. Hill Street and Navigation Street bridges, with their large and complex spans, were life-expired; indeed, by 1943, Hill Street had deteriorated into such a state that, despite wartime conditions, it was decided to put the replacement work in hand

Platform 3, looking west, showing the clutter of parcels trolleys, etc, on the platform and the steelwork for the new canopy taking shape. The new colour light signal at the centre of this platform is clearly visible below the footbridge, as is the diamond Rule 55 sign associated with the down direction signal on No. 4 platform. These photographs were taken on 1st January 1947 to record demolition of the last two trusses of the old roof. *L & GRP*

Work in progress in 1947 on erecting the new canopy to the west end of Platforms 2A and 3. The steelwork was obtained from the surplus stock of ARP steel stock held during the war to enable emergency repair or reconstruction of bomb damage to be effected quickly. The roof covering itself was corrugated asbestos sheets. Since the canopies were supposed to be temporary, pending the construction of a new permanent roof, no attempt at embellishment or aesthetics was made. Needless to say, nothing further was heard about the permanent roof, and the austere canopies remained in use until the station was rebuilt in the 1960s. ***Real Photographs***

As the first stage, a temporary bridge was built to allow work on Hill Street bridge to be started. It was, however, found to be unsafe for traffic to use the temporary bridge in the blackout, and despite the seriousness of the problem, work had to be suspended. It was eventually restarted in 1947, and the temporary bridge was at last brought into use on 28th February 1949, whilst the permanent bridge was completed about two years later.

As the end of the war approached, the LMS Signal Department began to consider the resurrection of some of the resignalling schemes which had had to be postponed in 1939. It was clear that shortages of money and resources (both men and materials) would prevent any extensive works being undertaken for an appreciable period after the end of hostilities. It was now a question of doing the work piecemeal, as and when the opportunity presented itself — usually as part of other essential works. The signal engineers therefore looked at how their hoped-for resignalling could be implemented in small stages, when the occasions arose, and adapted the scheme accordingly.

The first opportunity to make any real improvement came with the decision to take down the great roof. Clearly, No. 3 cabin could not be left as it was; with its open platform and level frames, it would be far too exposed to the weather. The installation of track circuiting, colour lights and electrical controls would make it possible to work the station area from the adjacent cabins (Nos. 1 and 5), allowing No. 3 to be closed. This would save the cost of replacing No. 3, and effect savings in manpower. The resignalling of the LNW side of the station area and the abolition of No. 3 cabin was therefore approved as part of the scheme to remove the great roof.

The crossovers between Nos. 1 and 2 sidings and the adjacent platform lines were taken out, and the semaphore signals at the centre of platforms 3, 4, 5 and 6 (new numbers) were replaced by two-aspect (red/yellow) colour lights; these were controlled by Nos. 1 and 5 cabins, as appropriate, as starting signals. Platform lines were track circuited, both to control the new signals and to give the signalmen a positive indication of the presence of trains and vehicles. The signals were provided with subsidiary aspects to allow a second train to enter an occupied platform, whilst control levers were provided in the two cabins for the bi-directional working on the up and down platform 4 line. The principal stage of the work was undertaken on Sunday, 13th October 1946, when the track circuits were brought into use, and No. 3 cabin was abolished. This cabin, complete with its distinctive clocks, was removed over the following couple of weeks.

The opportunity was taken as part of the scheme to install colour light signals and track circuits on the approaches to the station through the tunnel on the down LNW line at No. 1 cabin, and a new track circuit and colour light signal near No. 5 cabin on the up Wolverhampton line. This additional work allowed full use to be made of the potential of the track circuits in the platforms by introducing full control over the aspects displayed by the home signals, though it was not completed until May 1947. Economy was, however, an important consideration, and no work was undertaken on the Midland side of the station or on the Midland approaches to the station (these had to wait until 1952).

In the LNW side of the station it was decided not to convert the platform starting signals to colour lights. The majority, however, would not fit (nor would they be visible to drivers) under the new verandahs, and thus had to be altered. The elegant LNW timber signals, which of course had been designed for the lofty space of the old roof, were therefore cut down and fitted with new dolls and short arms (with intensified lights), so that they could be seen under the canopies. The resultant configurations were somewhat ugly and utilitarian.

As a final LMS promise of better things to come, it was announced at the company's shareholders' meeting in March 1946 that New Street was one of the stations the company intended to rebuild when normality returned.

BIRMINGHAM NEW STREET
DEPARTURES BETWEEN 4.30 P.M. AND 6.30 P.M. JULY 1890

Time	*Company*	*Departure*
4.35	MID	(1.15 slow from Bristol arr. 4.25), Saltley, Castle Bromwich, Kingsbury, Tamworth, Burton, Repton and Derby.
4.40	MID	Saltley, Water Orton, Nuneaton, Hinckley and Leicester.
4.40	MID	All stations via Five Ways to Kings Norton.
4.45	LNW	Stechford, Hampton, Kenilworth, Warwick and Leamington (direct).
4.45	LNW	Dudley Port, Wolverhampton, Penkridge, Stafford.
5.0	MID	All stations via Camp Hill to Kings Norton.
5.0	MID	(3.45 from Derby arr. 4.50) Bromsgrove, Droitwich, Worcester, Ashchurch, Cheltenham, Gloucester, Mangotsfield and Bristol.
5.5	MID	All stations except Bentley via Sutton Park and Walsall to Wolverhampton.
5.5	LNW	All stations via Dudley Port to Wolverhampton.
5.10	LNW	All stations to Leamington via Coventry.
5.15	LNW	All stations to Harborne.
5.15	LNW	All stations to Sutton Coldfield.
5.15	MID	Kings Norton and all stations via Redditch to Ashchurch.
5.18	MID	All stations via Camp Hill to Kings Norton.
5.25	LNW	Soho Road, Bescot and Walsall.
5.30	LNW	Kenilworth, Warwick, Leamington and stations via Marton to Rugby.
5.30	LNW	Smethwick, Dudley Port and Wolverhampton.
5.40	LNW	All stations to Walsall via Aston.
5.40	MID	Kings Norton and all stations to Cheltenham (picks up only at Church Road and Selly Oak).
5.45	MID	All stations via Five Ways to Kings Norton.
5.45	MID	(3.15 from Bristol) Burton and Derby, through coaches Bristol to Manchester (Cen), Liverpool (Cen), Sheffield, Leeds and Bradford.
5.50	LNW	Wolverhampton, express to Liverpool and Manchester.
5.55	LNW	All stations to Harborne.
5.55	MID	All stations to Nuneaton.
6.0	LNW	Sutton Coldfield, Four Oaks, Shenstone and Lichfield.
6.2	MID	All stations via Camp Hill to Kings Norton.
6.5	LNW	All stations via Dudley Port to Wolverhampton.
6.10	LNW	Stechford, Marston Green, Berkswell, Coventry, Brandon, Rugby and stations to Bletchley.
6.15	LNW	All stations to Sutton Coldfield.
6.20	LNW	All stations to Harborne.
6.20	MID	All stations via Sutton Park to Walsall.
6.25	MID	All stations via Five Ways to Kings Norton.
6.25	LNW	All stations via Aston and Bescot to Walsall and Wolverhampton.

BIRMINGHAM NEW STREET
DEPARTURES BETWEEN 4.30 P.M. AND 6.30 P.M. APRIL 1910

Time	*Company*	*Departure*
4.35	LNW	(2.30 from Euston, arr. 4.30) Wolverhampton.
4.40	LNW	Stechford, Hampton, Kenilworth, Warwick and Leamington (direct).
4.40	LNW	Monument Lane, Soho Road, Handsworth Wood, Walsall.
4.40	MID	Stations via Camp Hill to Kings Norton.
4.50	MID	Barnt Green, Blackwell, Bromsgrove, Droitwich, Worcester and stations to Great Malvern.
4.50	MID	(3.49 from Worcester, arr. 4.42) stations to Derby (except Branston and Pear Tree).
4.50	LNW	Stations to Harborne.
4.50	LNW	Sutton Coldfield and stations to Lichfield.
4.55	LNW	Smethwick, Dudley Port, Wolverhampton and Macclesfield.
5.0	LNW	(4.27 from Wolverhampton arr. 4.52) Euston (arr. 7.0) Tea Cars, carriage for Northampton (arr. 6.8) slipped at Blisworth.
5.0	MID	Kings Norton and stations to Redditch.
5.5	LNW	All stations to Wolverhampton.
5.5	LNW	Gravelly Hill and stations to Four Oaks.
5.6	MID	Stations via Camp Hill to Kings Norton.
5.10	MID	Stations to Nuneaton, Elmesthorpe, Hinckley and Leicester.
5.10	LNW	Stations to Hampton.
5.15	LNW	Stations to Harborne.
5.15	MID	Barnt Green and stations to Worcester and Hereford.
5.20	MID	Stations via Five Ways to Kings Norton.
5.20	LNW	Stations to Four Oaks.
5.20	LNW	Walsall (via Monument Lane).
5.25	LNW	Vauxhall and stations via Soho Road to Monument Lane.
5.30	LNW	Berkswell, Coventry, Brandon and Rugby.
5.30	LNW	Smethwick, Dudley Port and Wolverhampton.
5.30	MID	Stations via Sutton Park to Walsall (connection there via LNW train to Wolverhampton via Midland line).
5.33	MID	Stations via Camp Hill, Lifford and Five Ways to New Street.
5.35	LNW	Stations to Harborne.
5.37	LNW	Stations to Sutton Coldfield.
5.40	LNW	Monument Lane, Soho Road, Handsworth Wood, Bescot and Walsall.
5.40	LNW	Kenilworth, Warwick and Leamington (direct).
5.40	MID	(9.30 from Edinburgh, 9.20 from Glasgow and Bradford, Leeds and Newcastle, express arr. 5.35) Ashchurch, Cheltenham, Gloucester, Mangotsfield and Bristol (arr. 8.0).
5.43	LNW	Stations via Coventry to Leamington.
5.45	MID	(3.25 from Bristol). Through carriages to Manchester (Central), Halifax, Heysham and York. Also Bournemouth to York and Southampton to Derby), Tamworth, Burton, Derby, etc.
5.50	MID	Selly Oak, Bournville, Kings Norton and stations to Gloucester via Worcester, connection at Barnt Green for Redditch.
5.50	LNW	Wolverhampton, etc. to Liverpool and Manchester.
5.50	LNW	Stations via Vauxhall to Walsall.
5.55	MID	Stations to Tamworth and Nuneaton.
6.0	MID	Stations via Camp Hill to Kings Norton.
6.0	LNW	Rotton Park Road, Hagley Road and Harborne.
6.0	LNW	Sutton Coldfield and stations to Lichfield.
6.5	LNW	Adderley Park and Stechford.
6.5	LNW	Monument Lane and stations via Soho Road and Vauxhall to New Street.
6.10	LNW	Stations to Wolverhampton.
6.15	LNW	Stations to Harborne.
6.15	LNW	Gravelly Hill and stations to Sutton Coldfield.
6.18	MID	Stations via Camp Hill, Lifford and Five Ways to New Street.
6.20	MID	Stations via Five Ways, Lifford and Camp Hill to New Street.
6.20	LNW	(5.45 from Wolverhampton, arr. 6.11) Euston (arr. 8.20) dining car express.
6.25	LNW	Stations via Vauxhall to Walsall.
6.30	LNW	Hampton-in-Arden, Berkswell, Kenilworth, Warwick and Leamington (direct).
6.30	MID	Stations via Sutton Park to Walsall.

TRAINS STARTING AT MONUMENT LANE

5.5	LNW	Stations to Dudley.

TRAINS STARTING AT VAUXHALL

4.55	LNW	Stations to Four Oaks.
6.10	LNW	Stations to Four Oaks.
6.25	LNW	Stations to Four Oaks.

CHAPTER THREE

LOCAL PASSENGER SERVICES

THIS chapter looks in detail at the development of local passenger train services up to the 1960s, and adds to the brief review given in Volume Two. The changes to individual services are discussed on a route-by-route basis rather than chronologically, since this makes the process of development easier to follow. Express passenger services are described in Volume Four.

In the early days of railways, demand for travel was small. Most of the population (which in any event was far smaller than today) had little need to travel any distance, even on an occasional basis. Their lives and work were conducted within a fairly short distance of home, and most of their needs could be met within walking distance. There were no holidays with pay; indeed, for most working people, there were no holidays other than the occasional special day (such as feast days and bank holidays). Although rail fares were substantially less than the equivalent stage coach rates, they were still expensive — much higher in real terms than today. Trips by rail were limited to the wealthy, or to business and special occasions. Rail services reflected the resultant small demand, and were initially infrequent.

The railways did create new opportunities for travel which had not existed before. A combination of many factors brought about a steadily increasing demand for rail travel, and a few of these can be summarised here. Rail fares fell gradually in real terms throughout the Victorian period and through to the Great War, bringing travel within more people's reach. The prosperity of the country rose steadily, and there was a significant increase in the number of people within the relatively well-off middle class, who had more occasions and opportunities to travel.

The availability of transport enabled business to exploit new markets, and this in turn increased demand for business travel. Produce could be taken by train into the towns and cities, where better prices might be obtained and larger quantities sold; prior to the development of railways, the size of towns and cities was to a degree limited by the amount of food that could be brought in at reasonable prices. Land transport was too expensive and slow to be feasible over more than a few miles; rail transport changed all this, and made it possible for the rapid growth of urban areas. Slowly but steadily, train services improved to meet the increasing demand, as is evidenced by the tables accompanying this chapter (and in Volumes Two and Four).

In terms of development, Birmingham's local train services all generally followed the same pattern. There was a steady increase in frequency throughout the Victorian and Edwardian eras, with most services reaching a peak immediately before the outbreak of war in 1914. The Great War brought the growth to an abrupt end as the country turned its attention to the war, and the railway's priorities moved to the carriage of materials and men essential to the war effort. As a consequence, passenger services were curtailed; the reductions were small at first, but severe cuts were made in January 1917.

As described in Chapter 1, the war had a detrimental impact on Britain's manufacturing industry and prosperity, and with the country functioning at a lower economic level after the war than it had before, it was inevitable that the train services should reflect the change. Although there were improvements from 1919 onwards, most lines had somewhat fewer trains in 1922 than they had before the outbreak of war.

Despite the difficulties of the 1920s and 30s, as the years progressed, the LMS slowly managed to improve services on most lines, although there were exceptions. Even with the LMS improvements, the number of trains in 1938/9 generally remained a little below the numbers offered in 1910/14. The slow recovery in services was again abruptly brought to a halt with the outbreak of the Second World War.

Serious preparations for war had been under way since 1938. New emergency timetables offering drastically reduced services had been compiled and printed ready for issue in the event of war, and thus, in August 1939, the LMS had three sets of timetables to hand. The summer timetable was currently in use, and was due to expire on 24th September, whilst in the store cupboards and ready for issue were two other timetables: the 'peacetime' winter timetable for the period 25th September 1939 to 28th April 1940, and an undated 'emergency' timetable, ready for issue should everyone's worst fears be realised, and war be declared.

The peace efforts failed, and when war was declared on Sunday, 3rd September, the LMS immediately put in hand the emergency arrangements which had been carefully prepared over the preceding months. The summer timetable was cut short, and the 'emergency' timetables were brought into force on 11th September, the first practical Monday after the declaration of hostilities. The impact on passenger services was immediate and dramatic, with considerable reductions in the numbers of trains provided. Inevitably, the reductions varied significantly from line to line, with some services suffering relatively minor reductions, while others were reduced to skeletal levels. Something of the scale of the reductions can be judged from the fact that the unissued Midland Division winter 1939/40 passenger working timetable ran to 296 pages, while the 'emergency' timetable occupied just 163 pages.

The 'emergency' timetable was intended to reduce services to the minimum, commensurate with maintaining the essential activities of the country. It was designed to allow for the possibilities of serious dislocation through bombing, and to permit large numbers of extra trains to be run for military purposes and for evacuation of the great cities.

Once the initial objects had been achieved (and the feared bombing had not materialised), a new and slightly more generous timetable was brought into use on 25th September — the scheduled date for introduction of the winter timetable. This saw the reinstatement of some services and facilities, including a few of the dining cars, and further trains were restored over the following few weeks. Generally, the winter 1939 passenger services approximated to the levels which operated in the latter part of the Great War.

Nevertheless, further cuts were made in February 1941, mainly to local trains, and services stayed at the lower levels for the remainder of the war, and in most cases for a considerable period afterwards. The 1941 services (after the February cuts) shown in the accompanying tables illustrate the impact of the war on services in the Birmingham area. In a few cases, services were withdrawn altogether (such as that for passengers on the Camp Hill line), and in due course some stations were closed, including those at Five Ways and Soho Road.

For those local passenger services which did survive the Second World War, the 1950s and 1960s were a period of uncertainty and inconsistency. Most ser-

ARRIVALS AND DEPARTURES SEPTEMBER 1949

UP TRAINS—Weekdays

Train.	FROM	TO	Reporting No	Birmingham. Arr.	Birmingham. Dep.	Platform No.	REMARKS.
a.m. 4 0	Birmingham	Lowestoft	318	p.m. 3‡45	p.m. 4 0	3	(1) Lowestoft, (2) Yarmouth. Stops at Coventry, Rugby, Welford & K., Market Harboro', Rockingham, Seaton Jn., Kings Cliffe, Wansford, Peterboro,' Whittlesea, March, Brandon, Thetford, Attleborough, Wymondham, Norwich Thorpe then all stations. ‡—Mon. Lane.
4 5	Birmingham	Coventry	—	...	4 5	2	Calls at all stations.
2 20	Ashchurch	Birmingham	—	4 10	...	7	Forms 4‡15 p.m. Saltley (SX), 5.35 p.m. Walsall (SO).
12 15	Blackpool (N.)	Birmingham	264§	4 10	4‡23	3	(SO). ‡—To Vauxhall.
12	Birmingham	Burton	—	...	4 12	4	(Via Aston and Walsall.) Calls at all stations.
4‡15	Birmingham	Saltley	—	...	4‡15	7	(SX). Off 2.20 p.m. from Ashchurch.
4 18	Birmingham	Lichfield (C.)	—	...	4 18	1	(SO). Calls at all stations.
2 15	Bristol	York	276	4 28	4 35	7	Calls at Tamworth, Burton, Derby, Chesterfield, Sheffield, Rotherham and Pontefract.
4 5	Wolverham'ton	Euston	104 §	4 34	4 40	3	(SX). Euston only.
4 5	Wolverham'ton	Euston	108 §	4 37	5 0	4	(SO). Calls at Coventry, Rugby Northampton and Watford.
4 45	Birmingham	Cleethorpes	—	...	4 45	8	Stops at Nuneaton, Hinckley, Leicester, Loughboro,' Trent, Beeston, Nottingham, Rolleston Jn., Newark, Collingham, Lincoln, Market Rasen, Barnetby, Habrough, Grimsby Town and Docks.
4 48	Birmingham	Lichfield (C.)	—	...	4 48	1	(SX). (Via Sutton Coldfield.) Calls at all stations.
a.m. 9 30	Glasgow	Birmingham	98 §	4†50	5‡ 3	3	‡—To Vauxhall. †—P.B. 4.55p.m.
p.m. 5 0	Birmingham	Euston	108§	4‡54	5 0	4	(SX). Calls at Coventry, Rugby, Northampton and Watford. ‡—From Mon. Lane.
5 8	Birmingham	Leamington Spa	—	4‡59	5 8	4	(SX). Calls at Stechford, Marston Green, Hampton, Berkswell, Kenilworth and Warwick. ‡—From Monument Lane.
4 47	King's Norton	Leicester	—	5 4	5 10	7	Stops at all stations. Also conveys set for 5.35 p.m. Walsall (SX).
5 0	Mon. Lane	Lichfield (C.)	—	5 5	5 15	4	(SX). (Via Sutton Coldfield.) Calls at Wylde Green then all stations.
5 15	Birmingham	Derby	—	4‡55	5 15	8	Calls at all stations (except Coleshill, Whitacre, Elford, and Barton & W). ‡—From Kings Norton.
5 23	Birmingham	Rugby	—	...	5 23	2	Calls at all stations.
5‡21	Mon. Lane	Birmingham	—	5‡26	...	3	(SX). Forms 5.40 p.m. to Four Oaks.
5 26	Birmingham	Lichfield (C.)	—	5‡17	5 26	4	Calls at all stations. ‡—From Monument Lane (SX).
5 35	Birmingham	Walsall	—	...	5 35	7	(Via Streetly). Calls at all stations.
5 40	Birmingham	Four Oaks	—	...	5 40	3	(SX). Stops at all stations.
4 25	Worcester	Derby	—	5 40	5 50	7	Stops at Saltley, Castle Bromwich. Whitacre, Kingsbury, Wilnecote, Tamworth, Elford and Burton.
5‡37	Mon. Lane	Birmingham	—	5‡42	...	4	Forms 6.0 p.m. to Burton.
5 50	Birmingham	Coventry	—	...	5 50	2	Calls at all stations.
3 0	Manchester	Birmingham	236 §	5†52	...	3	Empty stock to Vauxhall at 6.12 p.m. †—P.B. 5.55 p.m.
5‡52	Mon. Lane	Birmingham	—	5‡57	...	4	Forms 6.7 p.m. to Rugeley (T.V.)
5‡45	Kings Norton	Birmingham	—	6‡ 0	...	7	(SO). Forms 6.10 p.m Leicester.
6 0	Birmingham	Burton	—	...	6 0	4	(Via Sutton Coldfield). Calls at all stations.
5 40	Longbridge	Birmingham	—	6 1	...	7	(SX). **Not advertised.** Forms 6.10 p.m. Leicester (SX).
6 7	Birmingham	Rugeley (T.V.)	—	...	6 7	4	(Via Aston and Walsall). Calls at all stations.
6 10	Birmingham	Leicester	—	...	6 10	7	Calls at all stations to Hinckley, then Leicester.
6‡12	Birmingham	Vauxhall	—	...	6‡12	3	Off 3.0 p.m. from Manchester.
5‡58	King's Norton	Birmingham	—	6‡15	...	8	(SX). Forms 6.40 p.m. to Walsall (SX).
5 30	Wolverham'ton	Birmingham	—	6 19	...	4	Forms 7.10 p.m. Rugeley.
6 24	Birmingham	Derby	—	...	6 24	8	(SX). Calls at all stations (except Coleshill, Elford, Barton & W., and Pear Tree & N.).
4 30 (SO) / 4 17 FSX	Stoke / Newcastle	Birmingham	—	6†28	...	3	(FX). Forms 7.0 p.m. Coventry. †—P.B. 6.30 p.m.
6 28	Birmingham (Via Leamington)	Rugby	—	6‡13	6 28	3	Stops at Stechford, Marston Green, Hampton - in - Arden, Tile Hill, Canley Halt, Coventry, Kenilworth, Warwick Leamington, Marton and Birdingbury. ‡—From Monument Lane.
4 17	Newcastle	Birmingham	—	6†29	...	3	(FO). Forms 7.0 p.m. Coventry. †—P.B. 6.30.
6 15	Birmingham (Cen.)	Birmingham	—	6 30	...	3 Siding	(SO). Parcels.
6 33	Birmingham	Rugeley (T.V.)	—	...	6 33	2	(SX). (Via Aston). Stops at all stations (except Brindley Heath)
6 33	Birmingham	Walsall	—	...	6 33	2	(SO) (Via Aston). Stops at all stations.

DOWN TRAINS—Weekdays

Train.	FROM	TO	Reporting No.	Birmingham. Arr.	Birmingham. Dep.	Platform No.	REMARKS.
p.m. 2 0	Stafford (via Rugeley)	Birmingham	—	p.m. 3 51	p.m. ...	5	Forms 5.0 p.m. Stafford.
1 40	Euston	Birmingham	101 §	3 55	4‡11	6	(SO). **"Q."** ‡—To Monument Lane.
12 5	York	Bristol	271	3 56	4 4	9	Stops at Ashchurch, Cheltenham, Gloucester and Mangotsfield.
4 5	Birmingham	Wolverham'ton	—	...	4 5	2A (SO) / 5 (SX)	Calls at all stations.
12 20	Euston	Birmingham	385	4 14	4‡20	5	‡—To Monument Lane.
4 20	Birmingham	Redditch	—	...	4 20	11	Calls at all stations.
4 35	Birmingham	Gloucester	—	4‡15	4 35	9	Stops at King's Norton, then all stations (except Northfield, Fernhill Heath, Cleeve and Churchdown). ‡—From Saltley.
2 48	Leicester	Birmingham	—	4 22	4‡42	10	(SO). ‡—To Kings Norton.
2 15	Euston	Wolverham'ton	103 §	4†34	4 40	5	Calls at Dudley Port. †—P.B. 4.35 p.m.
4‡38	Saltley	Birmingham	—	4‡45	...	10	Forms 5.8 p.m. Ashchurch and 5.32 p.m. Redditch.
4 50	Birmingham	Silverdale	277	4‡28	4 50	6	Stops at Smethwick, Dudley Port, Wolverhampton, Penkridge, Stafford then all stations to Stoke. Newcastle (except Wedgwood Halt). (Stops at Wedgwood Halt (SX). **Not advertised**). ‡—From Vauxhall.
3 20 / 4 15	Rugeley (T.V.) (SO). / Walsall (SX)	Birmingham	—	4 52	...	5	Forms 6.33 p.m. Walsall (SX) and 5.26 p.m. Lichfield via Sutton Coldfield (SO).
5 0	Birmingham	Stafford	—	...	5 0	2A	Calls at all stations.
4 16	Lichfield (C.)	Birmingham	—	5 7	...	5	Forms 5.26 p.m. Lichfield via Walsall.
5 8	Birmingham	Ashchurch	—	...	5 8	10	(Via Evesham.) Calls at all stations.
3 38	Derby	Birmingham	—	5 16	...	10	Forms 5.45 p.m. Bristol.
5 20	Birmingham	Wolverhampton	—	4‡58	5 20	6	(SX). Stops at Smethwick, Oldbury, Dudley Port and Deepfields. ‡—From Vauxhall.
4 0	Leamington Spa	Birmingham	—	5†17	5‡30	5	‡—To Monument Lane (SX). Forms 6.33 p.m. Walsall (SO). †—P.B. 5.21 p.m.
5 25	Birmingham	Worcester	—	5‡ 0	5 25	9	Stops at Blackwell, Bromsgrove and Droitwich Spa. ‡—From Saltley.
5 26	Birmingham	Lichfield (C.)	—	...	5 26	5	Calls at Bescot, Walsall, then all stations.
4 8	Leicester	Birmingham	—	5†30	...	10	†—P.B. 5.33 p.m. Forms 6.24 p.m. Derby (SX), 5.53 p.m. Kings Norton (SO).
5 32	Birmingham	Redditch	—	...	5 32	11	Stops at all stations.
5 40	Birmingham	Liverpool	279 §	5‡25	5 40	6	(1) Liverpool, (2) Manchester (FX). Calls at Wolverhampton, Stafford, Crewe, Hartford, Runcorn, Edge Hill ; Wilmslow, Stockport. ‡—From Vauxhall.
5 45	Birmingham	Bristol	—	...	5 45	10	Stops at Kings Norton, then all stations via Worcester (except Fernhill Heath and Cleeve).
4 40	Leamington Spa	Birmingham	—	5 46	...	5	Forms 5.57 p.m. to Stoke.
5 50	Birmingham	Manchester	281 §	5‡43	5 50	6	(FO). **Not advertised.** Calls at Wolverhampton, Stafford, Crewe, Wilmslow and Stockport. ‡—From Vauxhall.
2 8	York	Birmingham	225	5 41	5‡53	9	(FO). ‡—To Kings Norton.
5‡53	Birmingham	Kings Norton	—	...	5‡53	10	(SO). Off 4.8 p.m. from Leicester.
12 40	Newcastle	Bristol	223	5 55	6 5	9	Calls at Cheltenham, Gloucester and Mangotsfield.
5 57	Birmingham	Stoke	—	...	5 57	5	Stops at all stations (except Winson Green, Wedgewood Halt). Stops at Wedgewood Halt (TWO), to pick up. **Not advertised.**)
5 6	Lichfield City	Birmingham	—	6 0	...	6 (SO) / 5 (SX)	Forms 6.27 p.m. to Manchester (SO). 6.45 p.m. Four Oaks (SX).
5 12	Nuneaton	Birmingham	—	6 14	...	10	Forms 6.20 p.m., Redditch (SX) and 6.40 p.m. Walsall (SO).
5 24	Coventry	Birmingham	—	6 16	...	6	(SX). Forms 6.27 p.m. to Manchester.
5 45	Sutton Park	Birmingham	—	6 19	...	10	(SX). P.O. Mails.
6 20	Birmingham	Redditch	—	...	6 20	10	(SX). Stops at all stations.
5 38	Walsall	Birmingham	—	6 25	...	5	Forms 8.36 p.m. Lichfield (SO) and 9.25 p.m. Walsall (SX).
6 27	Birmingham	Manchester	407	...	6†27	6	Stops at all stations to Stockport (via Stoke) (except Gailey, Wedgwood Halt, Macclesfield (Cen.)), then Manchester. †—P.B. 6.24 p.m.
5 15	Derby	Worcester	—	6 28	6 35	9	Stops at all stations (except Selly Oak).
4 6	Bletchley	Birmingham	—	6 29	6‡43	6	‡—To Monument Lane.
5 22	W'hampton	Birmingham	—	6 38	6‡45	9	(Via Streetly). ‡—To King's Norton.
4 22	Euston	Birmingham	187 §	6 50	6‡55	5	"**Q.**" ‡—To Monument Lane.
4 30	Euston	W'hampton	125 §	6†55	7 4	6	†—P.B. 7.0 p.m.
5 37	Rugby	Birmingham	—	7† 1	7‡10	5	(SX). ‡—To Mon. Lane. †—P.B. 7.5 p.m.
3 30	Peterborough	Birmingham	—	7 5	...	9	Forms 7‡15 p.m. King's Norton (SX), 8.28 p.m. Derby (SO).
6 29	Four Oaks	Monument Lane	—	7 8	7 16	6	(SX). Light engine.
7‡15	Birmingham	King's Norton	—	...	7‡15	9	(SX). Off 7.5 p.m. arrival.
6 23	Lichfield (C.)	Birmingham	—	7 17	...	5	Forms 7.25 p.m. Wolverhampton.

vices continued at their skeleton wartime levels until the late 1950s; indeed, some were never improved before their (by then, inevitable) withdrawal in the 1960s. With the low levels of services offered on many lines at a time when road competition (both in public and private transport) was increasing rapidly, it is little wonder that traffic continued to be lost, and little new traffic was generated. However, some services were improved gradually, and in a number of cases (on the introduction of diesel multiple unit trains under the 1955 modernisation plan), massive improvements were made — usually to give a better service than had ever been offered before. But, hardly had these visionary services been introduced than railway policy took an about-turn, as Dr. Beeching published his plan 'The Reshaping of British Railways' in 1963. This set out to cure the difficulties of mounting financial losses by cutting out the portions of the system which were thought to be losing money, and concentrating on a profitable core.

The emphasis was now on cutting services rather than developing them. Lines were generally to fall into one of several categories: those where the passenger service was to be withdrawn (and the line limited to freight traffic only, or closed altogether); those where local stations were to be closed, leaving only long-distance services; and those which were to receive a modified service. The latter term was not explained, but in Birmingham it applied on the services to Lichfield (via Sutton), Leicester, Redditch (both of which had just benefited from improved diesel services), and Worcester. Service withdrawals included the Sutton Park line, and Walsall to Rugeley. In the event, the plan was only partly carried out.

At this point, it is appropriate to step back and look at how an important aspect of Birmingham's local passenger services developed. Today, city train services are perhaps most often thought of in terms of daily travel from the suburbs or surrounding districts into the centre to work. Such travel was unknown in the early days, and it was not until the last years of the nineteenth century that there were any real signs of this traffic beginning to develop in Birmingham. Victorian timetables reflected the situation, with no bunching of services at what have now become the morning and evening 'peaks'. The term 'commuter' for this type of passenger is, incidentally, of quite recent use in Britain, having originated in America; the railways here knew it as residential or suburban traffic.

The city was, of course, much smaller than it is now, and the majority of the residential districts known today were not developed until the 1920s onwards. The first lines to show any evidence of increasing suburban traffic were those which served the older residential districts, including the Harborne branch, the lines to King's Norton via Camp Hill and via Selly Oak, to Erdington and Sutton Coldfield, and to Perry Barr, Smethwick and Hampton-in-Arden. The initial traffic was therefore over quite short distances, though as the city grew and the better-off moved to 'nicer' areas further afield, the distances travelled gradually increased.

The railways did not have the suburban traffic to themselves for long; from around the turn of the century, a street tramway system developed in the city. Although far quicker than anything offered on the roads before, trams were not that fast, but what they did offer was convenience — the trams ran nearer to people's homes and to the places they wanted to go, while the railway stations were usually some distance away. The biggest advantages were the frequency of the service — far better than offered by the railway — and the cheap fares. Up to the Great War, the growth in demand for suburban travel was such that, except for short distances, both railway and tramway took their share, and rail suburban services continued to improve.

The reductions brought about by the Great War inevitably made the rail services less attractive. The main cuts had been made in the off-peak periods, with the result that most services had gaps of two hours or so between trains in the mornings, afternoons and evenings. After the return of peace, the railways were very slow to restore services, and much traffic was lost to the trams and the new buses, both of which proved much more responsive to passenger needs.

The changes in the fortunes of the suburban passenger train can be illustrated by looking at the Harborne Branch. In some ways this was a classic suburban line, running wholly within the conurbation, and designed to exploit local traffic. In other ways it was curious; one would hardly expect to find a single-track line so near to a city centre, while for parts of its length the surrounding landscape was surprisingly rural. The distance of the terminus from the city centre was also remarkably short (four miles by rail, and about three by road). The accompanying table shows the full service in selected years between 1877 and 1932. As early as

HARBORNE BRANCH TRAIN SERVICE

Trains from New Street to Harborne							*Trains from Harborne to New Street*					
1877	*1889*	*1905*	*1912*	*1922*	*1932*		*1877*	*1899*	*1905*	*1912*	*1922*	*1932*
	7.15	7.0	7.0	6.35						5.35	5.35	
7.45	8.0	7.45	7.35	7.22	7.24		6.55	6.45	6.35	6.35	6.19	6.24
											7.9	
9.5	9.25	9.20	9.0						7.25	7.25	7.27	7.29
10.5	10.15	10.15	10.10	9.55	9.27			7.45	7.48	7.39		
11.5	11.15	11.10	11.5						8.8	8.7	8.4	8.6
12.5	12.15	12.15	12.10	12.10	12.5				8.24	8.24	8.19	8.23
	12.55	12.50	12.50	12.50	12.50		8.35	8.30	8.33	8.36	8.32	8.37
			1.3*	1.4*				8.50	8.53	8.53	8.49	8.56
1.5	1.15	1.15	1.15	1.15	1.10			9.15	9.8	9.8	9.15	9.21
	2.15	2.20	2.8	2.7	2.4		9.30	9.50	9.43	9.33		
2.50			3.0							10.5		10.12
	3.15	3.15	3.25				10.30	10.45	10.40	10.42	10.32	
			3.58				11.30	11.45	11.40	11.30		
4.0	4.15	4.15	4.17	4.5	4.8		12.30	12.45	12.40	12.35	12.38	12.45
			4.50	4.50	4.45			1.45	1.50	1.50	1.45	1.50
5.0	5.15	5.15	5.15	5.15	5.15					2.3	2.8	2.6
		5.35	5.35	5.40	5.42		2.20	2.5	2.10	2.13		
	5.55		6.0	6.0	6.0			2.45	2.45	2.47	2.54	2.59
6.15	6.20	6.15	6.15	6.20	6.19		3.15	3.45	3.40	3.30		
		6.35	6.40	6.50	6.50					4.1		
		7.0	7.0							4.23		
7.20	7.15	7.20	7.20	7.15	7.18		4.25	4.45	4.40	4.42	4:36	4.38
		7.45	7.40	7.40	7.40				5.20	5.20		
	8.15	8.15	8.15	8.30	8.50		5.30	5.45	6.0	6.0		
8.40			8.50				6.50	6.45	6.40	6.45	6.25	6.26
	9.15	9.20	9.20	9.30	9.35				7.25	7.25	7.19	7.21
	10.20	10.0	10.0	10.0			8.0	7.45	7.50	8.6	8.15	8.13
		10.40	10.35	10.40	10.30			8.45	8.40	8.40	9.5	9.19
10.50			10.55		11.5		10.0	9.45	9.45	9.45		
	11.51	11.10	11.15					10.45	10.25	10.25	10.4	10.1
		11.30							11.3	11.5		
13	19	24	30	21	19	TOTALS	13	20	26	31	20	18

NOTES

*Starts at Monument Lane (not New Street) at time stated.

Line opened 10th August 1874.

The 1897 service was similar to 1889 with one extra late evening service from New Street (the last 3 trains being at 10.0 p.m., 10.45 and 11.30) and 2 additional trains from Harborne, one at 8.15 a.m. and a later last train at 11.5 p.m.

The 1910 service was similar to that of 1912.

Icknield Port Road station closed 18th May 1931 and the branch passenger service was withdrawn on 26th November 1934.

1877, the service was basically hourly, and this was developed into an almost even interval pattern by 1883, with departures at 15 minutes past most hours, a feature also evident in the 1889 timetable.

The lack of residential traffic in 1877 is evidenced by the fact that there was no change in the service frequency at the 'peak' times. Indeed, the 1889 and 1897 timetables show only the beginnings of such traffic with one extra morning train from Harborne in the former year, and two in the latter. The situation had changed markedly by 1905, with trains at every ten to twenty minutes from Harborne in the morning peak. The service had further developed by 1910, with about 30 trains each way during the day, a level which was sustained until the outbreak of the Great War.

The 1922 service shows the residual effects of the wartime cutbacks, with 21 trains from New Street and 20 trains from Harborne. The table demonstrates how the cuts had been made, with two-hour gaps between trains during the mornings and afternoons, an arrangement which, while perhaps dictated by economics, was hardly calculated to encourage off-peak travel.

The 1932 service demonstrates the relative lack of progress and the hard economic conditions found during the first decade of the existence of the LMS. Except for the disappearance of two trains each way, the service is much the same as that of 1922. By now, the great depression and the effects of bus and tram competition were having a considerable impact on the number of passengers carried on the branch, and hence its revenue. With the development of effective road competition, the branch was placed at a significant disadvantage, as the route from Birmingham was somewhat roundabout, and about a mile longer than by road. The limitations of a single line and the time taken to carry out crossing movements on the branch (especially if one of the trains was late) made it difficult to speed up the service, which at 15 to 20 minutes for the four miles was hardly fast.

At Harborne Junction, the line joined the busy double-track Stour Valley line for the run through Monument Lane and the North Tunnel to New Street. Out-of-course running of main-line trains could lead to appreciable delays to trains from Harborne waiting a path into New Street, or to depart from New Street (although delays from this cause in the 1920s and up to closure were said to be nowhere near as bad as they had been before the Great War). All these factors extended actual journey times even more, and for an increasing number of customers, road travel offered significant advantages over rail.

Apart from the non-improvement of the service after 1922, the first sign that circumstances had deteriorated came in 1931, when the tiny Icknield Port Road station, situated in a rather run-down area, was closed on 18th May. This did have the advantage of reducing the journey time between Birmingham and Harborne to a consistent (at least according to the timetable!) 15 minutes. Although the frequency of the service was not improved, the LMS did make attempts to retain and encourage traffic. Fares were progressively reduced until, by 1934, the price of a first class three-month season ticket had dropped from £2 2s 3d to £1 12s 6d, and third class singles had been cut back to 3d. Patronage continued to fall, however, and it was decided to close the line with effect from 26th November 1934, the last train running on Saturday, 24th November. There was no organised opposition to the closure, and Birmingham Corporation was content to respond by increasing the frequency of the bus service to Harborne.

A difficulty in reviewing train services on lines carrying both 'main line' and 'local' services is that the difference between the two types of service was not always clear-cut. Some long-distance trains called at local stations over the full length or on some portions of their route, while local services were further supplemented by calls at selected stations by what might otherwise be regarded as express trains. Examples of the latter practice included stops at Stechford and Hampton-in-Arden by certain Birmingham & London expresses, and stops by North expresses at Smethwick and Oldbury. As a general rule in this review of local services, trains which called at more than two local stations on the portion of route described are considered as forming part of the local services. Some services (for example, a number of those to Leamington) were in fact provided by connections rather than through trains. The review considers the general principles of the services only, irrespective of whether the service was offered directly, by trains which divided, or by connection, or where the train actually terminated. In any event, it is usually impossible to tell from public timetables how, in these respects, the services were provided.

In 1877, a service of eight local trains was offered between Birmingham and Coventry, three of which went through to Leamington, whilst there were two further short workings to Hampton-in Arden. By 1888, there were fifteen trains to Coventry, of which five went on to Leamington, while a further five ran to Leamington direct via Berkswell and Kenilworth. The number of trains to Coventry remained at about this level until the 1920s, and had increased to twenty-one by 1938. The increase was accounted for by the running of extra trains from Birmingham to Coventry in the early morning, and the 1938 timetable showed seven departures for Coventry between 6.30 and 9.0 a.m., compared with four in 1922. No doubt these extra trains were run for workers at the various factories associated with the motor industry which had been set up in the Coventry area. All these trains continued to run throughout the war and into the 1960s. The wartime cutbacks brought the service back to about 17 or 18 trains, and it remained at this level until the 1960s, when an increase to 23 or 24 a day occurred. After the Great War there was a loss of interest in the Leamington direct services, with only a token one or two trains running daily from New Street (until withdrawal in January 1965), although there were more trains in the reverse direction.

Of some interest is the appearance, by 1897, of a number of short workings from New Street to Stechford in the afternoon and early evening, indicating some demand for an 'inner suburban' service. These did not disappear until the Second World War.

The oldest line in the Birmingham area was the Grand Junction; this route was remarkable for passing through much of the West Midlands region, but not directly serving anywhere of any importance at all! It did, however, provide the link to Birmingham for the branches to Sutton and Lichfield, and to Walsall. After 1881, by the use of the short section of Midland track at Heath Town, the line provided an alternative route for LNW trains from Birmingham to Wolverhampton. The Soho lines enabled trains for Wolverhampton and Walsall to leave from either end of New Street.

Although the fact is perhaps forgotten today, Walsall was the third most important station (after New Street and Wolverhampton) on the LMS system in the West Midlands; it was a focal point for several services: LNW and Midland services by separate routes to Birmingham and Wolverhampton, and LNW services to Dudley, Lichfield (and hence to Burton-on-Trent and Derby), Cannock and Rugeley. The Rugeley line provided an alternative route to Stafford, Stoke and Manchester, and some trains from Birmingham to these places were run this way.

The line from Portobello Junction to Heath Town did not open until 1st March 1881, and prior to this, Wolverhampton could not be served directly from the Bescot line. Until 1873, GJ line trains had run to Bushbury, but from 1st January 1873 (to 1881) services from Birmingham terminated at Willenhall Bridge station (Willenhall until 1872, and from 1881, and renamed Willenhall, Bilston Street, in 1924). In 1877, a service of 17 trains ran from Birmingham to Walsall, a remarkable 13 of which also served Willenhall Bridge. By 1889, when the railway network was fully developed, there were 19 trains from New Street to Walsall, of which eight also served Wolverhampton, dividing or connecting at Bescot. This had increased to 28 and 13 respectively by 1912. The Second World War brought the Birmingham & Wolverhampton local service via Bescot to a virtual end, with only one train left in 1941; this, too, had gone by 1950. Trains to Walsall decreased in number to about 19, and this service, with its long morning and afternoon gaps, remained in force throughout the 1950s. Walsall was one of the lines to benefit positively from the introduction of diesel multiple units, a service of 22 trains from New Street being in force in 1962. Outside the peaks, trains were at hourly intervals, departing from New Street at 10 minutes past each hour. There were extra services at the peaks, and 17 trains continued on to the Rugeley line, although this was to succumb to closure on 18th January 1965.

Like the Harborne branch, the Sutton Coldfield line was conceived primarily as a passenger line, although it did carry some freight, mainly of a local nature. A service of 13 trains to Sutton was offered by 1877, and after the opening of the extension to Lichfield in 1884, this was effectively supplemented by eight extra trains to Lichfield. The residential district around Sutton developed quickly, and in the 1890s it became the practice to terminate some trains at Four Oaks rather than Sutton. The number of trains continuing through to Lichfield increased, too, and in consequence fewer trains terminated at Sutton. By 1912, there were just three trains terminating there, and the one service surviving in 1922 had disappeared by 1932. The reductions in service brought about by the Great War did not affect the line as badly as some, there being 31 trains in 1922 compared with 38 in 1912, and the total had struggled back to 34 by 1938.

The Second World War brought a much more dramatic change to the Sutton line, with the service in 1941 down to exactly half of its prewar level. In fact, it fell further during the early 1950s, to just 14 trains in 1954. The line, perhaps not surprisingly in view of the use made of it, had its service restored much earlier than most. An hourly steam motor train service between New Street and Sutton was introduced on 2nd May 1955, and this was extended to Four Oaks from 4th July. From 5th March 1956, the steam trains were withdrawn and replaced by brand-new, two-car lightweight diesel multiple units. These provided a half-hourly service to Four Oaks and hourly to Lichfield, journey times being reduced by up to six minutes. The new service offered 35 trains a day — just slightly better than in 1938. The benefit for passengers at the Lichfield end of the line was more marked, with 22 trains going through compared with 15 in 1938, and just 12 in 1912. British Railways stated that they hoped for a 200% increase in patronage — enough to turn a loss-making line into a profitable one. By the autumn of 1957, passenger carrying was up by 178%, and by April 1959 monthly patronage was up from 32,000 to 95,000, an increase of 297%.

The Stour Valley line theoretically served a much greater population than the Grand Junction, with stations situated in the towns of Smethwick, Oldbury, Dudley (at Dudley Port) and Tipton. Unfortunately, all of the stations were poorly located in industrial areas, away from the main centres of population and the town centres. Dudley, the most important town in the area, is awkwardly sited on top of a ridge, and had to be served by a 1¼-mile branch from Dudley Port. Even then, the station was in an inconvenient position at the bottom of the hill. At first, the LNW made an effort to provide a through local service from Birmingham to Dudley, to supplement the frequent shuttle connecting service on the branch, with six trains being offered in 1877 compared with ten trains to Wolverhampton. This had decreased slightly to five trains in 1889, while the Wolverhampton service had increased to 18. After this, the Dudley service had dwindled to just two by 1897, and it became accepted that passengers for Dudley had to change onto the shuttle service (often referred to as the 'Dudley Dasher') at Dudley Port.

The Stour Valley service suffered remarkably little during the Great War, the only significant differences between the 1922 and 1912 services being the loss of the two through Dudley trains, and the last train from Birmingham; the last departure was now 10.20 p.m. instead of 11.25. By 1938, there were 21 Wolverhampton trains, with a last departure from New Street at 11.8 p.m. and three Dudley trains. However, the story was different in the Second World War. The Dudley trains disappeared again, and the Wolverhampton service was reduced to 12 trains, with a last departure from New Street at 7.47 p.m. in 1941 (7.25 in 1950). The service changed very little until the mid 1960s, with most trains continuing to run at more or less the same times. The number of trains had increased slightly to 15 trains by 1966, and from the mid 1950s, the last departure from New Street was a little later, at 9.25 p.m.

With so many poorly-sited stations, closures inevitably took their toll on the Stour Valley line. Monmore Green disappeared as early as 1st January 1917, a casualty of the Great War, whilst Soho survived the Second World War, only to close on 23rd May 1949. Winson Green, the next station towards New Street, closed on 16th September 1957, and Monument Lane, by then the only station remaining between New Street and Smethwick, followed on 17th November 1958. The somewhat remote station at Albion closed on 1st February 1960, while Spon Lane ('For West Bromwich') and Ettingshall Road survived a few more years, both closing on 15th June 1964. Three weeks later, on 6th July 1964, the connecting 'Dasher' from Dudley Port (High Level) to Dudley was withdrawn, whilst other trains ceased to call at the town's station, leaving Dudley as one of the largest towns in Britain without a train service.

The Soho loop line, with its triangular junction connections to the Stour Valley and Grand Junction lines, offered opportunities for alternative routeing of some services. For example, trains to Wolverhampton and Walsall could start

SUTTON COLDFIELD AND LICHFIELD LINE
NUMBER OF TRAINS FROM NEW STREET

Year	*Number of trains terminating at:* Sutton Coldfield	Four Oaks	Lichfield	Total for route
1877	13	–	–	13
1889	12	–	8	20
1897	14	4	7	25
1912	3	23	12	38
1922	1	17	13	31
1932	–	15	17	32
1938	–	18	16	34
1941	–	8	9	17
1950	–	5	11	16
1954	–	4	10	14
1956	–	13	22	35
1958	–	10	26	36
1966	–	8	25	33

NOTES
Sutton Coldfield–Lichfield line opened 15th December 1884.
Lichfield total includes a few trains which continued beyond Lichfield and trains which terminated at Sutton Coldfield or Four Oaks but connected with a separate train from that station to Lichfield.

SOHO ROAD AND HANDSWORTH WOOD SERVICE CLOCKWISE INCLUDING SOHO/HANDSWORTH CIRCULAR TRAINS
(New Street–Monument Lane–Soho–Aston–Vauxhall–New Street)
Times in brackets indicate starting time of train from its starting point (or terminating time) when this is not New Street (see notes)

1889			*1897*			*1910*			*1922*			*1932*		
New Street			*New Street*			*New Street*			*New Street*			*New Street*		
dep.	*arr.*		*dep.*	*arr.*		*dep.*	*arr.*		*dep.*	*arr.*		*dep.*	*arr.*	
a.m.	*a.m.*		*a.m.*	*a.m.*		*a.m.*	*a.m.*		*a.m.*	*a.m.*		*a.m.*	*a.m.*	
7.45		B	7.35		E	7.25		D	(7.10)	(8.5)	FD	(7.10)	(7.41)	FD
			8.15		A	8.10	8.45		8.15		A	8.15		B
						8.20		A						
9.40		A	9.40		A	9.40		A	9.35		A	9.40		A
11.25		B	11.20		B	11.50		B						
p.m.	*p.m.*		*p.m.*	*p.m.*		*p.m.*	*p.m.*		*p.m.*	*p.m.*		*p.m.*	*p.m.*	
12.45		E	12.45	1.15		12.35	1.7		12.35	1.13		12.32	1.10	
						1.10	1.41		1.10		D	1.10		D
3.20		A	3.20		A	3.20		B						
						4.40		B	4.40		B	4.40		B
5.25		A	5.20		B	5.40		B	5.35		D	5.37		D
			6.20		E	6.5	6.37		6.5		D	6.5		D
						6.45	7.22							
7.10		A	7.30	8.5		7.25		C	7.5		D			
						8.5	8.40							
9.25	10.3		8.35	9.5		8.45	9.20		9.10		D			
			9.45	10.20		9.35	10.7		9.50		B	10.0		B
						10.30		B	10.35		D			
10.50	11.25		11.00	11.30		11.5	11.36							

NOTES
A to Wolverhampton
B to Walsall
C to Handsworth Wood
D to Vauxhall
E to Perry Barr
F from Monument Lane
G does not call at Handsworth Wood

ANTI-CLOCKWISE
(New Street–Vauxhall–Aston–Soho–Monument Lane–New Street)

1889			*1897*			*1910*			*1922*			*1932*		
New Street			*New Street*			*New Street*			*New Street*			*New Street*		
dep.	*arr.*		*dep.*	*arr.*		*dep.*	*arr.*		*dep.*	*arr.*		*dep.*	*arr.*	
a.m.	*a.m.*		*a.m.*	*a.m.*		*a.m.*	*a.m.*		*a.m.*	*a.m.*		*a.m.*	*a.m.*	
6.35	7.10		6.30	7.5		6.35	7.11							
8.2	8.32					7.18	7.52							
				8.25	C	(7.35)	8.8	D		8.9	B		8.10	BG
8.20	8.59						8.46	B		8.46	B		8.48	B
			8.20	8.55		8.27	9.3		8.27	9.22		8.27	9.22	
			9.0	9.30		9.0	9.30							
			9.40	10.15		9.30	10.5							
	10.43	A		11.12	B		11.12	B	10.45	11.22				
p.m.	*p.m.*		*p.m.*	*p.m.*		*p.m.*	*p.m.*		*p.m.*	*p.m.*		*p.m.*	*p.m.*	
	1.0	A		1.7	A		1.10	A		1.25	A		1.25	B
	2.17	C	1.40	2.16		1.35	2.13		1.35	2.14		1.37	2.13	
						1.55	2.30			2.47	B		2.41	B
			2.40	3.15		2.38	3.15							
	4.32	A		4.11	B		4.6	B		4.18	B		4.13	B
	5.46	A		5.35	A		5.30	A		5.28	A		5.33	A
						5.25		F				(5.52)	(6.22)	EF
	6.50	B		6.37	B		6.50	B		7.3	A		7.6	B
7.5	7.33						7.56	B		8.16	B		8.8	G
						10.20	10.53							

NOTES
A from Wolverhampton
B from Walsall
C from Perry Barr
D from Vauxhall
E from Aston
F to Monument Lane
G does not call at Handsworth Wood

from either end of New Street, while Wolverhampton trains could serve both Aston and Dudley Port or Monument Lane and Bescot. It also enabled a circular service, New Street to New Street via Soho Road and Handsworth Wood, to be operated. The accompanying table shows the full extent of the Soho Loop services in selected years from its full opening in 1889, to the 1930s. The services were somewhat erratic, and the circular one decidedly so; in 1889, there was just one train in the clockwise direction that made the full circle, and two in the reverse direction. The service reached its peak in the years leading up to the Great War, with nine trains completing both the clockwise and anti-clockwise circle.

The Soho services all but disappeared after the outbreak of war, and in 1922 only one train completed the clockwise circle, with a second running from Monument Lane to Vauxhall. Three trains made the complete journey in the reverse direction. There was little further change prior to the outbreak of the Second World War, and the few circular services survived the declaration of war by just three weeks, being withdrawn on 25th September 1939 (the day the revised winter wartime timetable was introduced). Soho Road and Handsworth Wood continued to be served by Walsall and Wolverhampton trains for nearly two more years, both closing on 5th May 1941. Some Walsall 'fast' trains continued to be routed this way.

The Birmingham and Gloucester (via Camp Hill) line of the Midland Railway passed through suburban districts as far as Northfield, and a good local service was developed to exploit this traffic. The trains involved were either purely local in character, terminating at King's Norton or Northfield, or services travelling further afield to Redditch, Worcester or Gloucester, or even to Bristol, though not all trains served all stations. By 1910, there were a very respectable 27 departures each day from New Street, of which 15 terminated at King's Norton or Northfield.

The 1922 timetable showed only 18 trains from New Street, with long gaps (over 2½ hours in this case) between trains in mid-morning and mid-afternoon, something which characterised most post-war services. There was hardly any change over the next 16 years, and in 1938 there was just one more train, the remaining 18 running at almost the same times as they had in 1922.

As with many other local services, the introduction of the wartime 'emergency' timetable brought a reduction in the number of trains to about half its former level, there being just ten in the

September 1939 'emergency' timetable, with some huge gaps in the morning, afternoon and evening. The LMS was far more concerned about congestion of traffic on the main line than with the needs of local passengers, and the service via Camp Hill was withdrawn altogether on 27th January 1941. The withdrawal was originally intended to be a temporary measure for the duration of war, but, like so many temporary arrangements, it effectively became final, and the closure was made officially permanent as from 27th November 1946.

The Birmingham West Suburban line was similar in character to the Camp Hill line as far as passenger services were concerned. The local stations were similarly served by trains terminating at King's Norton, Northfield or Halesowen, or by trains continuing to destinations south of Barnt Green. Indeed, the number of trains operated in 1910 was almost exactly the same as the Camp Hill line, with 25 departures from New Street (compared with 27 via Camp Hill). A reduced service of 19 trains was offered in 1922, again very similar to Camp Hill's 18. Unlike Camp Hill, however, the West Suburban service improved over the remaining years of peace, and a total of 24 departures were offered from New Street in 1938. Whereas the majority of the Camp Hill trains terminated at King's Norton, the majority of the West Suburban trains continued to destinations beyond Barnt Green.

The original promoters of the Birmingham West Suburban Railway had hoped to serve Harborne by a branch, and as a reminder of this intention,

CAMP HILL LOCAL SERVICE
DEPARTURES FROM NEW STREET

1890	*1910*	*1922*	*1938*
a.m.	*a.m.*	*a.m.*	*a.m.*
6.40 B	6.25 B	6.53 C	6.40 B
	7.0 C	7.5 B	6.47 C
	8.0 B	7.53 C	7.54 C
8.20 B	8.16 C	8.3 A	8.3 A
	8.37 A		
9.45 B	9.28 A	9.25 A	9.14 A
	10.50 A		
p.m.	*p.m.*	*p.m.*	*p.m.*
12.0 B	12.5 B	12.5 B	12.17 B
	12.46 A	12.40 A	12.38 A
1.0 A	1.0 A	1.0 A	1.0 A
	1.18 A		
2.10 B	1.55 B	2.12 A	2.12 A
2.30 A	2.30 A		
3.50 B	3.45 A		4.0 C
5.0 A	4.40 A	4.40 A	4.40 A
	5.6 A		
5.18 A	5.33 C	5.22 A	5.20 B
	6.0 A	5.45 A	5.42 A
6.2 A	6.18 C	6.15 A	6.12 A
6.40 A	6.44 A	6.48 A	6.48 A
	7.8 C		
	7.40 A	7.35 A	7.35 A
8.10 A	8.20 C	8.35 A	8.45 A
9.3 B	9.8 B		
9.40 A	9.40 A	9.35 A	9.45 B
10.25 B	10.12 B	10.30 D	10.50 A
11.8 A	11.20 A		
17	27	18	19

NOTES
A to Kings Norton or Northfield
B to Barnt Green or Redditch
C Circular Service
D to Hazelwell
Service withdrawn and stations closed 27th January 1941

Somerset Road station was described in the timetable as 'For Harborne'. As with the Harborne branch, some of the stations suffered badly from their locations, and from bus and tram competition; Church Road station closed on 1st January 1925, and Somerset Road followed on 28th July 1930.

Wartime service reductions were severe, with just nine trains remaining in 1941, only one of which terminated at King's Norton. The figures hide some curiosities, as only three of the trains from New Street called at Five Ways, but ten northbound trains called there (no doubt for ticket collection purposes). Almost inevitably, Five Ways' days were numbered; it struggled on until the end of the war was almost in sight, closing on 2nd October 1944.

In 1892, a curve had been built between the West Suburban and Camp Hill lines at Lifford, the main purpose of which was to provide a direct route from Lawley Street and the Derby direction to the new Central goods station. It also opened up the possibility of running a Midland circular passenger service from New Street to New Street via Bournville, Lifford and Camp Hill, and in 1910, five trains each way made the full circular journey, and a further train each way ran to Bournville the long way round. In 1922 and 1932 there were just two early morning trains in the clockwise direction,

LIFFORD CIRCULAR CLOCKWISE
New Street–Camp Hill–Lifford–Bournville–New Street

1910			*1922*			*1932*			*1938*		
New St. dep.	*Lifford*	*New St. arr.*	*New St. dep.*	*Lifford*	*New St. arr.*	*New St. dep.*	*Lifford*	*New St. arr.*	*New St. dep.*	*Lifford*	*New St. arr.*
a.m.	*a.m.*	*a.m.*	*a.m.*	*a.m.*	*a.m.*	*a.m.*	*a.m.*	*a.m.*	*a.m.*	*a.m.*	*a.m.*
7.0	7.22	7.45	6.53	7.19	7.42	6.48	7.14	7.42	6.47	7.14	7.42
8.16	8.41	A	7.53	B	8.41	7.54	B	8.34	7.54	8.16	8.34
p.m.	*p.m.*	*p.m.*							*p.m.*	*p.m.*	*p.m.*
5.33	5.56	6.25							4.0	4.22	4.43
6.18	6.41	7.2									
7.8	7.31	7.56									
8.20	8.43	9.3									

NOTES
A to Bournville
B does not call at Lifford

LIFFORD CIRCULAR ANTI-CLOCKWISE
New Street–Bournville–Lifford–Camp Hill–New Street

1910			*1922*			*1932*			*1938*		
New St. dep.	*Lifford*	*New St. arr.*	*New St. dep.*	*Lifford*	*New St. arr.*	*New St. dep.*	*Lifford*	*New St. arr.*	*New St. dep.*	*Lifford*	*New St. arr.*
a.m.	*a.m.*	*a.m.*	*a.m.*	*a.m.*	*a.m.*	*a.m.*	*a.m.*	*a.m.*	*a.m.*	*a.m.*	*a.m.*
7.3	7.23	7.47	7.10	7.36	8.7	7.10	7.41	8.6	7.10	7.42	8.6
8.0	8.22	8.46	7.52	8.17	8.51	7.52	8.17	8.44	7.52	8.18	8.41
8.55	9.20	9.44									
p.m.	*p.m.*	*p.m.*	*p.m.*	*p.m.*	*p.m.*	*p.m.*	*p.m.*	*p.m.*	*p.m.*	*p.m.*	*p.m.*
4.16	4.37	5.0	A	5.28	B	A	5.26	5.50	C	5.26	5.50
A	5.48	6.12									
6.20	6.43	7.6	6.0	6.21	6.35	6.5	6.21	6.44	6.5	6.24	6.52

NOTES
A from Bournville
B to Camp Hill
C from Selly Oak dep. 5.16

and three in the other, with a fourth train making part of the journey. By this time, the trains were mainly run for the benefit of Cadbury's workers who lived near Camp Hill line stations, for whom there were no convenient bus services. The clockwise service had increased to three trains by 1938. This sparse service was withdrawn at the same time as that on the Camp Hill line.

Worcester was served mainly by local trains calling at most stations, but also by a few of the West of England expresses which were routed via Worcester Shrub Hill, rather than using the direct line via Dunhampstead. Apart from wartime, the number of trains remained remarkably constant at around 17 each way. Journey times were hardly spectacular, with most trains taking between 45 minutes and an hour for the 26 miles; even the best expresses required about 40 minutes for the journey.

Before leaving the Midland lines south of Birmingham, the Redditch branch deserves some mention. As with services to Lichfield on the other side of the city, the 1922 timetable was similar to that of 1910, with 13 trains from New Street compared with the 14 of 1910 (and the 13 trains to Lichfield). Again, as with Lichfield, the number of trains increased a little, reaching 17 in 1938 (which equated closely with Lichfield's 16). Wartime conditions reduced the service to just seven trains in 1941, and this had only increased to nine by 1950, again not dissimilar to Lichfield. Unlike that line however, the Redditch timetable did not improve in the 1950s, and was still running nine trains in 1959. The following year, there was a remarkable change for the better: with the introduction of diesel multiple units on 25th April 1960, radical changes were made to the service, which became approximately hourly, with 18 trains a day from New Street. By contrast, the service southwards from Redditch was reduced from five to three trains each way, and remained steam-worked (except on Sundays); not surprisingly, it did not survive much longer, and was withdrawn on 1st October 1962.

The bold experiment with hourly trains to Redditch unfortunately did not last long, and came to an abrupt end in 1966, perversely shortly after it was announced that Redditch was to be the location of a new town, when the timetable was reduced to just six trains, departing from New Street at 8.20, 13.35, 16.35, 17.10 17.40 and 18.15. Perhaps this was a taste of what was meant by the term 'modified service' in Beeching's report. Although up to this time, the Redditch service had largely paralleled that to Lichfield, the situation on the two lines was now entirely different.

North of Birmingham, the Midland's main line to Derby was never blessed with a good local service, and the number of trains provided changed remarkably little over the years. The eight trains from New Street of 1910 became seven in 1922, nine in 1938, eight again in 1941 and ten in 1958. As some of the trains were longer-distance services which called only at selected stations, the number of trains and quality of service varied somewhat from station to station.

The Midland had gained access to Walsall and Wolverhampton via its Sutton Park line, and an alternative ser-

SUTTON PARK LINE
Birmingham New Street–Castle Bromwich–Sutton Park–Walsall

Trains from Birmingham				*Trains to Birmingham*			
1890	*1910*	*1922*	*1941*	*1890*	*1910*	*1922*	*1941*
a.m.	*a.m.*	*a.m.*	*a.m.*	*a.m.*	*a.m.*	*a.m.*	*a.m.*
7.0	6.32			7.12	7.16		
7.55	7.40	7.20	7.18	8.12	8.0	7.55	7.8
9.6	9.5	8.7	8.13	8.54	8.54	9.0	8.10
				9.12			
10.0	10.37	10.42		9.40	9.35	9.48	
p.m.	*p.m.*	*p.m.*	*p.m.*				
12.35				11.24	11.13	10.55	
1.8	1.5	1.10	1.8	*p.m.*	*p.m.*	*p.m.*	*p.m.*
1.55	2.0			1.20	1.26	1.45	1.40
3.43	4.2	4.5		2.30	2.53	3.23	
5.5	5.30	5.30	5.35	4.47	4.55		5.43
6.20	6.30	6.30	6.35	6.30	6.21	6.36	
7.20	7.30	7.15	8.5	7.52	8.14	7.22	
8.35	9.2	9.10		9.7	9.22	8.53	
	9.50			10.15	10.15		
10.55	11.10	10.47			11.9	10.38	

NOTES

For trains to Birmingham, the times given are the arrival times at New Street.

With minor changes, the 1922 service continued in force until the outbreak of war in 1939.

With the exception of the 8.5 p.m. from Birmingham, which had been discontinued by 1950, the 1941 service continued in force with only minor changes until the trains were withdrawn on 18th January 1965.

Redditch Branch — *Number of trains from New Street*

West Suburban Line — *Trains from New Street serving one or more of the stations between New Street and Kings Norton*

Year	*Number of trains*	*Number of trains terminating at Kings Norton or Northfield*	*Number of trains terminating at Barnt Green or beyond*	*Circular services*	*Total No. of trains*
1890	10	15	1	–	16
1910	14	16	6	3	25
1922	13	7	9	3	19
1932	13	4	15	3	22
1938	17	5	16	3	24
1941	7	1	8	–	9
1950	9	1	8	–	9
1954	9	1	8	–	9
1958	9	3	8	–	11
1961	18	2	19	–	21
1965	18	–	20	–	20
1966	6	–	6	–	6

NOTES

Redditch Branch trains which call at West Suburban stations are included in both tables.

Kings Norton and Northfield total includes trains to Halesowen.

Church Road Station closed 1st January 1925.

Somerset Road Station closed 28th July 1930.

Five Ways Station closed 2nd October 1944. In 1941 only 3 down trains (but 10 up trains) called at Five Ways.

Line beyond Redditch closed to passengers 1st October 1962.

In 1890 also 1 train to Selly Oak.

vice from New Street to these towns was offered by this route. The accompanying table shows the basic service offered to and from Birmingham. Not all trains went through to Wolverhampton, and some of those that did used the LNW route from Walsall rather than the Midland one. The ten trains each day of 1922 changed very little until the introduction of the 'emergency' timetable in 1939. The six trains of 1941 had been reduced to five by 1950 with the withdrawal of the last train from Birmingham, and those remaining trains continued with only minor changes until the service was withdrawn on 18th January 1965.

The Midland's branch from Whitacre to Nuneaton connected there with the LNW line to Leicester. By use of this line, over which it had running powers for 'coaching' (passenger) traffic, the Midland was able to offer a service from Birmingham to Leicester, and onwards (usually by connections) to Nottingham and Lincoln. The line carried a variety of stopping and fast trains, the stopping patterns varying somewhat before or after Nuneaton. The service fell into three categories: local trains that called at most stations to Nuneaton, a small number of semi-fast trains that called at one or two stations before Nuneaton, and a further small number of fast trains that were first stop Nuneaton. In addition, a few trains ran through to Nottingham and Lincoln.

The number of trains on the Nuneaton line varied little over the years between 1910 and 1938: there were nine locals in 1910 and nine in 1938. The number of semi-fast trains had increased slightly from one to three over the same period, and the total number of trains from 13 to 16. Curtailment of services in the Second World War was drastic, with just six trains in 1941, though recovery afterwards was much quicker than on most lines, with the total back to 14 in 1950 and 16 by 1958, the same figure as in 1938. The local service had further improved by 1962 with the introduction of diesel multiple units, and an even-interval service of trains departing at 15 minutes past most hours was offered. There were now 16 local trains, nearly twice the prewar number, but only one fast train, though that number had increased to three by 1966. The remaining local stations between New Street and Nuneaton (except Water Orton) closed in March 1968.

A long-standing feature of the timetable, appearing by 1922 and continuing through to 1966, was the apparent provision of a late-night service to Leicester only, leaving New Street somewhere between 10.30 and 11.00 p.m. Closer examination of the timetable revealed that this service was 'via Derby' (the first leg of the journey, as far as Derby, being on the Bristol–Newcastle Mail), and the journey time offered varied between 2½ and 3½ hours. To add insult to injury on this hardly attractive service, a footnote declared that a higher fare would be charged for the privilege of using it!

Two tramcars on Hill Street, near New Street station, in October 1949. Routes 37 and 39 took commuters from South Birmingham to the station and, of course, home again in the evenings. The tramcar service just outlived the great overall roof of the station, finally ending in 1953.

T. J. Edgington

DETAILS OF CONTROL REPORTING ARRANGEMENTS IN THE AREA AROUND NEW STREET IN THE 1950s

CONTROL REPORTING POINTS

MIDLAND DIVISION

Signal Box	To Be Reported
Saltley Sidings	Departure of empty coach trains and light engines from Saltley Carriage Sidings via Camp Hill or Birmingham (New Street).
Saltley Junction	Arrival, departure and passing of passenger trains, also passing of freight trains and light engines from Lawley Street and Duddeston Sidings.
Lawley Street 'A' Box	Arrival of all trains.
Landor Street Junction	Arrival, departure or passing of all trains to and from Bordesley (WR), also freight trains to and from Grand Junction.
St Andrew's Junction	Arrival, departure and passing of all trains and light engines to and from Exchange Sidings and Birmingham (New Street).
Bordesley Junction	Arrival, departure or passing of all trains and light engines to and from Bordesley (WR), also the time trains are ready to leave Bordesley (WR).
Camp Hill Station	Arrival, departure or passing of all trains and light engines.
Church Road Junction	Arrival, departure or passing of freight trains, light engines and passenger trains; also arrival and departure of parcels trains at and from Birmingham (Central).
Bournville Station	Arrival of engines off freight or special empty coach trains for MP Depot; also departure of engines from MP Depot when gonging off late.

WESTERN DIVISION

Signal Box	To Be Reported
Stechford No. 1	Arrival, departure or passing of freight trains and freight light engines; also of special passenger trains to and from the Aston line.
Birmingham New Street No. 1	Arrival and departure of selected and special passenger trains.
Sheepcote Lane	Arrival, departure or passing of selected and special passenger trains.
Harborne Junction	Arrival, departure or passing of freight trains and freight light engines, to or from the Soho Road Line.
Soho Soap Works Junction	Arrival, departure or passing of freight trains, special passenger trains and freight light engines, to and from the Soho Road Line.
Aston No. 1	Arrival, departure or passing of freight trains and special passenger trains.
Perry Barr South Junction	Arrival, departure or passing of freight trains, selected and special passenger trains to and from the Soho Road Line.
Perry Barr North Junction	Arrival, departure or passing of freight trains, selected and special passenger trains.
Sutton Coldfield	Arrival, departure or passing of freight trains, arrival and departure of special passenger trains.

No signal box in the Western Division control area was required to report all passenger trains.

REPORTS TO CONTROL BY TRAFFIC YARDS

The following yards were required to report the arrival and departure of freight trains and time of release of engines from freight work:

MIDLAND DIVISION

Yard	Person Responsible
Duddeston Sidings	Yard Foreman (Shunter when no Yard Foreman in attendance).
Lawley Street Marshalling Sidings	Yard Inspector.

WESTERN DIVISION

Yard	Person Responsible
Aston Goods	Inspector or Foreman.
Curzon Street	Inspector or Foreman.
Exchange Sidings	Shunter.
Monument Lane	Yard Foreman or Shunter.

The signalman and yard staff listed above were also responsible for reporting the loadings of freight trains arriving and departing. In addition, the following had also to report freight train loadings:

Yard	Person Responsible
Camp Hill	Shunter.
Kings Norton Marshalling Sidings	Yard Foreman.
Selly Oak	Shunter.
Stechford	Inspector.
Adderley Park	Shunter.
Soho Pool	Foreman or Shunter

DELAYS TO TRAINS

The place at which delays to trains occurred had to report the delay and its cause direct to control. However, because they were so busy, the following signal boxes were exempt from the requirements to report signal delays:

Birmingham New Street — all signal boxes.
Proof House.
Sheepcote Lane.
Aston No. 1 For all passenger trains.
Grand Junction — For all passenger trains.

NOTE these details are an abstract from the Birmingham control arrangements and only cover the area immediately around New Street and Curzon Street.

CHAPTER FOUR
BIRMINGHAM TRAIN CONTROL

THE period up to the Great War was one of almost continuous expansion in the volume of rail traffic. This growth was accommodated in two ways: by the expansion of physical features — construction of additional running lines and sidings, and enlargement of stations and yards — and by improvements in traffic working, made possible by such features as the introduction of the block system and telephones, the availability of larger and better engines (and rolling stock), and better braking systems. The capacity of the railway, measured in terms of the volume of traffic that could be handled in a set period, both in total and on each line of rails, continually increased.

Despite the continuous improvements, on the busier sections of line the increases in capacity only just kept pace with the increasing traffic, with the result that freight traffic often suffered from considerable delays through congestion, and all too frequently this spilled over to affect the running of passenger trains. The cost of the delays, in additional engine time, wages and overtime payments, poor rolling stock utilisation and late deliveries, was considerable. Part of the problem was that, although there was a central authority for day-to-day operation through the working timetable and associated instructions, in the operating department (whatever it might be called on a particular railway) there was no ready means available which allowed for daily operating needs and problems to be met quickly. The railway lacked a means of making rapid decisions in a strategic way which allowed the solutions to best meet local needs without causing problems elsewhere on the system, and at minimum overall cost.

Most problems had perforce to be solved locally by the people on the spot — notably yardmasters and stationmasters — and inevitably, this could have adverse repercussions elsewhere. For example, an excess of passenger traffic might require stations to add extra vehicles to a train, resulting perhaps in delay (and extra cost) while a pilot engine and crew were found; in additional delays at stations further on, because the train was now too long to be accommodated in station platforms; or further hold-ups while some of the extra vehicles were detached, perhaps because the train was no longer made up in the most sensible order for later stations or workings. Similarly, late-

EXTRACT FROM MIDLAND DIVISION SIDE STRIP LINE OR CONTROL DIAGRAM FOR MAIN LINE THROUGH BIRMINGHAM

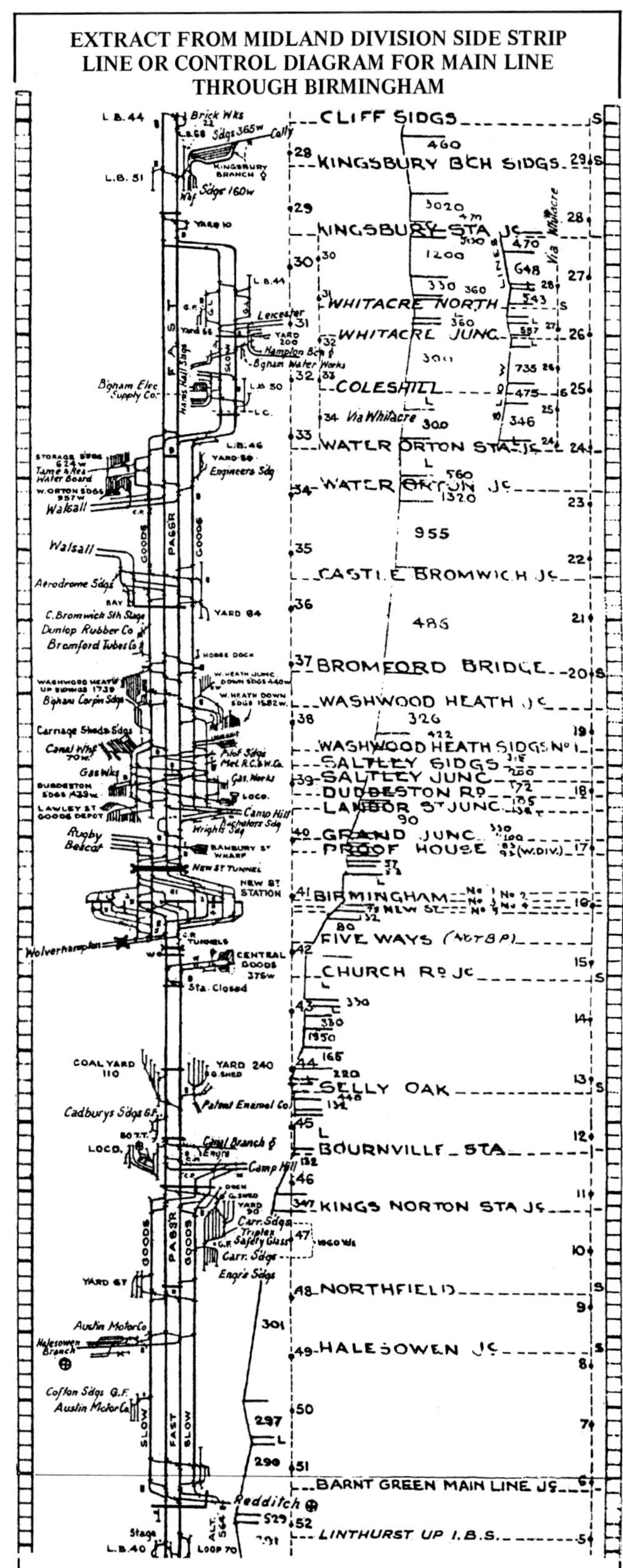

The Midland issued a set of 'Side Strip' or Control Diagrams for the use of its Control Office staff (they were also used by the timetable planners, hence the compressed and constant vertical scale). Illustrated here is a portion of one of the diagrams (slightly reduced in size) showing the section of the main line from Kingsbury to Barnt Green via New Street. The sheets give a diagrammatic indication of the running lines and sidings on the route together with operating information such as yard and siding capacities and the locations of private sidings. There were enlargements for the more complex areas. The Midland Control offices were not provided with detailed wall-mounted maps of the control area, these sheets being used instead.

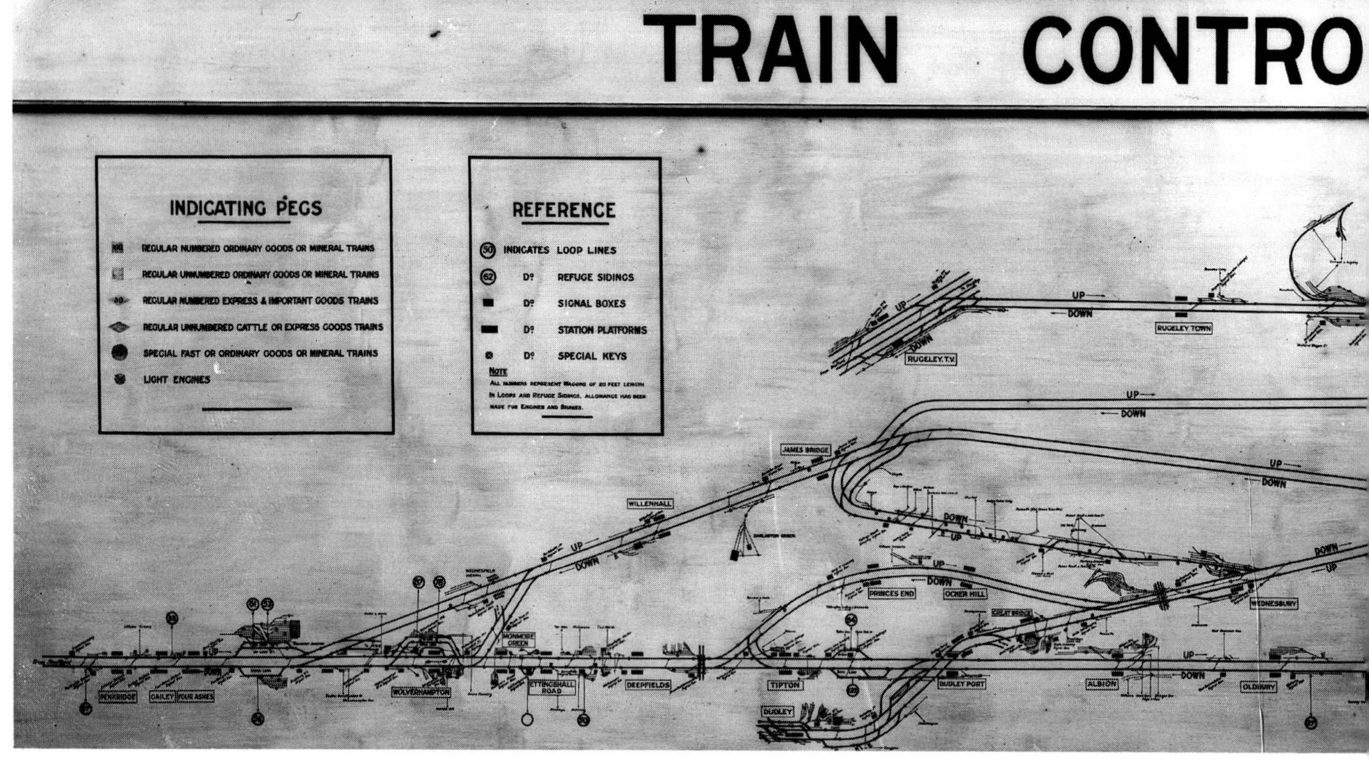

The LNW, in its control offices, provided details of its routes and their track and siding capacities in the form of large wall-mounted diagrammatic maps. This photograph shows the control map for the Bescot area as introduced in 1912. The majority of the maps were prepared in this long, narrow format and it must have required considerable skill on the part of the draughtsmen concerned to adjust the geographical layout of the railways to fit into the space. This diagram illustrates very clearly the problem and how it was overcome. The place-to-place scale was distinctly variable! The notes on the left indicate coding of the indicating pegs which were stuck in holes in the diagram to indicate the positions of the trains. The diagram or train board therefore gave a good visual indication of the state of the traffic at any point in time. The numbers in circles indicated the capacity of loop lines and refuge sidings in numbers of wagons. *National Railway Museum*

TRAIN AND TRAFFIC CONTROL INSTRUCTIONS

OBJECTS OF CONTROL

L1. The fundamental principle of efficient train and traffic operating is that the scheduled timings of trains in the working time tables, notices, etc. be maintained, the booked workings for Guards, Enginemen and engines be adhered to, and that the instructions relating to the classification, marshalling and loading of freight trains be complied with.

L2. The main objects of Control are to maintain the booked arrangements to the maximum possible extent, to guide the working back to normal when out-of-course, and to modify the arrangements when necessary to meet fluctuations in traffic.

L3. The Control in conjunction with other Operating and Motive Power staff engaged in train and traffic working will have the following general aims :—

(*a*) To ensure the expeditious working of traffic including empty stock.

(*b*) To plan and organise the current working of Passenger and Freight trains so as to avoid delay.

(*c*) To obtain the maximum work from engine power and trainmen by :—

(*i*) Punctual working.

(*ii*) Using the fewest locomotives possible.

(*iii*) Securing the maximum authorised loading.

(*iv*) Incurring the minimum amount of light mileage or unrequired assistance.

(*v*) Releasing engines promptly after completion of work.

(*vi*) Making the best use of unbalanced engines.

(*d*) To regulate the working of trainmen to ensure economical working and avoid excessive hours.

L4. All staff associated with the working of trains and the movement of traffic must carry out instructions given from the Control and must co-operate at all times to the fullest extent, by information, consultation and suggestion to overcome difficulties.

L5. Station Masters, Yard Masters, Supervisors and the Staff under them are not relieved of their responsibility and must use their initiative in carrying out laid down arrangements.

A summary of the primary objects of the control system as set out in a control instructions book of 1953.

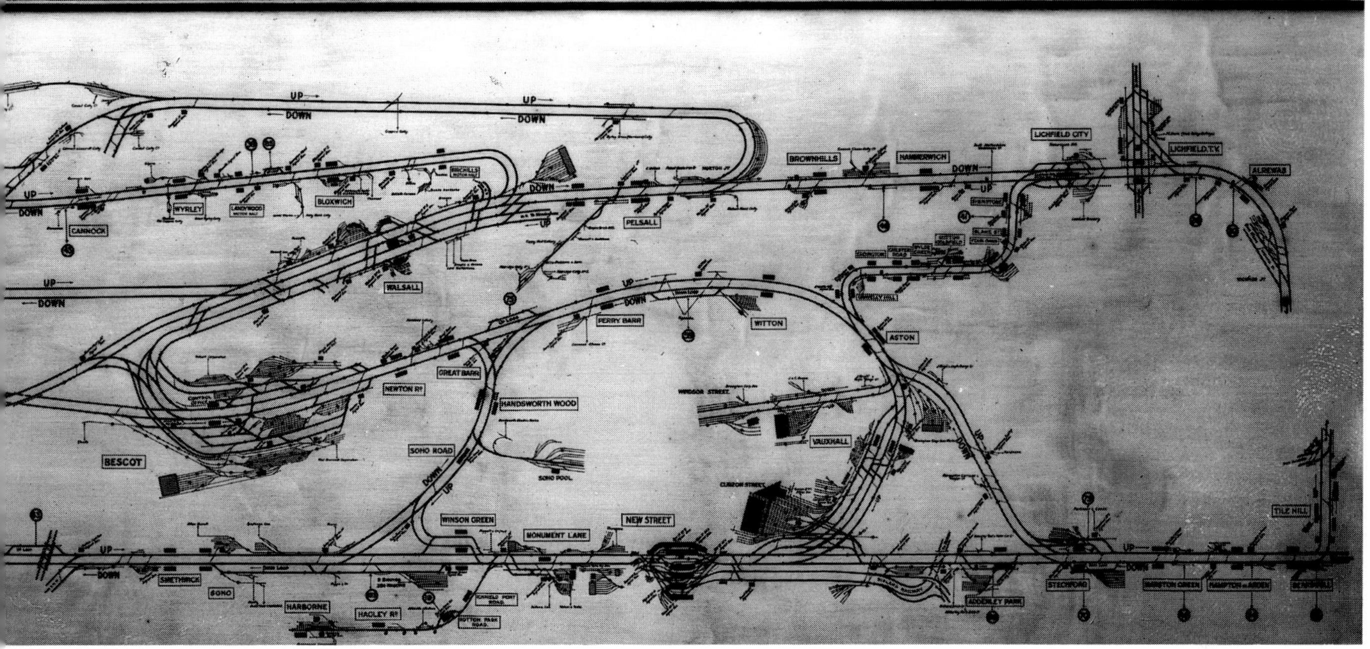

running freight trains could delay following trains, and other services with which they connected.

In the case of freight traffic, the working timetable had of necessity to cater, by means of regular and conditional services, for something approaching the maximum normal volume of traffic. The lack of real knowledge of the situation elsewhere could mean that if traffic was low, some trains would be run unnecessarily, when their loads could have been combined with others. Conversely, if a yard became overwhelmed with traffic, there was no easy way of deciding on the spot which traffic should be held back, and which should be diverted elsewhere. Similarly, if there was too much traffic for a particular train, the surplus would, through lack of assured alternatives, often have to be held over to the next day.

The principal difficulty was that the staff who had to make the decisions were only familiar with the circumstances in their immediate area. Their view of the position further afield was invariably vague or incomplete, and there was noone else to ask who was in possession of anything like a full picture of the situation. By far the greatest difficulties occurred with the goods traffic; passenger trains were, in the main, far easier to deal with, and were generally managed satisfactorily. If an overview of the whole goods traffic situation was available, it would then be possible to use that knowledge to combine lightly-loaded trains together, divert traffic away from congested areas — to other yards or routes — and to find accommodation on other services for excess traffic. The ability to make strategic decisions of this sort would clearly speed up the traffic and effect economies in the working.

The Midland Railway was the first company to get to grips with the efficient management of day-to-day traffic operation. The origins of the control system lay in a pressing need to reduce the excessive hours that many goods and mineral train crews were working as a result of delays to their trains. Relief arrangements had to be set in motion by the men themselves, and with limited information on the running of the trains, it was often difficult to ensure that men were available, and were sent to the right place to afford relief in a reasonable time. A relief office was therefore set up in July 1907 at Rotherham Masborough, in the area with the worst record for long hours. This took over responsibility for calling for and arranging relief, and within six months, Masborough moved from the worst place in the 'long hours league' to the best.

The Midland was already looking at train working with a view to devising some means of controlling the freight traffic, and the success of the Masborough relief office gave additional impetus to the process. This led to an expansion of the Masborough operation, experimentally, to cover the control of freight trains in the area. The results were most encouraging, and from 4th January 1909 an enlarged control organisation was brought into use to cover the lines from Cudworth to Toton. The improvements and savings effected were quite marked, and it was soon decided to extend the arrangement to cover the whole system, this work being completed in 1912. The impact on reducing delays can be seen from the following figures:

Year	*Weekly Average Hours of Delay*
1907	21,869
1909	11,680
1911	8,959
1913	7,749

The three principal purposes of the train control system in respect of freight train operation were established as:

1. To save engine and train miles
2. To load wagons and trains to full capacity
3. To move them as quickly as possible

The control system (as set up) was based on a central office at Derby, with 23 local offices situated at important traffic centres. An office at Saltley covered the Birmingham area of the Midland, and its responsibilities extended along the main line from Kingsbury (near Tamworth) to Pirton Siding (near Ashchurch). Adjacent districts were controlled from offices at Burton, Coalville, Leicester, Gloucester and Swansea.

Clearly, the key to success of the control operation was information, and the first action taken was to set up adequate telephone communications between the control offices and a range of important locations in each district. A selection of strategically-located signalboxes formed the core of the system, each being responsible for reporting the progress of the trains. There were also telephone links with stations, yards and engine sheds.

The control office became responsible for deciding priorities in running, arranging engine power, train crews and crew relief. They decided where assisting engines were required, and from the information they had on train loading, were able to cancel or combine lightly-loaded trains to save on line occupation and costs. Wagons could also be diverted to other yards, to make best use of all the services available. The overview of the whole system enabled services to be quickly rearranged or diverted in the event of difficulties, such as lines blocked by derailments. Stations and yards provided details of the traffic and empty wagons they had on hand each day, as well as their requirements for wagons to meet traffic demands. The control offices were then able to arrange the efficient distribution of suitable wagons to match requirements as nearly as possible, and could avoid sending any more wagons to yards which were already full!

In view of its pioneering role in the development of train control, it was perhaps logical that the Midland should take the system further than any other company. From 1st January 1917, the system was extended to cover important passenger trains, resulting once again in useful improvements to train working.

Other railway companies with substantial freight traffic quickly realised the potential and advantages of the control system, and considered introducing arrangements on their own lines. The initial priority was for those areas with complex freight operations involving much marshalling and trip working. The London & North Western saw the control system as being primarily for freight, and set up control districts in areas where freight working was either difficult or particularly important. The control areas were introduced rather more gradually than had been the case on the Midland, partly to allow for the installation of the additional telephone circuits necessary to ensure that the communications were good enough to make the system work. At some of the reporting signalboxes on the main line, this involved the construction of separate telephone annexes to house the instruments, and the employment of special attendants; in many instances the signalmen were too busy to take on the extra work, and give reporting the priority and attention it required.

Not surprisingly, the LNW decided to site its West Midlands control office at Bescot, the focal point of much of the district's freight operations. Commencing operations in December 1912, Bescot covered the area from Stafford (TV) Junction to Coventry No. 3, and as far east as Wichnor, (but excluding the lines to Leamington). It eventually interfaced with adjacent controls at Stafford and Nuneaton. Until the Great War, when its hours were extended, the control was open between 6 a.m. Monday and 6 a.m. the following Sunday.

Inevitably, there were appreciable differences in the methods used at the LNW control offices when compared with the Midland. Perhaps the most noticeable was the provision of large wall-mounted diagrams in LNW control offices, showing in detail all the lines covered by that control. This included representations of the number of running lines, and track layouts at each station or yard. In the Midland offices, small paper side-strip or section line diagrams, specially prepared for control and timetabling purposes, were used for reference. As with the Midland, the LNW control system was based on a series of districts with an office at a central point in each, although the districts were generally a little larger than on the Midland; consequently, there were slightly fewer offices on the LNW. However, the basic functions of control — to ensure the efficient, expeditious and economical operation of freight traffic, together with the ability to react swiftly to events — were the same as on the Midland.

The Grouping brought the LNW and Midland together under the umbrella of the LMS. For various reasons, Midland ideas and men predominated in the operating department, and inevitably the LNW system was adapted to accord more closely to that of the Midland. The Midland had opted for a heavily-centralised form of management, with all the traffic organisation and control offices reporting to a central authority at Derby. This practice was adopted by the LMS,

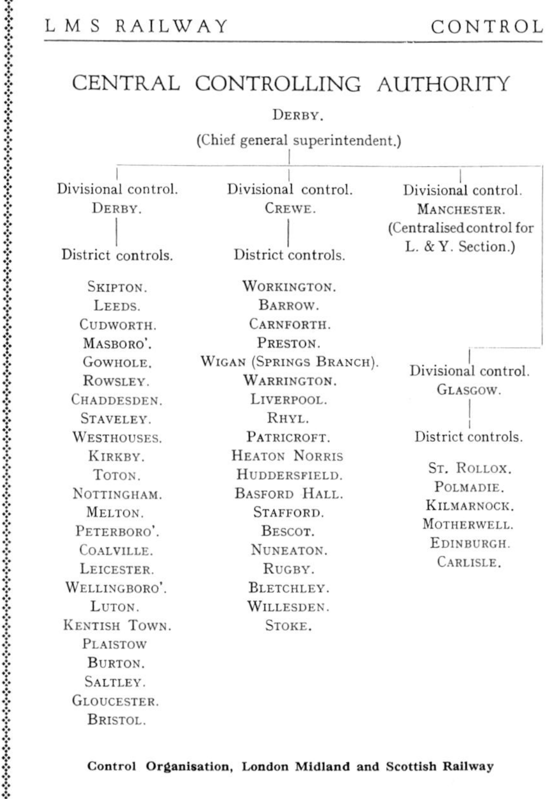

L M S RAILWAY — CONTROL

CENTRAL CONTROLLING AUTHORITY

Derby.

(Chief general superintendent.)

Divisional control. Derby.
District controls.
Skipton. Leeds. Cudworth. Masboro'. Gowhole. Rowsley. Chaddesden. Staveley. Westhouses. Kirkby. Toton. Nottingham. Melton. Peterboro'. Coalville. Leicester. Wellingboro'. Luton. Kentish Town. Plaistow Burton. Saltley. Gloucester. Bristol.

Divisional control. Crewe.
District controls.
Workington. Barrow. Carnforth. Preston. Wigan (Springs Branch). Warrington. Liverpool. Rhyl. Patricroft. Heaton Norris Huddersfield. Basford Hall. Stafford. Bescot. Nuneaton. Rugby. Bletchley. Willesden. Stoke.

Divisional control. Manchester. (Centralised control for L. & Y. Section.)

Divisional control. Glasgow.
District controls.
St. Rollox. Polmadie. Kilmarnock. Motherwell. Edinburgh. Carlisle.

Control Organisation, London Midland and Scottish Railway

PAGE TWENTY

LMS control organisation in 1923. Note the large number of control districts on the Midland Division which contrasts sharply with the one office on the Lancashire & Yorkshire section, illustrating quite different methods of achieving broadly the same object.

After the Western Division Control Office was destroyed in an air raid in 1940, work was put in hand to repair the building and rebuild the control office. In the difficult wartime conditions it was not until 1941 that the work was completed. This photograph was taken in April 1942 shortly after the office re-opened. There were three area controllers: 'A' section nearest the camera controlling the South Staffordshire District (Dudley, Walsall, Lichfield); 'B' section covered the Stour Valley Line (New Street was at the right-hand end of the board) and Wolverhampton–Bescot; 'C' section covered the lines south of New Street (bottom left on the board), the Sutton–Lichfield line and the Grand Junction line north to Bescot. The boards were in the white-on-black style favoured by the LMS Signal and Telegraph Department at this period for illuminated signal cabin diagrams. Note the telephone key switchboards at each position. From right to left, the men on duty were: Frank Whalley (Office Relief Controller) in charge of the 'A' section, Norman Rothwell on the 'B' section, and Arthur Harris on 'C' section. Furthest from the camera was Fred Carter, Freight Rolling Stock Controller, who normally worked in the next office but had been brought in specially to fill up the photograph!
British Railways

and the posts of district superintendents (the titles varied from company to company) which had existed on most companies were abolished (except in areas where there was no control office). In practice, the district controllers took on much of the responsibilities of the old district superintendents, and eventually the post of divisional superintendent (equivalent of the old LNW Superintendent of the Line) reappeared.

An early (and major) change was the decision that the LMS control system should cover both freight and passenger trains, and it was therefore necessary to extend the LNW control operation to include the latter. In Birmingham, the focus of freight operations was Bescot, whilst the passenger services were centred on New Street station; a new, combined passenger and freight control office for the Western (LNW) Division was therefore set up on the top floor of the office block on platform 6, in 1925, and the old office at Bescot was closed. By contrast, the previously-established Midland Division combined control office remained at Saltley. This was originally located on the station platform, but in about 1937 it moved to a new office outside Saltley engine shed, opposite Duddeston Road Junction signal box. Despite the fact that they were part of the same company, the Western and Midland divisional traffic operations in the West Midlands hardly impinged on each other, except at a couple of exchange points. Even at New Street, few trains crossed from one side to the other; to all intents and purposes, it functioned as two 'independent' stations, side by side.

In these circumstances, there was not much interaction or overlap between the two Birmingham control offices, and thus there was no great incentive to combine the two operations. Hence, Birmingham retained its two LMS control offices.

The control system and its offices were essential to the efficient operation of the railway at the best of times, but in adversity, such as wartime, they took on even greater significance. It was recognised by the LMS that the control system had to be capable of functioning under all conditions throughout the war. The control offices, situated as they were in busy yard and station areas, were clearly very vulnerable to bombing; in 1939, a programme of constructing bomb-proof bunkers, in which to house the control offices and any other essential functions, was therefore set in motion. Each control office was equipped with all the essentials, and was capable of being brought fully into use within a few minutes once the control office staff (and any papers they were able to bring with them) had arrived. Thus, transfer could be effected quickly, either during periods of air raids or in the event of damage to the original office. Duplicate telephone lines were provided from the emergency control office, linking into the control telephone circuits some distance from the main office, as a precaution against the lines being lost at the same time as those in the main office.

At New Street, a protected emergency control office was constructed under platform 1A, just to the west of Navigation Street bridge. The need for the office to be blastproof was amply demonstrated on 16th October 1940, when No. 5 signal cabin, only a few yards away, was almost totally destroyed by the blast from a bomb which fell nearby. Just a few days later, on 28th October, a fire bomb damaged the platform 6 office block, and rendered the Western Division control office unusable — it was, of course, somewhat exposed in its position on the top floor. The control staff reconvened in the emergency bunker, and the control had to remain there for some time.

The emergency control office at New Street was of substantial construction, designed to withstand a direct hit from bombs of up to 500 pounds in weight. The basic structural design of the standard control office shelter consisted of two concrete walls, one 3ft thick and the other 1ft 6in thick separated by a 4ft cavity filled with sand. The roof was 10ft thick, comprising two layers of reinforced concrete, one 4ft and the other 2ft, again with a 4ft layer of sand between. The actual constructional details were modified somewhat to suit the location. Inside was an entrance air lock, the control room, and three small rooms: one to house a generator, the second a battery room, and one for a telephone switchboard. There were up to seven controllers' positions in the control room itself, though it was very cramped and claustrophobic. While the intention was to allow the control function to continue during air raids and emergency conditions, the buildings were not really suited to continuous operation, and it was there-

The two photographs on this page show the Western Division control office in 1948. The top photograph was taken in January and the bottom one on 5th August. *T. J. Edgington*

NEW OPERATING ORGANISATION STRUCTURE

DISTRICT OPERATING MANAGER

ASSISTANT DISTRICT OPERATING MANAGER

ASSISTANT TO DISTRICT OPERATING MANAGER

CONTROL OFFICE

GENERAL SECTION

DISTRICT INSPECTORS

CHIEF STAFF CLERK

STAFF SECTION

NEW OPERATING DISTRICTS

London (Western)
London (Midland)
Rugby
Birmingham (Midland)
Birmingham (Western)
Crewe
Stoke
Manchester (Western)
Liverpool
Chester
Swansea
Preston
Barrow
Leicester
Nottingham
Derby
Gloucester
Rotherham
Wakefield
Leeds

fore necessary to construct a new permanent control office to replace that which was destroyed.

Rather surprisingly, in view of the vulnerability of the original location on the top floor of the platform 6 buildings, the decision was taken to rebuild it in the same location. Of course, there were good reasons for keeping the office at New Street: it was accessible for the staff, and all the telephone circuits were concentrated there. Moving away from New Street would have meant a lot of work in laying new cables — not an easy thing to do in wartime, even if the materials could have been found. Once the decision had been taken to keep the office at New Street, there was not a lot of choice but to put it back where it had been. In wartime conditions the reconstruction work took quite some time, and it was not until about October 1941 that the work was complete, allowing the staff to be transferred to the new office from their claustrophobic bunker. Fortunately, by this time the worst of the air raids were over, and there was no more damage caused to New Street.

By 1939, the control system had been in use (with relatively little change) for over 20 years, and the time had come for some changes to bring the system up to date. With the general improvements in communications and other developments that had taken place over the years, the most obvious and productive change would be to make the control areas larger, thus obtaining economies of scale, and reducing the problems of operations across control boundaries. It was also felt that the highly-centralised organisation inherited from the Midland was too rigid, and stifled initiative. Proposals were therefore put forward in 1939 for a new operating organisation, based on a system of district operating managers (thereby effectively recreating the old district superintendents). The control offices were to report to the district managers, with the number of offices and their boundaries adjusted to suit. The war intervened before anything was done, and rather than risk any disruption in a national emergency, the proposals were deferred for the duration.

The destruction of the New Street office, did, however, provide an opportunity to try out new ideas. The result of the studies into operational efficiency and future needs led to a new and simplified office layout, with the section controllers and their control boards laid out along one wall, with the guards, loco and passenger controllers occupying a curved row of desks behind and facing the control boards, whilst overseeing everything from further back still sat the head controller. The resultant layout was considered successful enough to be adopted as the basis for future installations.

With the end of the war in 1945, the 1939 proposals for a new operating organisation were resurrected. The aim was to achieve some degree of decentralisation by placing operating staff (formerly controlled from headquarters), along with the local staff, under the supervision and control of district operating managers. The control offices, formerly under a district controller and responsible to a divisional central control, were also placed under the district operating managers. The control areas were to be adjusted where necessary to correspond with the new operating districts.

In England and Wales, there were to be 20 new operating districts, 18 under district operating managers and two small ones under district traffic managers. The existing 42 control districts were rationalised into the 20 new districts, and the number of control offices was reduced, generally to one per district. At the same time, opportunity was taken to modernise those control offices that were to remain, and as far as possible these were moved so as to occupy the same building as the district operating manager and his headquarters staff. In all, the new arrangements cost about £1 million to implement.

Despite the unification of the LNW and Midland some 20 years previously, and the introduction of larger traffic management districts, it was still found necessary to have two district operating managers in Birmingham, one to cover the ex-LNW lines, and one to cover the ex-Midland; this in turn necessitated two control offices. A start towards integration was made by locating the two operating manager's offices together in the buildings on platform 6 at New Street. Since the Western Division control office was a modern installation and already located on the top floor of this building, it was decided to retain it unchanged, whilst a new control office for the Birmingham (Midland) Division was established in a nearby room.

The Birmingham (Western) district became the first of the district operating manager's districts to be set up, a contributory factor being that there was no control office to equip. Mr. A.R. Thomson, the former district controller, was appointed district operating manager in March 1945, and in 1946, his district was responsible for 1,839 passenger trains a week, together with 22,776 freight train miles and 694,000 wagon miles. By coincidence, the last link in the new operating manager's organisation was also forged in Birmingham; the last district operating manager's district to be set up was Birmingham (Midland), which commenced to function on 3rd March 1947. The old Midland control office at Saltley was then closed, and the staff moved to their new office at New Street. In 1949, the train boards in the Western Division control office were renewed, the three LMS sectional boards with their black backgrounds giving way to two sectional boards with a light olive green background.

Despite their proximity, there was little interaction between the new control offices or their staffs. Although the LMS control system had supposedly been unified since the 1920s, there were still differences in practice between the Midland and Western controls. The Midland control was deeply involved in the regulation of the running of the trains, whereas the Western left more of the work to the signalmen; something of the difference can be seen by studying the train reporting arrangements. As was often the way with different groups of people, the atmospheres in the two offices were also quite different — one was quiet and rather staid, the other more relaxed and talkative. The outside staff sometimes had a rather sceptical view of some of 'control's' decisions and, in circumstances when they did not agree, would refer to the controllers derogatorily as, for example, 'The Brains Trust'. This lack of respect stemmed from the practice of recruiting the control assistants from the

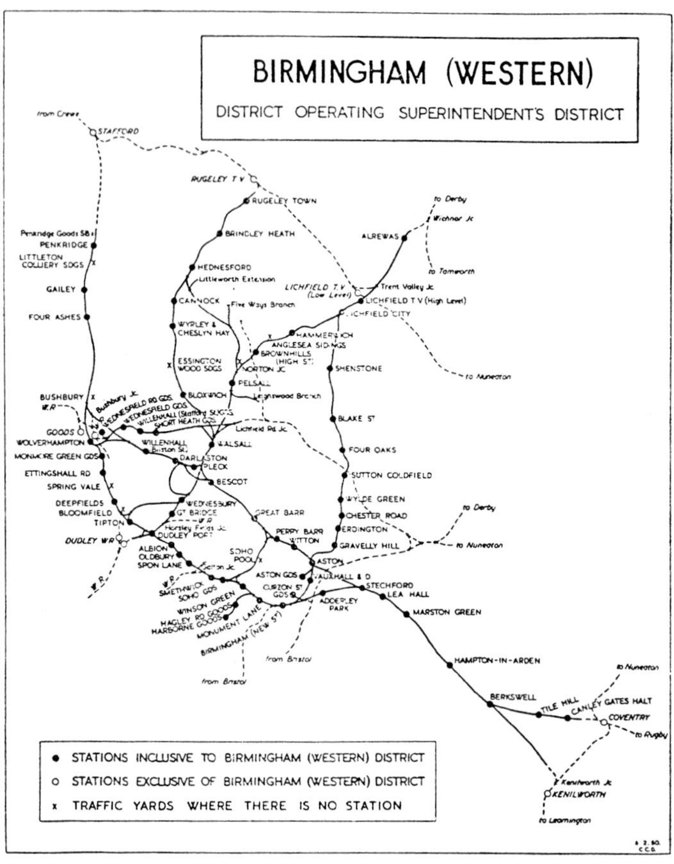

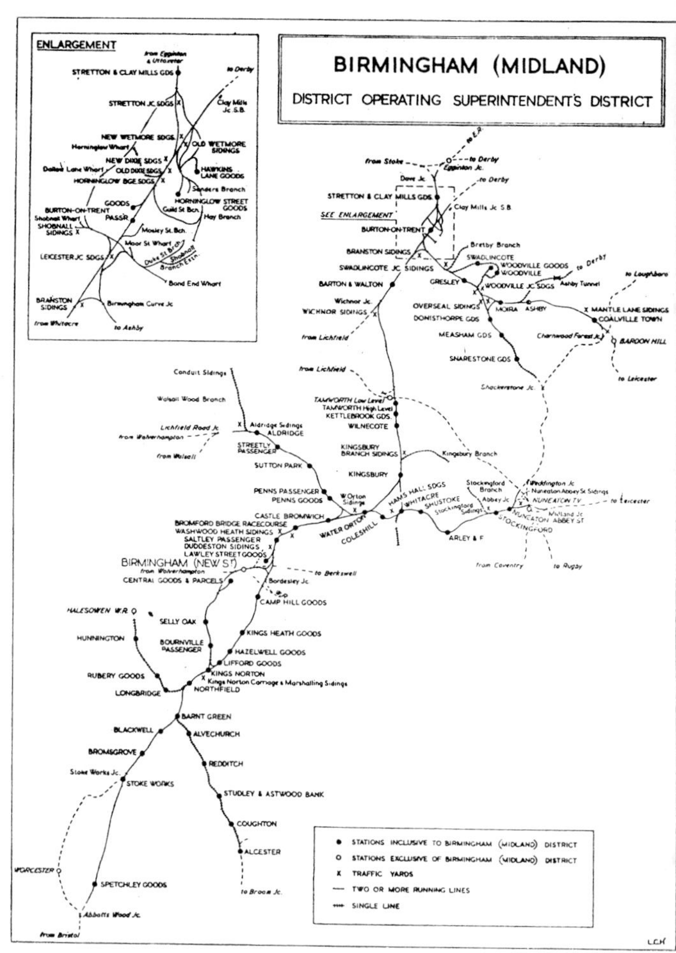

Maps showing the Birmingham Western and Midland Control areas as at 1950. These areas dated from the 1945 reorganisation.

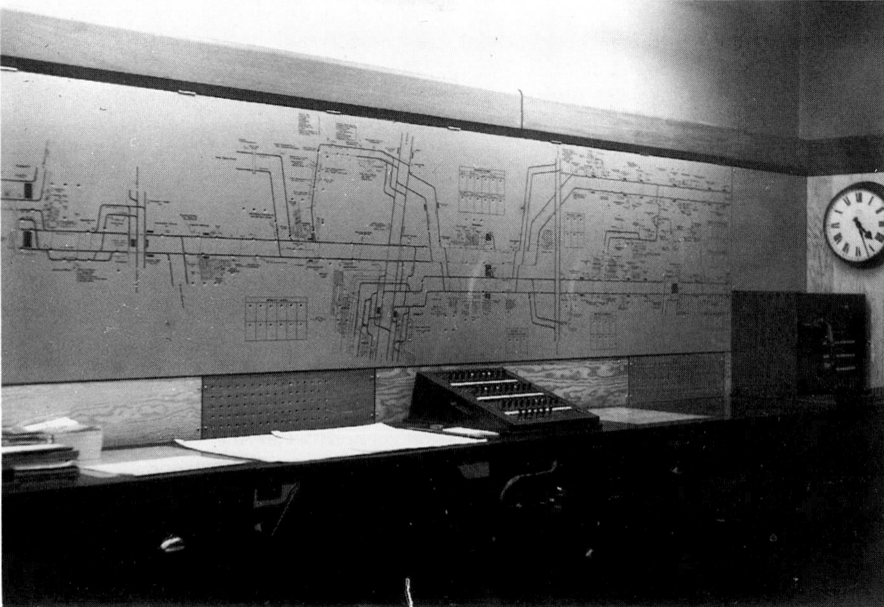

These two photographs (above and top right) show the new Western Division control boards on 9th February 1949, immediately after installation. Indeed the work was not quite complete as the woodwork still had to be varnished and the boards were not yet in use. These boards were a light olive green in colour and the tracks were coloured, red for main lines, yellow for slow lines and blue for goods lines. Comparison with the earlier photographs shows that only the boards had been changed and the clocks moved, the desks remained unchanged. In the new arrangement there were only two sections of board. This photograph shows the South Staffordshire section with Dudley on the left and Walsall in the centre, the Walsall–Rugeley line top right and the Walsall–Lichfield line bottom right. *T. J. Edgington*

railway clerical grades, rather than utilising staff with operating experience (such as signalmen). Inevitably, some of the men (perhaps previously a parcels clerk) had a somewhat limited knowledge of the operating practices and geography of their district, and some of their decisions betrayed this.

In addition to the staff in the control office itself, a number of control personnel were outstationed at various points as regulators, to assist in the working. Thus, on the Midland Division, there was a regulator at Duddeston Road signalbox whose duties were to plan and regulate the movements of trains and engines between Washwood Heath Junction and King's Heath Station, and to and from Grand Junction. An assistant controller was stationed at Water Orton Station Junction to assist the signalman, and carry out the train reporting. Those new to control work would often spend their first 12 months there as a means of getting to know the area and the job.

Another assistant controller was stationed at Bromsgrove South, and occupied a small cabin near the foot of the signalbox steps. His main purpose was to

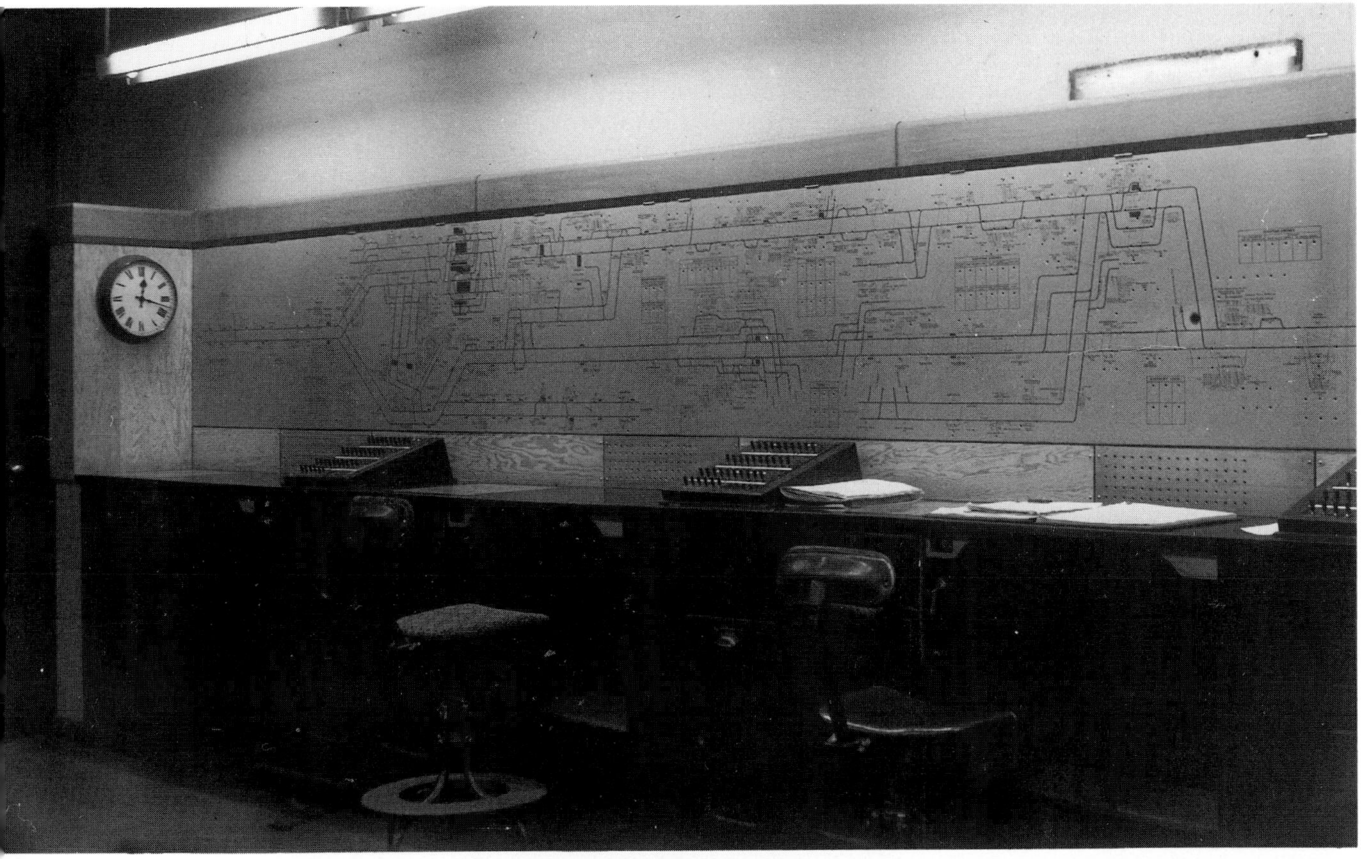

The Main Line control board. The Stour Valley line ran along the top with New Street on the left and Wolverhampton on the right. The Lichfield line appears at the bottom left and the Midland Walsall line at bottom right. *T. J. Edgington*

A close-up of part of the Main Line control board covering the New Street, Curzon Street and Aston area, with Ron Cole, the duty controller, placing a train location peg and its identifying tag into one of the train position locating holes in the board, in this case on the up Western line at Proof House Junction. Note the spaces for engines on shed, as well as those for banking engines. Pegs not in use (e.g. trips which did not run at that time of day) were kept in the rack below the board. The Perry Barr banker peg bore the number 132, its trip working number (this had remained the same since at least 1938). The photograph was taken in December 1952. *Birmingham Post & Mail*

organise the relief and changeover of train crews, being in BR days near the regional boundary. The controller liaised with the WR at Gloucester and with Birmingham control on the crew requirements and the running of the trains. Here, as well as being in touch with the running of trains and the crewing and relief requirements, the controller had to be familiar with the different terminology used by men from different companies or regions. The freight trains fitted with vacuum brakes were known as 'fitted' to the LMR men and 'vacuum' to the WR men; 'Engine and brake' on the LMR was 'engine and van' on the WR.

The scheme to reconstruct New Street station meant that the two control offices had to be moved to allow demolition of the buildings. The offices therefore moved, in 1959, into the Birmingham divisional offices, then in Gloucester House on Smallbrook Ringway. Here at last, the two controls came together in the same room — not that it made a great deal of difference in the first instance: the Western men went about their business at one end of the room, and the Midland men at the othe Gradually, however, integration wa achieved, and the unified control wa generally known as 'Ringway Control' b the outside staff. From January 1963, th ex-GW lines in the Birmingham area hitherto part of the Western Regio were transferred to the London Midlan Region. The Western Region control a Snow Hill was moved to Glouceste House to join the LMR control — anoth er set of men with, initially, little in com mon with the others.

With the completion of the reconstruc tion of New Street and the electrificatio of the ex-LNW lines, the majority of th trains which had used Snow Hill statio — including all of the expresses — wer either withdrawn or transferred to Ne Street. When Broadgate House on Broa Street (later known as Rail House, an now as Quayside Tower) opened, the con trol office, combined at last, moved there In recent years, in connection with th restructuring of the railway industry further changes have been made in th control organisation and the location o the offices.

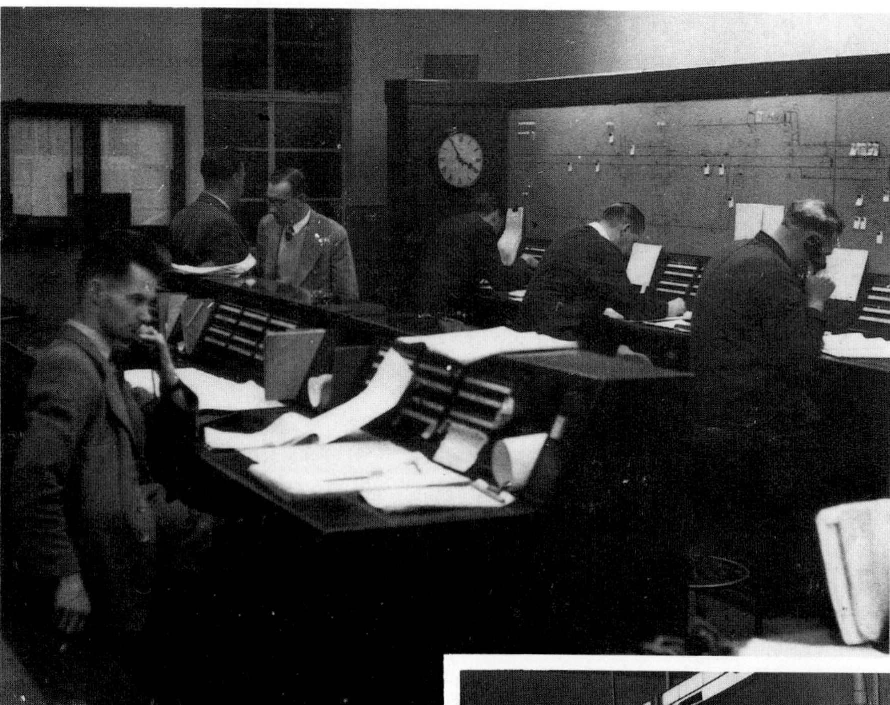

These photographs were taken in the Midland Division control office in 1952 or 3. The office was just along the corridor from the Western Division office and opened in March 1947. The view above shows the control desks and part of the control boards, with, on the left, George Walker, the Guards Controller, and in the centre, with the spectacles, Steve Hughes, the Saltley Area engine controller. In the background, the portion of the control board visible covered the King's Norton to Bromsgrove and Redditch section. *Right:* A section of the control board with some of the controllers posing for the camera. The Kingsbury branch sidings show nearest the camera with the four-track Water Orton–Saltley section beyond, and the Water Orton to Walsall and Wolverhampton line at the top. A number of train pegs and tags can be seen on the board giving an indication of how these were used. Arnold Kingman, the Leicester/Burton and Water Orton section controller, is shown on the right, followed by Vic Pigeon, Saltley section engine controller; Bill Blakeman, Washwood Heath section controller; and Ray Brotherton, assistant controller Kings Norton and Bromsgrove.

Cty. R. Brotherton

Two views of the 'A' and 'B' or Bromsgrove–Kings Norton and Washwood Heath section of the Midland control board, the picture below showing controller Bill Blakeman and assistant controller Ray Brotherton on duty on the Washwood Heath and Bromsgrove–Kings Norton sections respectively.

Cty. R. Brotherton

GOODS

CHAPTER FIVE

CURZON STREET GOODS STATION

THE dominant role of Curzon Street was as a receiving point for a huge volume of general goods traffic, both incoming and outgoing, much of which travelled by overnight express goods trains which linked all the major centres. The day's work fell into two distinct phases: the mornings, when the incoming goods trains were received and unloaded, and the goods sorted and delivered; and the afternoons, when goods were brought in from the surrounding areas for loading into the outward goods trains for overnight despatch to their destination. The scale of the operations at Curzon Street is demonstrated by the fact that, in 1914, there were nearly 2,000 men employed there; in addition, there were 600 horses housed in the stables. Fifty-four small fixed cranes, mostly inside the various warehouses and sheds, were to be found in the depot, the majority of which were hydraulically powered.

Within the depot, the men and the work were divided into distinct functions, and the degree of overlap between them was quite small. Relatively few of the uniformed men changed from one functional area to another, and not many had any detailed knowledge of how work in other parts of the depot was carried out. At the railway end were the signalmen, shunters and capstanmen who dealt with the incoming and outgoing trains. Next were the goods shed staff, who loaded and unloaded the railway wagons and delivery vehicles, and sorted and checked the goods. At the other end of the shed were the cartage staff, who delivered or collected the goods around the town.

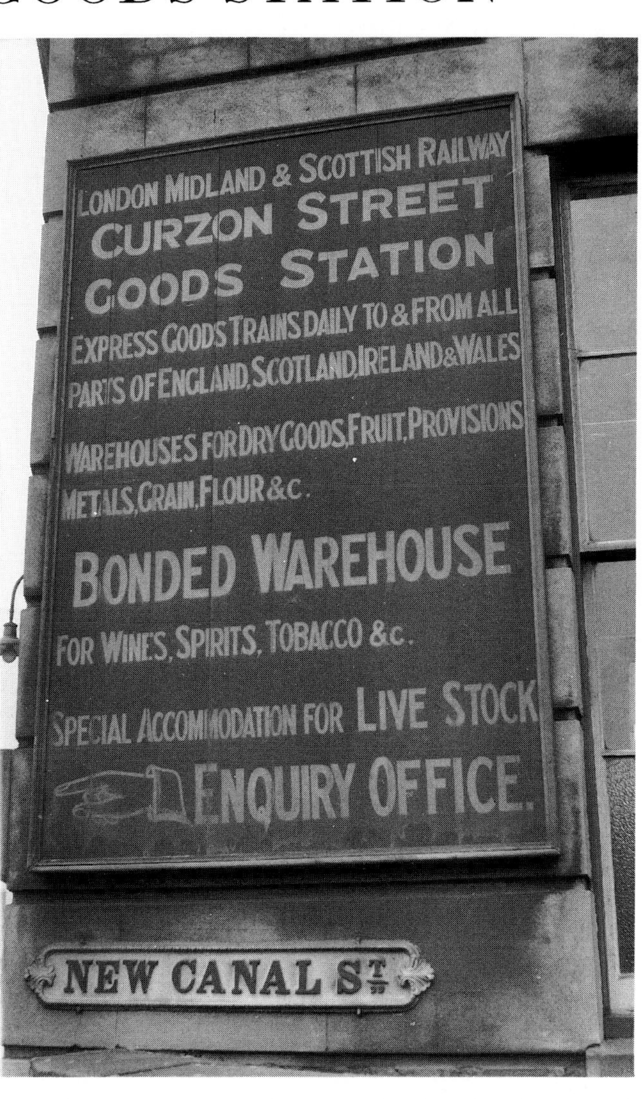

Notice board on the Curzon Street end of the hotel extension block of the main building. This notice was still extant in the 1950s. There was previously an equivalent LNW notice in a similar position. ***Collection R. Carpenter***

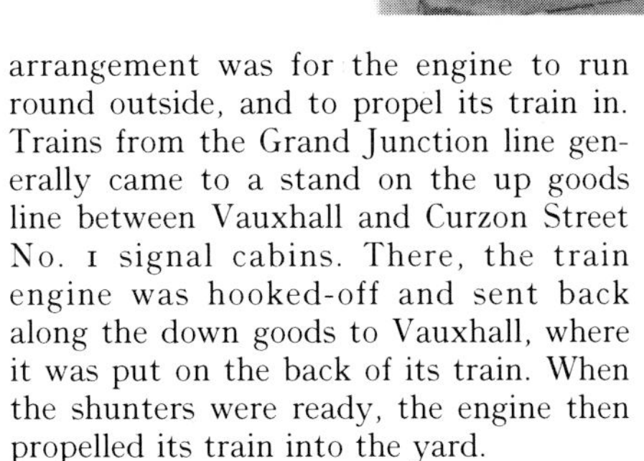

Opposite: **The New Canal Street frontage of the goods offices, photographed on 19th August 1932. The gaggle of small boys sitting on the plinth gives an appreciation of both the size of the building and the size of the individual blocks of stone used in its construction.** ***Birmingham Libraries***

The Curzon Street site was extremely cramped, and hardly big enough for the traffic handled. The sidings were short and there was little space for the marshalling of trains, in consequence of which the work at Curzon Street was closely linked with various marshalling yards. The principal link was with Exchange Sidings, but yards further afield, such as Stechford, Adderley Park and Bescot, also had important roles to play.

A feature of the layout at Curzon Street was that only one of its sidings was long enough to accommodate a full-size train; this was Siding No. 2 (the 'Excursion Line'), though even this did not have any provision for running round, and could be occupied by other traffic. As far as possible, therefore, the practice of running trains directly into the yard was avoided; instead, the normal arrangement was for the engine to run round outside, and to propel its train in. Trains from the Grand Junction line generally came to a stand on the up goods line between Vauxhall and Curzon Street No. 1 signal cabins. There, the train engine was hooked-off and sent back along the down goods to Vauxhall, where it was put on the back of its train. When the shunters were ready, the engine then propelled its train into the yard.

For trains from the south there was no goods line, and so they simply stopped on the down main line at Grand Junction. The engine ran round via the up main, crossing over again at Exchange Sidings signal cabin, and then propelled the train into Curzon Street. This could be a very time-consuming process if the engine had to wait for a path on the up main, or if the shunters were not ready for the train. A further complication was that the roads outside the goods shed (roads 4 to 23) were quite short, most only holding about ten wagons, and so if trains were to be put directly into the shed sidings (as the men would try to do, to save time and shunting later) they could not generally be disposed of in one shunt. Several movements were usually necessary to divide the train between the various sidings, thus adding to the time that the main line could be occupied; the down and up mains could therefore be blocked for an appreciable period. Special authority was given for these propelling movements into Curzon Street from the down main line and from Exchange Sidings.

To facilitate the working of down freight trains, the LNW issued the following instruction in 1913:

'Stechford must advise Curzon Street the loading of all goods trains, and Curzon Street on *receipt* of this information must

LONDON MIDLAND AND SCOTTISH RAILWAY COMPANY.

(WESTERN DIVISION).

BIRMINGHAM CONTROL AREA

NOTICE.

SEPTEMBER 26th, 1938, until further notice.

No. 26—CURZON STREET YARD SHUNTING ENGINE.

Class 3 Freight Tank Engine.

5.52 a.m. (SX) to 4.2 a.m.

5.52 a.m. (SO) to 8.52 p.m.

No. 142—BESCOT, WALSALL, CURZON STREET TRIP ENGINE.

Class 2 Freight Engine.

	arr. (SO)	dep.		arr. (SO)	dep.
	p.m.	p.m.		p.m.	p.m.
Bescot	...	4 24 L.E.	Exchange Sidings	8 10	8 38
Walsall	4 32	5 18	Adderley Park	8 43	11 15
Bescot	5 27	7 8	Stechford	11 25	11 40
Curzon Street	7 47	8 5	Bescot	12 15 a.m.	...

No. 150—STECHFORD TRIP ENGINE.

Class 2 Freight Engine.

	arr.	(SX)	dep.
	p.m.		p.m.
Aston Shed	...		1 25 L.E.
Stechford	1 33	(shunt)	6 33 L.E.
Exchange Sidings	6 40		6 55
Curzon Street	7 10		7 30
Exchange Sidings	7 35		8 36
Adderley Park	8 41		9 36 L.E.
			a.m.
Vauxhall	9 46		2 27(MX)
	a.m.		
Aston Shed	2 31		...

	arr.	(SO)	dep.
	a.m.		a.m.
Aston Shed	...		11 30 L.E.
			a.m.
Curzon Street	11 37		11 50
			p.m.
Exchange Sidings	11 55		12 41
	p.m.		
Adderley Park	12 46		1 13
Stechford	1 23	(shunt)	5 48
Albion	8 17		8 30 L.E.
Ettingshall Road	8 42		9 22
	a.m.		a.m.
Exchange Sidings	1 34		1 46 L.E. (Sun.)
Aston Shed	1 57		...

No. 152—CURZON STREET, BANBURY STREET, VAUXHALL, AND ADDERLEY PARK TRIP ENGINE.

Class 2 Freight Engine.

	arr.	(SO)	dep.
	a.m.		a.m.
Aston Shed	...		5 52 L.E.
Curzon Street	5 59	Shunt	5 0 (Sun.)
Exchange Sidings	5 5		5 30
Curzon Street	5 45	Shunt	11 10 L.E.
Aston Shed	11 17		...

	arr. (SX)	dep.
	a.m.	a.m.
Aston Shed	...	5 52 L.E.
Curzon Street	5 59	...
		a.m.
Curzon Street	...	2 0 L.E. (MX)
Aston Shed	2 7	...

No. 158A—BESCOT, STECHFORD AND BUSHBURY TRIP ENGINE.

Class 6 Freight Engine.

	arr.	(SX)	dep.
	p.m.		p.m.
Bescot	...		9 40
			a.m.
Stechford	10 16	(shunt)	12 21 L.E.(MX)

	arr.	dep.
	a.m.	a.m.
Curzon Street	12 31	2 20
Soho Pool	2 48	3 0
Bescot	3 20 L.E. to Shed	

No. 158—CURZON STREET, EXCHANGE SIDINGS, AND ADDERLEY PARK TRIP ENGINE.

Class 2 Freight Engine.

	arr.	(SX)	dep.
	p.m.		p.m.
Aston Shed	...		11 0 L.E.
Exchange Sidings	11 11		11 45
			a.m.
Adderley Park	11 50	(shunt)	1 55 (MX)
	a.m.		
Stechford	2 5		2 20

	arr. (MX)	dep.
	a.m.	a.m.
Bescot	2 57	4 30
Vauxhall	4 55	5 28
Curzon Street	5 43	5 55 L.E.
Aston Shed	6 1	...

No. 166—VAUXHALL, BESCOT, SUTTON LINE & GREAT BARR TRIP ENGINE.

Class 6 Freight Engine.

	arr.	(MX)	dep.
	a.m.		a.m.
Aston Shed	...		3 5 L.E.
Curzon Street	3 12		3 40
Bescot	4 36		...
		(MO)	
Aston Shed	...		4 25 L.E.
Bescot	4 45	(daily)	5 15
Norton Junction	5 40		6 32
Lichfield	6 55		8 26
Shenstone	8 41		9 42
Four Oaks	10 8		11 5
Sutton Coldfield	11 10		12 13

	arr.		dep.
	p.m.		p.m.
Chester Road	12 17		12 50
Erdington	12 55	shunt	4 10
Aston Goods	4 25	(SX)	5 17 E. & B.
Witton	5 28		6 30
Bescot	6 53		7 25 Daily
Witton	7 43		7 55 L.E.
Aston Shed	7 58		...
Aston Goods	4 25	(SO)	5 17 E. & B.
Great Barr	5 36		6 15
Bescot	6 28		...

No. 169—BUSHBURY, SPRING VALE, BESCOT & CURZON ST. TRIP ENGINE.

Class 6 Freight Engine.

	arr. (MO)	dep.
	a.m.	a.m.
Aston	...	3 25 L.E.
Stechford	3 33	3 55
Ettingshall Road	7 0	7 8 L.E.
Bushbury	7 23	8 30
Bescot	8 54	9 50
Curzon Street	11 10	11 50
	p.m.	p.m.
Stechford	1 40	2 52
Dudley Port	5 5	5 16
Tipton	5 21	5 30
Aston Shed	6 35 p.m.	

	arr. (MX)	dep.
	a.m.	a.m.
Aston	...	2 25 L.E.
Stechford	2 33	3 40
Wolverhampton	4 59	5 27 L.E.
Bushbury	5 32	6 40
Bescot	8 48	9 50
Curzon Street	11 10	11 23 L.E.
Aston Junction	11 31	...

No. 173—ASTON, STECHFORD, AND CURZON STREET TRIP ENGINE.

Class 2 Freight Engine.

	arr.	(SX)	dep.
	p.m.		p.m.
Vauxhall	...		6 55 L.E.
Aston Goods	7 4		7 20
Stechford	7 41		8 53 L.E.
Aston Gas Works	9 5		9 40
Aston Goods	9 50		...
	p.m.	(SO)	p.m.
Aston Goods	...		6 30
Stechford	6 56	(shunt)	9 0

	arr. (SO)	dep.
	p.m.	p.m.
Adderley Park	9 10	9 35
Exchange Sidings	9 40	10 10
Curzon Street	10 25	10 55 L.E.
Exchange Sidings	10 57	11 33
		a.m.
Stechford	11 45	12 45 (Sun.)
Aston Goods	1 9	... L.E. to Shed.

No. 187—WITTON AND GREAT BARR SHUNTING ENGINE.

Class 4 Freight Engine.

	arr. (SX)	dep.	arr. (SO)	dep.
	a.m.	a.m.	a.m.	a.m.
Aston Shed	...	10 26 L.E.	...	10 26
Witton	10 31	11 35	10 31	11 35
Perry Barr	11 41	11 49	11 41	11 49
	p.m.	p.m.	p.m.	p.m.
Bescot	12 20	1 23	12 20	1 25
Great Barr	1 38	4 10	1 40	3 35
Perry Barr	4 18	4 39	3 43	3 53
Witton	4 43	5 13	3 58	4 12
Curzon Street	5 36	5 55	4 35	5 0 Light to Shed
Exchange Sidings	6 0	6 17 L.E.	...	...
Aston Shed	6 28	...	5 9	...

No. 201—CURZON STREET, ADDERLEY PARK, AND STECHFORD TRIP ENGINE.

Class 6 Freight Engine.

	arr. (daily)	dep.
	p.m.	a.m.
Aston Shed	...	11 55 L.E.
		p.m.
Stechford	12 3	12 20
Exchange Sidings	12 30	12 40
Curzon Street	12 45(SX)	2 10
Exchange Sidings	2 15	2 52
Adderley Park	2 55	6 13 L.E.
Curzon Street	6 17	7 10
Adderley Park	7 19	8 34 L.E.
Curzon Street	8 37	9 40
Exchange Sidings	9 45	9 57

	arr. (SX)	dep.
	p.m.	p.m.
Stechford	10 7	10 45
Adderley Park	10 55	11 25
	(MX)	a.m.
Exchange Sidings	11 30	12 1
Stechford	12 10	12 27 L.E.
Aston Shed	12 35	p.m.
Curzon Street	...(SO)	1 3 L.E.
Aston Shed	1 10	...

(Commencing 18-10-38)

After working 12.1 a.m. from Exchange Sidings, works as under :—

	arr.	(MX)	dep.
	a.m.		a.m.
Stechford	...		12 30 L.E.
Adderley Park	12 40	(shunt)	4 0 L.E.
Aston Shed	4 20		...

No. 202—CURZON STREET, VAUXHALL, EXCHANGE SIDINGS, ADDERLEY PARK, AND STECHFORD TRIP ENGINE.

Class 2 Freight Engines.

	arr.	(Sundays)	dep.
	p.m.		p.m.
Aston Shed	...		10 35 L.E.
		(MO)	a.m.
Curzon Street	10 42	shunt	12 45 L.E.
Exchange Sidings	12 47		1 0
Curzon Street	1 15		7 48
Exchange Sidings	7 53		9 45
Adderley Park	9 50	shunt	
	p.m.	(SX)	p.m.
Aston Shed	...		10 0 L.E.
Curzon Street	10 7		10 20
			(MX) a.m.
Exchange Sdgs.	10 25	shunt	12 13 L.E.
	a.m.		
Curzon Street	12 15	shunt	7 48
Exchange Sidings	7 53		9 45
			(Daily) p.m.
Adderley Park	9 50	shunt	12 10 L.E.
Curzon Street	12 15		1 25LE(SX)
Vauxhall	1 30	shunt	3 45 (SX)

	arr.	(SX)	dep.
	p.m.		p.m.
Curzon Street	3 50		5 30
Adderley Park	5 40		8 0 L.E.
Aston Shed	8 14		...
		(SO)	
Curzon St.	12 15	shunt	6 42
Adderley Park	6 51		7 25 L.E.
Exchange Sdgs.	7 28		7 55
Adderley Park	7 58		9 15 L.E.
Exchange Sidings	9 18		10 25
Curzon Street	10 40	shunt	12 0
		(Sunday)	
	a.m.		a.m.
Exchange Sdgs.	12 5		12 45
Curzon Street	1 0		2 55
Exchange Sdgs.	3 0		3 30
Stechford	3 40	shunt	7 45 light to Shed
Aston Shed	7 53		...

No. 203—CURZON STREET, EXCHANGE SIDINGS, ADDERLEY PARK, AND STECHFORD TRIP ENGINE.

Class 4 Freight Engine.

	arr. (MO)	dep.
	a.m.	a.m.
Aston Shed	...	4 45 L.E.
Stechford	4 53	5 0
Aston Goods	5 22	5 40 L.E.
Curzon Street	5 52	6 0
Exchange Sidings	6 5	6 20
Adderley Park	6 25	8 5
Stechford	8 15	8 20 L.E.
Adderley Park	8 25	9 33
Stechford	9 42	10 17 L.E.
Adderley Park	10 22	10 42
Stechford	10 52	11 18 L.E.
Adderley Park	11 23	11 51
	p.m.	p.m.
Stechford	12 1	12 30 Light to Shed
Aston Shed	12 56	...

	arr.	dep.
	p.m.	p.m.
New Street	(SX)	8 48 L.E.
Aston Goods	9 2	9 55
		a.m.
Stechford	10 30	12 45 (MX)
	a.m.	
Aston Goods	1 10(MX)	1 50 L.E.
Stechford	2 2	3 35
Exchange Sidings	3 45	4 40
Curzon Street	4 45	5 25
Exchange Sidings	5 30	6 50
Adderley Park	6 55	8 5
Stechford	8 15	8 20LE(MX)
Adderley Park	8 25(MX)	9 33
Stechford	9 42	10 17 L.E.
Adderley Park	10 22	10 42
Stechford	10 52	11 18 L.E.
		p.m.
Adderley Park	11 23	12 18 (SO)
	p.m.	
Stechford	12 28	1 21 E & B
Metro Sidings	1 28	1 33
Robinson's Sidings	1 36	1 46
Aston Goods	1 56 L.E. to Shed.	
		(MSX) a.m.
Adderley Park	...	11 51
		p.m.
Stechford	12 1	12 47
Aston Goods	1 9	...

No. 207—MONUMENT LANE, SOHO, AND SMETHWICK SHUNTING ENGINE.

Class 4 Freight Engine.

	arr.		dep.
	a.m.		a.m.
Mon. Lane Shed	...		4 55 L.E.
Smethwick	5 7	(shunt)	5 55 L.E.
Soho	6 0	(shunt)	7 58
Smethwick	8 3	(shunt)	10 17 L.E.
Soho	10 22		...
	a.m.	(SX)	a.m.
Soho	...		11 33 L.E.
Mon. Lane Shed	11 40		2 53 L.E.
Spon Lane Basin	3 5		4 52 L.E.
Oldbury	4 55	(shunt)	7 16
Spon Lane Basin	7 20		7 40 E.&B.
Oldbury	7 45		9 25

	arr.	(SX)	dep.
	p.m.		p.m.
Spon Lane Basin	9 30		9 56 L.E.
Oldbury	9 58		10 49 L.E.
Albion	10 53		11 33
	a.m.		a.m.
Exchange Sidings	12 37		12 50(L.E.(MX)
Monument Lane	12 58		...
	p.m.	(SO)	p.m.
Soho	...		12 28 L.E.
Oldbury	12 38	(shunt)	4 15
Spon Lane Basin	4 20	(shunt)	6 0 L.E.
Mon. Lane Shed	6 13		...

No. 209—CURZON STREET, EXCHANGE SIDINGS, AND VAUXHALL TRIP ENGINE.

Class 4 Freight Engine.

	arr.	(SX)	dep.
	p.m.		p.m.
Aston Shed	...		4 45 L.E.
Curzon Street (Wharf)	4 52	(shunt)	8 0 L.E.
Vauxhall	8 5	(shunt)	11 36 L.E.
Aston Shed	11 40		...

No. 241—ASTON, BESCOT, STECHFORD AND MONUMENT LANE TRIP ENGINE.

Class 6 Freight Engine.

	arr. (SX)	dep.
	p.m.	p.m.
Aston Goods	...	9 35
Bescot	10 2	11 5
		a.m.
Stechford	11 45	2 5(MX)

	arr. (MX)	dep.
	a.m.	a.m.
Exchange Sidings	2 15	2 25
New Street	...	2 31
Monument Lane	2 37	3 5
Aston Goods	3 42	3 50 L.E.
,, Shed	3 55	...

No. 306—WITTON AND ASTON TRIP ENGINE.

Class 2 Freight Engine.

	arr.	(SX)	dep.
	p.m.		p.m.
Aston Shed	...		12 53 L.E.
Witton	12 57	(shunt)	6 7
Aston Goods	6 18		8 5 Bank
Aston Jn.	8 17 L.E. to Shed.		
(Commencing 31-10-38)			
Aston Jn.	8 17	(SX)	8 35 L.E.
Witton	8 40	(shunt)	11 10 L.E.
Aston Shed	11 15		...

	arr.	(SO)	dep.
	p.m.		p.m.
Aston Shed	...		12 53 L.E.
Witton	12 57	(shunt)	5 32 L.E.
Perry Barr	5 34		7 5 L.E.
Aston Shed	7 12		...

No. 313—ASTON, BESCOT, AND EXCHANGE SIDINGS TRIP ENGINE.

Class 4 Freight Engine.

	arr. (SX)	dep.
	a.m.	a.m.
Aston Loco Shed	...	9 15 train
Aston Goods	9 22	9 50
		p.m.
Stechford	10 12	12 7
	p.m.	
Bescot	1 1	2 0
Perry Barr	2 21	2 33
Aston Gas Works Sdg.	2 42	2 52
Curzon Street	3 11	3 28
Exchange Sidings	3 33	4 30
Curzon Street	4 35	4 40 L.E.
Aston Shed	4 47	...

	arr. (SO)	dep.
	p.m.	p.m.
Bescot	...	2 0
Perry Barr	2 21	2 33
Aston Gas Works Sdg.	2 42	2 52
Curzon Street	3 11	3 28
Exchange Sidings	3 33	3 58 L.E.
Aston Goods	4 16	5 0
Bescot	5 27	...

No. 350—BUSHBURY, BESCOT, STECHFORD, AND MONUMENT LANE TRIP ENGINE.

	arr.	(SX)	dep.
	p.m.		p.m.
Bushbury	...		8 35
Darlaston Green	8 53		9 32
Bescot	9 44		11 13
			a.m.
Aston Goods	11 45		1 30 (MX)
	a.m.		
Bescot	1 54		3 10 (MX)
Aston Goods	3 50		... L.E. To Aston Shed

	arr. (SO)	dep.
	p.m.	p.m.
Aston Shed	...	3 45 L.E.
Curzon Street	3 52	4 13
Adderley Park	4 23	6 33
Curzon Street	7 10	8 17
Aston Junction	8 26 L	8 28
Bescot	8 50	11 13
		a.m.
Aston Goods	11 45	12 30 (Sun.)
	a.m.	
Bescot	12 55	1 40
Curzon Street	2 21	2 45 L.E.
Aston Shed	2 52	...

The following are the Trips running between Curzon Street Goods Yard (Birmingham) and the Exchange Sidings with the LMS Railway (Midland Section)

Trips from Curzon Street to Exchange Sidings.		Trips from Exchange Sidings to Curzon Street.	
Trip.	Worked by	Trip.	Worked by
2.55 a.m. (Sundays) ...	Trip Engine No. 202.	12.45 a.m. (Sundays) ...	Trip Engine No. 202.
5.0 a.m. (Sundays) ...	Trip Engine No. 152.	1.0 a.m. (MO)	Trip Engine No. 202.
5.25 a.m. (MX)	Trip Engine No. 203.	4.40 a.m. (MX)	Trip Engine No. 203.
6.0 a.m. (MO)	Trip Engine No. 203.	5.30 a.m. (Sundays) ...	Trip Engine No. 152.
7.48 a.m.	Trip Engine No. 202.	10.37 a.m.	Trip Engine No. 349.
11.50 a.m.	Trip Engine No. 150. (SO) No. 169 (MO) No. 354 (MSX)	4.30 p.m. (SX)	Trip Engine No. 313.
3.28 p.m.	Trip Engine No. 313.	6.55 p.m. (SX)	Trip Engine No. 150.
5.55 p.m. (SX)	Trip Engine No. 187.	10.10 p.m.	Trip Engine No. 147 (SX), No. 173 (SO)
8.5 p.m. (SO)	Trip Engine No. 142.		
9.40 p.m. (SX)	Trip Engine No. 201.		
10.20 p.m. (SX) ...... / 12.0 night (SO)	Trip Engine No. 202.		
10.55 p.m. (SO)	Trip Engine No. 173.		
11.12 p.m. (SO)	Trip Engine No. 128.		

CLASSIFICATION AND MARSHALLING OF LOCAL FREIGHT TRAINS.

MARSHALLING OF TRAINS INTO JUNCTIONS.

The Freight Train marshalling shewn herein, unless otherwise indicated, reads from front to rear of the train.

Unless otherwise shewn the following must be taken as the standard marshalling for all Trains to the following points :—

Trains into Curzon Street—

From Bescot—
- Midlands
- Curzon Streets

Through train loads to be made to the Midland Line via Stechford and Exchange Sidings when possible.

TRAINS.

No. 128—1.30 a.m. (MX), Curzon Street to Dudley (via Stour Valley).

- Engine
- North Stour Stations
- South Stour Stations
- Dudley
- G. W. Line
- Brake Van

North Stour wagons to be detached at Dudley Port and worked forward by 2.58 a.m. Stechford to Wolverhampton.

No. 128—10.10 p.m. (SX), Bescot to Curzon Street

- Curzon Street Goods Traffic
- Curzon Street Coal (20 Wagons)

No. 139—8.20 a.m. (SX), Curzon Street to Coventry.

From Curzon Street—
- Coventry and Rugby Road Van
- Leamington Road Van
- Adderley Park
- Stechfords
- Coventry Roaders

Attach at Adderley Park
- Stechford Up Side traffic

From Stechford—
- Road Vans
- Marston Green
- Hampton
- Berkswell
- Tile Hill

No. 150—6.55 p.m. (SX), Exchange Sidings to Curzon Street.

To convey traffic from Midland Section to connect at Curzon Street with the 8.5 p.m. (SX), Curzon Street to Camden train.

No. 150—9.22 p.m. (SO), Ettingshall Rd. to Exchange Sidings.
No. 159—9.30 p.m. (SX), Bushbury to Washwood Heath.

To be restricted to a single engine load from Bushbury to Wolverhampton.

To convey from stations where timed traffic for the Midland Section, via Exchange Sidings; also Aston and Curzon Street wagons.

No. 151—2.58 a.m. (MX), Curzon Street to Coventry.

- Midland Exchange
- Stechford Exchange
- Coventry
- Coventry Exchange
- Leamington

No. 157—1.50 a.m. (MX), Bescot to Exchange Sidings (via Stechford).

- Brake Van
- Banbury Street
- Midland Division

Not to exceed 45 including brake vans.

To convey from Stechford loads of empties for Bournville off the 6.15 p.m ex Camden.

No. 162—12.10 p.m., Lichfield City to Curzon Street

To be put in marshalled order at Shenstone.

To clear all up line outwards wagons from Sutton, except Chester Road wagons and Cannock Chase empties. After detaching at Erdington to attach Curzon St. traffic and exchange only.

Not to convey empty goods wagons from Shenstone which must be worked to Lichfield for Wichnor.

To convey live stock traffic from Four Oaks when required.

No. 166—8.26 a.m., Lichfield City to Erdington.

To shunt Goods Yards at Four Oaks, Sutton, Chester Road and Erdington, and to convey to Sutton the wagons shunted out at Four Oaks.

To leave Sutton Coldfield with traffic for Chester Road and Erdington only: The engine of this train to place Curzon Street traffic on No. 1 Siding at Erdington for the 12.10 p.m., Lichfield City to Curzon Street to attach.

No. 169—9.50 a.m., Bescot to Curzon Street.

- Witton
- Aston Gas
- Curzon Street
- Banbury Street
- Adderley Park

To convey additional brake van from Bescot daily for 11.35 a.m., Witton to Bescot.

No. 187—1.23 p.m. (SX), 1.25 p.m. (SO), Bescot to Curzon Street

To leave Great Barr marshalled—
- Midlands
- Adderley Park and Souths
- Curzon St., Banbury St. & Vauxhall (in one Section).

No. 182—8.5 p.m. (SX), Aston to Curzon Street.

From Aston Goods Yard.
- Engine
- Brake Van
- Curzon Street
- Midland Division
- Vauxhall Cripples

No. 201—9.40 p.m. (SX), Curzon Street to Stechford.

- Broad Street (fitted)
- Camden (fitted)
- Camden
- Camden Exchange

To attach important Willesden traffic at Exchange Sidings to connect at Stechford with 1.30 a.m. (MX) ex Stechford.

No. 201—10.45 p.m. (SX), Stechford to Exchange Sidings.

Not to convey rough and unimportant traffic for Curzon Street or Vauxhall, such traffic must be held back at Stechford for the 1.15 a.m., Peterboro' to Curzon Street.

Nos. 202 (SO) 10.25 p.m., 147 (SX)—10.10 p.m., Exchange Sidings to Curzon Street.

To convey traffic for Crewe, Chester, etc., to be worked forward on the 11.14 p.m., Curzon Street to Preston, and Cambridge traffic for 10.55 p.m., Curzon Street to Sudbury Jn.

No. 306—6.7 p.m. (SX), Witton to Aston Goods

- Windsor Street Gas Works
- Aston Goods
- Sutton Line
- Nechells
- Curzon Street
- Exchange Sidings

The Sutton Line wagons to go forward on trip, Aston Goods to Curzon Street, to connect with 8.20 a.m., Curzon Street to Sutton Line.

No. 340—8.45 p.m. (SX), Curzon Street to Bescot.

- 4 fitted Leeds (N.E.)
- Huddersfield fitted
- Huddersfield
- Edgeley Exchange (including Broadheath, Oldham, Denton, Stockport, and Ashton)
- L.N.E. (G. C. Section)
- Leeds and N.E. Section
- South Stafford Line Goods traffic including Sheffield via Wichnor, Lichfield City meat, & Rugeley T.V
- Midland Division, via Wichnor
- Burton (including Derby traffic)

No. 350—8.17 p.m. (SO), Curzon Street to Bescot.

- Sheffield
- Derby
- L. & N. E. (G. N. Section)
- Midland Division via Wichnor
- South Stafford Line Goods traffic
- Burton

Details of the local shunting engine and trip freight workings affecting Curzon Street as they were in September 1938. Details of the order in which traffic had to be marshalled on some of the local trip workings were also given. Not all services which called at Exchange Sidings were included.

Photographs of the goods trains which served Curzon Street are unfortunately rather rare. The principal goods trains ran at night and the local freights and the myriad of inter-yard trips were a part of the workaday railway scene which most photographers did not notice. Thie photograph shows the 6.15 p.m. Camden–Curzon Street 'Maltese Cross' express goods train in 1939. The express goods trains were usually worked by large passenger or mixed traffic engines and here 'Claughton' No. 6004 of Camden shed was accelerating the train along the down slow line at Kilburn. There were three scheduled trains a day from Camden to Curzon Street in 1939, the other two being 'Fitted Freight 2s' departing at 8.33 and 10.55 p.m. At this time there were only five 'Maltese Cross' trains from Camden each week night. ***Locomotive Publishing Co.***

advise Adderley Park or Exchange Sidings whether it will be necessary for the engine to run round and propel its train into Curzon Street or whether it may run into the yard engine first.'

If time was critical and the main line had to be cleared, the train would have to be propelled into the excursion line in one movement, and shunted into the shed roads later. Alternatively, although this was said to be a rare occurrence, the train could be stopped at Exchange Sidings and set back into Adderley Park yard to wait until Curzon Street was ready to accept it. Once on the through siding, it could be broken up and run round there, or at Exchange Sidings, so as to be ready to be propelled into Curzon Street.

Fortunately, most of the main trains arrived in the early hours of the morning when there were few passenger trains about. If a goods train arrived at Grand Junction with a passenger train close behind, the goods was (if possible) run direct into Curzon Street on the 'Excursion Line' so as to clear the main line. In this case, the Curzon Street shunting engine was put on the back of the train and drew it out again (either onto the shunting neck or one of the goods lines towards Vauxhall) to release the train engine. The shunting engine then propelled the wagons into the appropriate sidings. However, as even the 'Excursion Line' was limited in length, this could only be done with relatively short trains; a long train would stand foul of the goods line, or even the main line, connections.

In addition to the trains which terminated at Curzon Street itself, a substantial proportion of the traffic arrived in the area as part of the loads of through freight trains, or trains terminating at other yards. Since, even at night, few freight trains passed through New Street, these wagons were left at a convenient yard, such as Stechford or Bescot. There were regular trip freights between the various yards by which wagons could be transferred to their destination station, though wagons from Stechford were generally tripped first to Exchange Sidings to allow some sorting before arrival at Curzon Street.

Exchange Sidings had two primary functions. The first, and most important (and from which the yard took its name), was to exchange wagon traffic between the Midland and LNW. Its other function was to act as a marshalling point for Curzon Street, and this included holding traffic when there was insufficient siding space for it in the yard there. Wagons for the LNW line and Curzon Street from the Midland were collected in the Midland yard at Lawley Street, and then tripped to Exchange. The method of working these trips was particularly interesting: the train was made up at Lawley Street with the train engine facing east (which suited the yard arrangements there). Once the train had drawn out of the yard onto the running lines, a pilot engine was attached at the rear, and this engine then hauled the train (with the train engine now at the back) round the curve from Landor Street to Grand Junction. The train was stopped between Grand Junction and Proof House Junction, where the pilot detached and returned light engine to Lawley Street. The train engine then drew the train into Exchange Sidings from the Grand Junction end, and then if required, shunted the train as necessary and propelled those wagons destined for Curzon Street across into the sidings there. More usually (and always in pre-grouping days), a LNW/Western Division engine did the shunting, and undertook the trips across to Curzon Street.

The Exchange Sidings shunter arranged these moves with the Curzon Street shunter by telephone. It was important, for instance, that he ascertained how many wagons were to be placed on each road, so that the train could be cut in the correct places. Some of the shunts would be into roads which already contained wagons: as none of them were very long, if too many wagons were sent across, time could be wasted in further dividing the train, and putting the excess wagons into another road.

If the direct Midland line to Grand Junction was blocked or required for passenger trains, the Lawley Street trips were turned onto the Camp Hill line at Landor Street Junction, again with pilot leading and the train engine at the rear. The train stopped with the train engine at St. Andrew's Junction, where the pilot was detached. The train engine then drew the train round the Gloucester line curve and into Exchange Sidings at the east end; the shunters did not like this arrangement, since the engine was then at the wrong end of the train to do the shunting. Therefore, either the engine had to run round, or another trip engine had to be found to do the work (Exchange did not normally have a pilot engine of its own). Depending on how the train had been put together at Lawley Street, there could be additional shunting too, since

MIDLAND DIVISION FREIGHT TRAINS AND ENGINES PASSING THROUGH NEW STREET STATION JULY 1927

New Street dep.	*Time*	*Day*	*Class*	*From/to*
				DOWN TRAINS
a.m.	*a.m.*			
3.32	3.15	MX	TF	Washwood Heath to Central.
5.32	5.13	MX	TF	Washwood Heath to Central.
6.25	6.10	MX	LE	Washwood Heath to Central. After working 12.5 a.m. from Normanton.
6.59	6.42	MX	LE	Washwood Heath to Central. After working 4.40 a.m. from Central.
p.m.	*p.m.*			
8.1	7.50	SX	LE	Duddeston Road Junction to Central. To work 8.50 to Water Orton.
11.14	11.50	SX	LE	From Water Orton.
				UP TRAINS
a.m.	*a.m.*			
1.35	1.15	MX	TF	Central to Water Orton.
2.30 a 2.35 d	2.20	MX	F	Central to Lawley Street (worked by engine & men off 7.40 from Bristol).
4.10	2.0	MX	TF	Worcester to Washwood Heath. (Five Ways arr. 3.53. dep. LE 4.2). LE Five Ways to Washwood Heath via New Street, Grand Junction & St. Andrew's Junction (4.9).
4.53 a 4.54 d	4.40	MX	LE	No. 12 Trip Engine, Selly Oak–Lawley St.
7.10	6.55	SX	LE	Central–Washwood Heath (picks up guard at New St).
10.38	10.28			No. 24 Trip Engine, Church Road Jcn–Washwood Heath West End. Dep. Five Ways 10.26 (from Washwood Heath via Lifford. arr. there 10.20).
p.m.	*p.m.*			
7.56	7.17	SX	TF	Bournville (E & B to Cadbury's Sdgs. arr. 7.20, dep. 7.39).
9.13 a 9.15 d	8.50	SX	TF	Central to Water Orton.
12.10	11.50	SX	EF	Central to Bath.

WESTERN DIVISION FREIGHT TRAINS AND ENGINES PASSING THROUGH NEW STREET STATION SEPTEMBER 1929

Trip	*Time at New St. arr.*	*dep/pass*	*Starting time*	*Day*	*Class*	*From/to*
						DOWN TRAINS
	a.m.	*a.m.*	*a.m.*			
	12.15		12.5		LE	Aston to New St. (to work 12.35 to Curzon St.).
208		12.44	12.40	MX	LE	Exchange Sidings to Monument Lane.
	12.55		12.50	MX	FF No. 2	Curzon St. to New St.
167		1.31	1.3	MX	TF	Adderley Park to Dudley Port.
		2.17	2.10	MX	EF	Exchange Sidings to Crewe (via Bescot).
187		9.4			LE	New St. to Witton (after working 8.35 a.m. passenger from Harborne).
		p.m.				
312		2.7		SX	LE	New St. to Harborne Jcn.
323		6.33		SX	LE	New St. to Smethwick (to work 7.22 a.m. Express Freight to Bushbury after working 4.19 p.m. passenger from Wolverhampton).
						UP TRAINS
	a.m.	*a.m.*	*p.m.*			
208		12.20	11.23	SX	F	Spon Lane Basin to Exchange Sidings.
		12.27	7.55	SX	+EF	Manchester to Exchange Sidings.
		12.35		MX	EF	New St. to Curzon St. (arr. 12.40).
		1.5		MX	LE	To Stechford (after working 11.16 p.m. passenger from Rugby) (works 2.0 a.m. Express Freight Stechford to Rugby).
		1.15		MX	LE	New St. to Aston (after working 12.50 a.m. from Curzon Street).
159		2.38	9.30	SX	TF	Bushbury to Exchange Sidings.
			a.m.			
170	3.15	3.25	3.5	MX	F	Monument Lane to Curzon St.
		4.35	4.30	MX	LE	Monument Lane to Lichfield City.
		p.m.				
203		8.48		SX	LE	New St. to Aston Goods (after working 7.40 passenger from Walsall).

EF Express Freight
F Freight
FF Fitted Freight
LE Light Engine
\+ Maltese Cross

the train arrived the opposite way round to the normal arrangement. If it was known in advance that the train was to go via St. Andrew's, the Exchange Sidings shunter would try to persuade Lawley Street to 'set' the train accordingly to save time and work.

During the winter months, a number of the propelling movements into Curzon Street from Vauxhall and Exchange took place in darkness, especially those involving trains worked in from the down main line (the majority of the long-distance goods trains arrived during the night). To act as a marker for the wagons, and as a warning of their approach, a white light was attached to the coupling of the first wagon; a lamp man was booked on at nights to undertake this work. As a rule Exchange Sidings were not used for storing wagons, and vehicles were only held there to wait for the trains that would take them forward, or for space to be made available for them in Curzon Street or Banbury Street yards. The six sidings which were all accessible from both ends had a total capacity of 200 wagons.

Strictly speaking, half of the Exchange yard (sidings 1 to 3) was LNW, and the other half Midland (sidings 4 to 6), hence the two shunting necks at the Grand Junction end. Wagons were left in the sidings of the company for which they were destined, although the distinctions became blurred after 1923, and in later years at least the shunters preferred (as far as possible) to use the Midland shunting neck, since it was better aligned than the LNW one. The sidings were on a high embankment, making the location very exposed. Other than the small shunters cabin, which was sited near Grand Junction signal cabin, there was no shelter. Enginemen therefore usually stayed with their engines, though this could be very unpleasant in winter when freezing cold winds whipped rain or snow into the cabs. The staff had their own graphic name for the place: Siberia!

Curzon Street No. 1 signal box was the key to the operation of the goods yard controlling the entry into the main portion of the yard and all the points into the shed area. It also controlled the goods lines, working with Curzon Street No. 2 Grand Junction and Proof House Junction. Working of goods trains to and from the Grand Junction line was easier than from the London line since the trains could stand on the goods lines to await acceptance, clear of the passenger lines. The sections were short, however and Curzon Street No. 1 slotted No. 2's home signals as its home signals; this necessitated the use of the special bell signal 'Take off slot, train waiting', although not all the No. 2 signalmen bothered to send this, on the grounds that the No. 1 signalman ought to have seen the train! Services for the yard normally stopped at these signals for the engine to run round. In addition to goods trains, the goods lines were used for some empty coaching stock trains and light engines to and from New Street. Vauxhall would, however, send the carriages on the main line whenever possible since the carriage shed was on that side, and it saved the problem of crossing the train over to the goods line.

Curzon Street No. 1 was a class 1 signalman's job, and rather unpopular because of the shunting work that kept the men on the go most of the time. In addition, the work was difficult due to the problems of communicating with the shunters, and in knowing what they wanted to be done next. Meals usually had to be snatched while on the go. The signalman had to be familiar with the locations of all the yard points to avoid derailments, as he changed them between successive shunts, often while wagons were still on the move. There was no radio or tannoy system for communication, and the box was too big and high for the signalman to be able to hear shouts from the shunters. A system of hand semaphore signals was used during the day, and as so many different signals were necessary (there were 23 shed sidings under the signalman's direct control), representations of them were chalked on the end wall of the signal cabin as an aid to the signalman. At night, the shunters used lamp signals, but again there were too many different signals for the usual combinations of colours, 'up and down' and 'side to side' movements of the lamp etc. to cover all the requirements, so half-and-half signals also had to be used: for example, a half-red, half-green light waved up and down would apply to a specific road. Some signalmen found it all too much to master, and did not stay long. An experienced man eventually learnt, by observing the wagons, to anticipate some of the moves, and was able to set up some of the roads before the shunter had given his signal.

A particularly difficult movement was to transfer wagons from Curzon Street to Banbury Street. Although only a few yards away, the shunt had to go to Grand Junction and stop on the up Western line from New Street, blocking that line. It then set back across the long crossover into the yard, blocking the down Western, and the up and down Midland lines. It was obviously difficult to find a margin in which to undertake the shunt, and having completed it, the whole move had to be done again, in reverse, in order to get the engine back to Curzon Street. Needless to say, it was not done very often — usually only once a day!

A wagon in the process of being turned from the turntable line onto one of the sidings outside the main goods shed at Curzon Street on 19th June 1935. The photographer had his back to the main shed and the shadow of the roof can be seen in the foreground. The roof of the grain warehouse shows in the background, above the wagons. The capstanman on the right had his right foot on the control pedal of a powered capstan and was drawing the wagon round with the rope. The way in which the rope was attached, by means of the hook, to the wagon axle-guard can be clearly seen. The man on the left was the hooker-on, who was riding on the turntable, and is shown with his right foot on the turntable stop key ready to drop this into its slot as soon as the turntable came into line with the siding. The wagon would then be despatched along the siding, leaving the men to turn their attention to the next wagon on the cross line. Compare this picture with that on page 88 of Volume 2. *LMS*

In the main portion of Curzon Street yard, the shunters worked in pairs; the man in charge of each pair was a class 1 shunter, and he had a class 3 shunter working under him. The head shunter arranged the moves, while the under shunter's primary responsibility was to protect the turntables. He ensured that all the shunting movements onto the goods shed roads (sidings 4 to 23) were stopped short of the turntables, and worked in conjunction with the capstanmen to ensure the wagons were left where the capstanmen wanted them. The head shunter determined which roads the wagons were to be put onto, using his knowledge of what was already in the sidings (and hence the space available on each road), and whereabouts in the shed the wagons were required. As far as possible, the train engines of incoming freights were used to put away the wagons in the correct sidings. Any wagons that could not be dealt with this way, and those which arrived on the trip freights, were disposed of by the pilot engines that worked in the yard (or the trip engines). Usually, there was at least one pilot or trip engine in the yard all the time, whilst at busy periods there could be several.

The shunter first checked the incoming train, and decided (from experience, and the information on the wagon labels) how he wanted it divided up between the various shed sidings. He then communicated the information for each successive shunt to the engine driver and signalman (who worked all the points in the main yard area).

Once the inward traffic had been placed on one of the roads outside the shed, it waited until the capstanman was ready to deal with each particular wagon, and take it into the shed. Just outside the main goods shed there was a row of twenty-one wagon turntables, which took the turntable line across into the fruit shed. Only nine of the sidings extended into the main shed; these were cattle sidings 4, 7 and 8, City Road sidings 13, 14 and 15, Cheapside sidings 16 and 20, and Whitechapel siding 22.

The capstanman's job was to bring empty wagons out of the shed roads and replace them with full ones, so that the shed staff could unload them (or vice versa, for loading). Between the shed and the turntables were four capstans, which were hydraulically powered, and operated by means of foot treadles. Again the men worked in pairs, each capstanman being assisted by a 'hooker-on'. To draw a wagon out of the shed, the hooker-on placed a metal hook attached to the end of a hemp rope on a suitable part of the wagon underframe (usually near one of the axle boxes), whilst the other end of the rope was passed a couple of turns around a convenient capstan. When ready, the wagon brake was released, and the capstanman operated the capstan by means of the foot treadle to pull the rope tight and draw the wagon out. The momentum of the wagon enabled it to run past the capstan and onto the turntable outside the shed. If the road beyond the turntable was empty or being used for storing empty wagons, the hooker-on lifted or knocked the hook off (if necessary) to allow the wagon to roll down the siding, and then stopped it with the hand brake at a suitable place. More usually, the hook was placed so that it would drop off the wagon when the rope went slack as it passed the capstan.

It was more likely, however, that the wagon would need to be transferred to a different siding. In this case, the wagon was stopped on the turntable. The hooker-on lifted out the turntable stop key to free it, and the capstanman used the capstan and rope to pull the wagon round through 90 degrees onto the turntable road. The hooker-on replaced the turntable key to secure it, and the capstanman drew the wagon off and onto the turntable at the required road, moving to a different capstan if necessary (the process is illustrated on page 88 of Volume 2). There were also unpowered 'dummy' capstans to help guide rope and wagon. The procedure of turning the wagon was then repeated, and the wagon run out onto the required siding. A skilful team could accomplish this whole process in a couple of minutes, sometimes without the wagon having stopped moving.

The capstan work required considerable skill and vigilance to ensure that one capstan team (there could be four pairs working at the same time) did not interfere with or cause danger to any of the others. In addition, the work had to be coordinated with that of the shunters to ensure that both did not try to use the same siding at the same time, and to avoid accidents. There were further turntables inside the shed to enable wagons to be moved in or out without interfering unduly with adjacent wagons which were still being dealt with.

Inside the shed, the whole area (other than the sidings) had a flat floor set just below wagon floor level; this platform was called 'The Deck'. The platforms alongside the sidings were divided into 'bays', each being simply an area of the open deck, defined by custom, and by notices hanging from the roof. A team of men were responsible for each bay, and normally consisted of three or four people: a checker, a loader, and one or two porters. Usually, there would be about 15 teams at work at any one time. The first step in unloading was for the checker to find the packet of invoices belonging to the wagon, which listed the contents of the particular load. He then checked off each item as the loader unloaded the wagon, after which the porters took the goods away and placed them at the front of the deck ready for loading onto the delivery vehicles. This loading area was also divided into bays, and the goods were placed as far as possible in the correct area for the particular delivery round.

The checker reported any differences between the invoices and the goods in the wagon. Goods without invoices had to be put on one side until an invoice could be found, while enquiries had to be made with the originating station in the case of invoices for which there were no goods. It was by no means uncommon for wagons to turn up with no paperwork at all,

CURZON STREET STATION
LMS CARTAGE FIGURES

	HORSE CARTAGE				*MOTOR CARTAGE*			
Period 6 months to	*Weight carted Tons*	*Average number of horses working per day*	*Average number of horses not working per day*	*Average cost per ton* s. d.	*Weight carted Tons*	*Average number of motors per day*	*Average cost per ton* s. d.	*Total weight carted Tons*
June 1923	95,936	173	10	3–7	63,708	46	2–6¾	159,644
Dec 1923	97,441	173	11	3–2½	67,132	46	2–5	164,573
June 1924	98,406	177	9	3–2¾	72,013	51	2–6	170,419
Dec 1924	96,317	177	9	3–1¾	72,873	51	2–5½	169,190
June 1925	98,239	177	10	3–3¾	75,593	54	2–5¾	173,832
Dec 1925	99,561	176	10	3–3	73,113	51	2–6¼	172,674
June 1926	93,697	162	25	3–2	67,405	46	2–5¼	161,102
Dec 1926	97,771	172	14	3–3¼	74,970	51	2–5	172,741
June 1927	100,751	172	15	3–1¾	79,217	53	2–5	179,968
Dec 1927	97,711	173	12	3–1¾	77,972	55	2–5½	175,683

The June 1926 figures are depressed by the General Strike in May, when the average number of horses at work was only 98 and the average number of motors was 26.
The total weight carted figures given here can be compared with those for the 1905-1910 period given on page 106 of Volume 2.

CURZON STREET GOODS STATION
SUMMARY OF GOODS HANDLED 1923–1927

Period	*Number of consignments excluding tranships*	*Number of invoices handled*	*Handled tonnage Forwarded and received*	*Tranships*	*Cost per ton* s. d.	*Cattle traffic Tons*	*Gross tonnage excluding coal & coke*	*Coal and coke received excluding forwarded*	*Goods average load per wagon tons Shed*	*Yard*	*Total weight carted Tons*
1923	1,506,107	–	362,553	85,553	2–3¾	–	615,973	187,930	3.25	6.91	324,217
1924	1,461,756	544,236	380,272	86,730	2–4½	18,878	619,296	196,067	3.30	7.99	339,609
1925	1,512,490	572,815	390,594	80,852	2–4½	18,383	639,328	208,750	3.19	7.32	346,506
1926	1,197,678	515,163	357,733	73,806	2–3¾	17,529	579,215	204,593	3.04	6.41	333,843
1927	1,481,709	534,020	364,717	73,989	2–3¾	20,695	605,013	251,259	2.70	7.48	355,651

NOTES
1926 figures low due to General Strike.
Includes Curzon Street, Banbury Street, Vauxhall and Adderley Park, but NOT Monument Lane, Aston or Soho Pool, or the various ex-Midland depots in the city.

either because the packet had fallen off in transit or, more likely, there had not been time to get it ready before the train left. In these cases, the wagon had to be left until the invoices had appeared — late invoices usually arrived at New Street by passenger train, and replacement invoices generally arrived the same way. The shipping office clerks made the necessary enquiries.

At the cart loading bay end of the shed, another team of men further sorted the goods into the various rounds, and loaded the carts or lorries. Once again, each item was checked against the paperwork by a checker, and was weighed if necessary.

In the morning, the process of delivery began as the cartage staff booked on duty. Once his vehicle was ready, the carter left on his round. Most of the men worked the same round each day, perhaps being moved from time to time to another one, so that they would always be familiar with several rounds. If the round was a short one (usually those on the station side of the city), the carter would return to the depot when he had finished. If required, he would take out another load, and so on until the work was done. The process of dealing with the inwards traffic continued generally until the early afternoon, and as the work was completed, the men changed over to deal with the outwards traffic. After the introduction of the 8-hour day, the change coincided approximately with the 2 p.m. shift change for the yard staff.

Each carter usually did a collection round as well as a delivery round. For those working some distance from the depot, the collection round was generally begun as soon as they had finished delivering, or before if it would save time and there was room on the cart. The majority of collection calls were regular, calling at the same places each day and collecting whatever (if anything) the customer had, though the carter would be notified of any special calls. Since the carters were paid a small bonus on the tonnage they carried, there was an incentive to collect as much as they could. In addition, since the men normally did the same round (which was also in the same area as the delivery round), it was in their interest to strike up a good relationship with the customers, so that they would be encouraged to use the railway for more of their traffic. The company was well aware of the importance of the men's relationship with the customers, and encouraged the carters to be helpful and reliable so as to build up the customers' trust.

As the afternoon wore on, the cartage yard at Curzon Street became busier and busier as the carts returned in greater numbers, and the yard inspectors became increasingly engaged in organising matters. Usually, there would be a steady stream of phone calls from traders and factories asking if special collections of large consignments and urgent goods could be made. This meant finding a man and vehicle to do the extra work, though this was not usually a problem; the carters' wages were very low, and there was always someone anxious to earn a bit of overtime.

The carts were unloaded onto the outer end of the goods shed deck for sorting, and it was here that the bay system really came into its own. The whole deck was divided into bays, each of which was labelled up by means of notices hung from the roof for a specific destination or series of destinations. Deck porters transferred the goods from the edge of the deck to the appropriate bay, where the consignments were sorted and loaded into the railway wagons, as far as possible in the order in which the trains were to leave. As the wagons were loaded, the checkers prepared sheets detailing what had been received, and into which wagon each item had been loaded, and placed these in a rack. The sheets were collected by a messenger at regular intervals and taken to the shipping or despatch office — this office was situated above the deck in the roof of the shed, and was reached by a spiral staircase from the deck.

After each round of the deck, the messenger numbered all the notes he had collected, and divided them up into different destination districts for the clerks. There were between ten and twenty clerks in the shipping office, and they were divided into two groups. The first group, each of whom dealt with a particular area, worked out the rates for each item and passed them to the next room. Here, the clerks made out the invoices, either on a typewriter (which produced carbon copies) or by hand, in which case copies were produced on a special hand duplicating machine. This triplicate system of invoicing was first introduced in Birmingham on 1st May 1910. The completed invoices were then returned to the first office, and placed in slots in a rack system for the various destinations, to await collection.

At first sight, a curious aspect of the work on the deck at Curzon Street was that a significant proportion of the goods handled had neither originated in Curzon Street's collection area, nor was destined for anywhere in it. Indeed, most of this traffic had nothing to do with Birmingham at all. This situation arose because of the nature of much of the traffic — single, often small packages, sometimes referred to as 'smalls', with starting points and destinations mostly outside the city.

To deal with this type of traffic, a 'tranship station' was nominated in each area, and all the small consignments were gathered at these places for sorting and reloading. In many cases, this accumulated enough items to make up reasonable wagon loads, though in other instances the consignments for a particular area were gathered together, and sent on to another depot in the right direction in a tranship van. To collect the consignments from the smaller stations and bring them to the tranship station, as well as to distribute those arriving there and destined for other stations in the locality, a system of 'road vans' (railway wagons carrying local traffic) were operated on many lines. These worked to their own timetable, and were normally included in the daily pick-up freight trains.

Curzon Street was the tranship station for most of the central district. There were in fact very few lines in the district that had a road van service, since virtually every station in Birmingham and the Black Country was sufficiently busy to justify its own direct wagon services for 'smalls'. In 1921, only stations on the Sutton/Lichfield line, and between Bloxwich and Hednesford on the Cannock line, had road van services. The former van was sent out from Curzon Street (loaded with the day's consignments for the stations on that route) on the morning trip working. It came back with 'smalls' for Curzon Street to deliver locally, or tranship for other destinations. The 'Cannock and Hednesford' vans came, one each from London Broad Street and Camden depots, on the 10.40 p.m. service. Curzon Street despatched (and received) eight or nine other road vans each day to places outside its tranship area where traffic warranted them. The arriving vans had to be unloaded, and the individual items sorted for delivery or reloading into other vans for onward transport to (or towards) their destination. This work took up an appreciable amount of labour and space in the goods shed. The invoices for small consignments, incidentally, went with the wagon for intermediate checking, and not direct to destination.

By the turn of the century, traffic had grown to the extent that Curzon Street was having difficulty in coping with all the work. Just in time, the LNW opened a large, new central tranship station at Crewe, and from November 1901, a certain amount of the work was transferred there. For the central district, this meant that tranships from stations north of Crewe, and from the Shropshire, South and Central Wales districts destined for

THE TRANSHIP SYSTEM

The railway merchandise traffic, particularly that handled by the 'collected and delivered' service, was characterised by the fact that much of it came in small quantities (numbers, not necessarily weight — some single items could be very heavy), often single packets, parcels or packing cases, with widely differing starting points and destinations. In many instances, the number of items for one destination collected at a goods station each day did not justify the provision of a wagon direct to that place, and so some means had to be found of combining sufficient consignments together to make up a wagon load — or at least as much of a load as possible.

The problem can be illustrated by taking an example of the producer of, say, jam for the grocery trade. To avoid excessive use of storage space — and having to pay for large quantities of jam, some time before they could sell it — grocers would order in small batches at quite frequent intervals. Thus, while the produce would leave the factory in large quantities — whole cart loads — and hence an economic unit, when it got to the goods station the load could be split into dozens of small packages, all with separate destinations. While packages for large places, say Manchester, could join other consignments to form a full wagon load, this was unlikely to be the case for small places, or locations further afield. Apart from the pots of jam, it was unlikely that there would be anything else at all to hand (let alone enough to make up a full wagon load) for, say, Rhayader or Ravenglass.

The economics of rail transit and the ability of the railway to offer low rates for transport of goods lay in its ability to join large numbers of units together — goods wagons and goods trains — for the majority of the journey. The difference between profit and loss lay in keeping the individual units — the wagons — as full as possible, and the total number as small as possible. It was generally considered that a load of less than one ton was not an economic use of a wagon, and if possible, the load should be significantly greater than this. Thus, the idea of sending the jam to Rhayader in its own wagon, simply because there was nothing else, was out of the question.

The solution lay in the 'tranship' system. Here, a large goods depot (such as Curzon Street) in each area was designated as a tranship station. All consignments destined for the whole area served by one tranship station could be gathered together to make up one or more wagon loads. If there was still not enough for a wagon load, the consignments could be combined with others for districts beyond the tranship station to make up a load (provided these, too, did not justify a wagon of their own direct to the district tranship station). If there was enough for more than one wagon, as far as possible the packages would be separated, with one wagon for the consignments to the goods station itself ('town') and one for its tranship area; this clearly aided the work at the destination. Some consignments might require transhipping several times during their journey (see page 103 of Volume 2). The jam for Rhayader would probably go in a tranship van to Shrewsbury, and that to Ravenglass in a Carnforth tranship van.

For small stations the problem worked both ways, as neither the inwards nor the outwards traffic in small consignments was enough to justify the provision of wagons destined for that station only. To serve stations of this sort, it was the practice on many routes to include one or more 'road vans' in the daily stopping goods train(s). The working of these vans was timetabled in the same way as the train service, and any station could load 'smalls' into these vans to be carried to any other, or receive consignments by it. In most cases, the itinerary of the van included larger or junction stations where the consignments could be transferred or transhipped, giving links with other parts of the network. At the heart of each area lay the tranship station and by a combination of direct wagons, road vans, and the tranship system, a daily service was provided for all stations in the area.

The volume of all types of goods traffic handled by the railways increased enormously during the last twenty years of the 19th century. By the late 1890s, stations like Curzon Street were becoming choked with traffic, with the consequent problems of inefficiency and delay. At places which were also tranship stations, the ever-increasing volume of tranship work disrupted the basic work of the depot more and more. The LNW took bold steps to solve the problems, and in 1901 opened a large new central tranship shed at Crewe. From 4th November of that year, a considerable quantity of the tranship work was transferred there, giving valuable relief to the existing goods stations and allowing resources to be concentrated more on local traffic. Some stations were freed of tranship work, but the majority still had to deal with the traffic which related to their own tranship district.

After the addition of the central tranship station at Crewe, the LNW tranship system operated with increasing effectiveness, a fact reflected in greater average loads of wagons (and consequent savings in the number of wagons required), and reduced congestion at other main goods stations. It continued in operation, without further major modification, into the LMS period. After amalgamation with the Lancashire & Yorkshire Railway in January 1922, the ex-L&Y tranship stations were integrated into the network, and some alterations were made to the road van services.

There was little change in the tranship working after the grouping of 1923, other than a change to the use of the Midland term 'tariff van' instead of road van, and some minor changes in boundaries to reflect the new common ownership. In due course, the LMS did make changes by introducing a network of 'Sub-Transit Stations' within the tranship zones. These may be thought of as functioning as tranship stations in their own right, except when the forwarding station did not have sufficient weight of merchandise to justify through-loading to it — in which case, those consignments would have to be included in a load to the parent tranship station.

stations (LNW and foreign) to the south of Stafford were dealt with at Crewe instead of Curzon Street, Monument Lane or Wolverhampton. This gave valuable relief to the shed and yard work at Curzon Street, freeing resources to be concentrated more on local traffic, which had been in danger of being disrupted by the ever-increasing tranship work. Nevertheless, Curzon Street continued to deal with a significant amount of tranship traffic.

After the opening of the goods shed at Aston in September 1901, some tranship work was carried out there as well, affording further relief, though it only operated as an adjunct to Curzon Street. Aston sent wagons direct to only a limited number of larger depots; the remainder of the traffic, and all the road van services, continued to be despatched from Curzon Street.

Despite the amalgamation of the LNW and Midland into the LMS in 1923, there were no great changes. The ex-LNW tranship zone based on Curzon Street/Aston remained separate from the ex-Midland zone based on Lawley Street; since the two areas were only connected at Exchange Sidings and Walsall, there was little scope for integration.

Eventually, the LMS did make changes by developing a system of sub-transit stations, one of which was established at Walsall, and Curzon Street, Aston and Lawley Street were all considered as parents to it. A wagon could be sent to whichever was most convenient for the destination — all three sent and received loads to and from Walsall daily. Walsall sub-zone included depots on the South Staffordshire and Cannock lines (formerly in the Curzon Street zone), as well as some stations on the ex-Midland line to Wolverhampton.

Goods in less than a whole wagon load arriving at Curzon Street destined for Lawley Street, or vice versa, were unloaded and carted to the other depot, involving double handling. To prevent this, forwarding stations were encouraged to utilise other transfer points (for example, Bedford, Manchester or Lancaster, as appropriate) to ensure that, if possible, the wagon would arrive at the correct Birmingham depot, and thus avoid the transfer process.

The LMS also created an additional tranship station at Coventry, covering stations to the east of Berkswell (exclusive). However, Curzon Street retained daily direct loadings to all stations in the Coventry group, except those on the Rugby & Marton line. The Wolverhampton area depots were transferred to the Lawley Street zone.

CURZON STREET GOODS STATION
SUMMARY OF FACILITIES – 1923

Number of warehouses	8	Capacity 2 to 10 tons	2 manual
Total warehouse floor space	129,798 sq ft	Capacity 2 to 10 tons	1 steam
Shed deck – Wagon berths	98	Number of hydraulic capstans	21
Cart berths	57	Siding accommodation	
Shed and warehouse cranes		Wagons in position for loading/unloading	820
Capacity up to 1 ton	11 friction	Wagons awaiting attention	791
Capacity 1 to 5 tons	24 manual	Cattle dock	
Capacity 1 to 5 tons	12 hydraulic	Wagon berths	27
Number of electric platform trucks	28	Number of pens	29
(4 more added during year and 3 more added in 1924)		Stable accommodation	178 horses
Yard cranes		Accommodation for clerks	141
Capacity up to 1 ton	1	(increased to 160 in 1924)	

WORKING OF ROAD VANS.

No. of Road Van.	Labelled TO	Trains worked by: Time of Departure	From	To	Stations served.	Remarks.
	The days on which the vans leave the starting point are shewn in the "Remarks" column.					
	From Birmingham (Curzon St.)					
16	Brackley	10 50 p.m. 1 30 a.m. 10 15 a.m.	Curzon St ... Stechford ... Bletchley ...	Stechford ... Bletchley ... Brackley ...	Swanbourne, Winslow, Verney Jct. & Met. Rly., Padbury, Buckingham, Fulwell & Westbury, Brackley.	Daily. To be run irrespective of weight.
17	Cambridge	10 50 p.m. 1 30 a.m. 8 50 p.m. (SO) 2 0 a.m. (MO) 7 15 a.m. 4 35 p.m.	Curzon St. ... Stechford ... Curzon St. ... Rugby......... Bletchley ... Bedford	Stechford (S) Bletchley ... Rugby......... Bletchley ... Bedford ...... Cambridge ...	Bedford, Blunham, Willington, Girtford Sdg., Sandy, Potton, Gamlingay, Old North Road, Lord's B'ge, Cambridge	Daily. Goods for Fenny Stratford WoburnSands, Ridgmont & Millbrook to be sent to Bletchley for transfer.
18	Daventry	3 15 a.m. 6 45 a.m. 8 50 p.m. (SO) 1 15 a.m. (Sun.) 12 20 p.m. 12 0noon	Curzon St. ... Coventry...... Curzon St. ... Coventry...... Warwick ... Warwick......	Coventry...... Warwick ... Coventry...... Warwick...... Southam (S) Southam (SO)	Leamington Milverton, Southam, Napton & S. Flecknoe, Braunston, Daventry	Daily.
19	Lichfield City ...	8 55 a.m.	Curzon St. ...	Lichfield City	Blake Street, Shenstone, Lichfield	Daily.
20	Llandovery	10 5 p.m. 11 45 p.m. 10 0 p.m. (M) 2 50 a.m. (MO) 9 50 a.m. 1 45 p.m.	Curzon St. ... Bescot ...... Burton ...... Salop .... (detach at Knighton ... Llandrindod Wells	Bescot (S) ... Stafford ...... Swansea ...... Swansea ...... Knighton) Llandrindod Wells Llandovery...	Broome, Hopton Heath, Bucknell, Knighton, Knucklas, Llangunllo, Llanbister Road, Dolau, Penybont, Llandrindod Wells, Builth Road, (Cambrian and Neath and Brecon Stations via Builth Road), Cilmery, Garth, Llangammarch Wells, Llanwrtyd Wells, Cynghordy	(Mons., Tues., Weds., and Fridays only)
21	Llanelly	10 5 p.m. 11 45 p.m. 10 0 p.m. 2 50 a.m. 8 0 a.m.	Curzon St. ... Bescot ...... (M) Burton... (MO) Salop... Llandovery... * detach at	Bescot ...... Salop .... Swansea ...... Llandovery * Pontardulais Llandovery.	Llandovery, Llanwrda, Llangadock, Talley Rd., Llandilo, Derwydd Road, Llandebie, Tirydail, Cross Hands, Pantyffynnon, Pontardulais, Llangennech, Bynea, Llanelly, Ammanford, Garnant, Brynamman Clydach-on-Tawe, Glais, Pontardawe, Ystalfera Gwys, to be loaded for Swansea for transfer. Goods for Golden Grove, Dryslwyn, Llanarthney, Nantgaredig, Abergwili, Carmarthen, also for G. W. and M. & M. Line Stations, via Carmarthen, to be loaded Crewe for transfer.	(M W F O) Goods for Mumbles Road, Dunvant, Killay, Gowerton, Pen clawdd, Llanmorlais, Gorseinon, Llansamlet, Morriston,
22	London (King's Cross)	1 5 a.m. 8 50 p.m. (SO) 5 35 a.m. 8 15 a.m.	(M) Curzon St Curzon St. ... Rugby......... Mkt.Harboro'	Peterboro' ... Rugby......... Mkt.Harboro' Peterboro' ...	Peterboro' to King's Cross	Daily. G.N. Van. Labelled Peterboro' (G.N.) to be overhauled

WORKING OF ROAD VANS—continued.

No. of Road Van.	Labelled TO	Trains worked by: Time of Departure	From	To	Stations served.	Remarks.
	From Birmingham (Curzon St.)—continued.					
23	Loughboro'	10 50 p.m. 1 42 a.m. 9 10 a.m.	Curzon St. ... Coventry...... Nuneaton ...	Coventry (S) Nuneaton (M) Loughboro'...	Market Bosworth, Coalville, Shepshed, Loughboro'	(MWF). Goods for Stoke Golding, Shackerstone, Heather Hugglescote, Whitwick, Snareston Measham, & Donisthorpe, to be sent to Nuneaton for transfer.
24	Luton	10 50 p.m. 1 30 a.m. 8 50 p.m. (SO) 2 0 a.m. (MO) 8 15 a.m. 6 10 p.m. 9 40 a.m.	Curzon St. ... Stechford ... Curzon St. ... Rugby......... Bletchley ... Leighton ... Dunstable ...	Stechford (S) Bletchley ... Rugby......... Bletchley ..... Leighton ... Dunstable ... Luton	Leighton, Stanbridgeford, Dunstable, Luton	Daily.
25	Oswestry	1 5 a.m. 5 40 a.m. 10 45 a.m. 5 30 a.m. 12 0noon	Curzon St. ... Bushbury ... Crewe .... Whitchurch Ellesmere ...	Bushbury ... Crewe .... Whitchurch Ellesmere ... Oswestry ...	Fenns Bank, Bettisfield, Welshampton, Ellesmere, Overton-on-Dee, Bangor-on-Dee, Marchwell, Frankton, Whittington Oswestry, Llynclys, Pant, Llanymnech, Llansaintffraid, Llanfechain, Llanfyllin, Four Crosses, Pool Quay	(M W F O) Load with Ellesmere traffic to come out at that station To come out at Oswestry Label compo Ellesmere Oswestry.
26	Rugby	8 20 a.m. 11 0 a.m. (next day)	Curzon St. ... Coventry......	Coventry...... Rugby	Adderley Park, Stechford, Marston Green, Hampton, Berkswell, Tile Hill, Coventry, Brandon, Rugby.	Daily. To be run irrespective of weight
27	Stamford	1 5 a.m. 8 45 a.m.	Curzon St. ... Rugby	Rugby ...... Peterboro' ...	Market Harboro' (Welford traffic to come out at Market Harboro'), Clipstone and Oxenden, Kelmarsh, Lamport, Brixworth, Pitsford & Brampton, Hallaton, East Norton, Tilton, John o' Gaunt, Great Dalby, Melton Mowbray Scalford, Long Clawson, Harby & Stathern, Redmile, Barnston, Medbourne, Ashley & Weston, Rockingham, Seaton, Uppingham, Wakerley, King's Cliff, Nassington, Morcott, Stamford.	Daily. Goods for Clifton Mill, Yelvertoft, Theddingw'th & Lubenham to be sent to Rugby for transfer.
28	Thrapston, via Northampton	10 50 p.m. 4 30 a.m. 9 45 a.m.	Curzon St. ... Rugby ...... Northampton	Rugby ...... Northampton Peterboro' ...	Billing, Castle Ashby, Wellingboro', Ditchford, Irthlingboro', Ringstead, Thrapston, Goods for Thorpe, Barnwell, Oundle, Elton, Wansford, Orton Waterville, to be loaded to Northampton for transfer.	(Sats. excepted)

Details of Road or Tranship Van workings from Curzon Street in October 1922, showing destinations, stations served and working details. Arrangements in the reverse direction were different in some cases.

These photographs were taken in about 1933 to illustrate the methods used on the main deck at Curzon Street for handling the merchandise traffic. The first shows a typical deck gang loading a wagon from an electric trolley of LMS origin. The men had collected the goods from the bay alongside the road vehicle unloading dock and brought them across the deck to the appropriate van. Note the destination card hooked on the wagon above the trolley driver's head. This shows that the wagon was destined for Birkenhead. The man in the centre with the paperwork was a checker, whilst the loader is shown in the process of taking the package off the trolley prior to loading it into the van. The third member of the team was driving the trolley which was of a different design from those first used at Curzon Street. It was steered by the handle on the left and driven by the foot treadle. The large black box was the battery. All the Curzon Street batteries had letter codes prominently painted on them like this. It enabled the battery room staff to keep a record of the whereabouts and charging rates and times of the battery stock. At the end of each turn of duty, the batteries were removed and sent to the charging room and a newly charged battery substituted so that the trolley could continue work. The small trailer on the left, containing further goods, could be hooked onto the electric trolley to increase its carrying capacity. One of the deck cranes also features on the left. *National Railway Museum*

Another view of a gang in the process of loading a van, labelled for Croydon (misspelt Croyden!), not perhaps a destination one would associate with the LNW or LMS or which might be expected to require a whole van. It does serve to illustrate the wide variety of destinations that Curzon Street loaded for. No doubt this van would have travelled by one of the overnight express freights for London and be detached at Willesden. From there it would have gone forward on another service to reach the Southern via the West London Railway and would probably have gone initially to Norwood Yard, which covered former London Brighton & South Coast Railway destinations. The cases of Ty-phoo tea were marked 'G & W Collins, Fonting Street, St. Helens, Lancs'. The trailer with the trolley on the right was loaded with cases of jam from Ledbury in Herefordshire. No doubt both these commodities had arrived at Curzon Street on other services for transhipment. *National Railway Museum*

Once loaded, a wagon of tranships for a single destination tranship station would be despatched on the express goods trains, in exactly the same way as any other loaded wagon. Road vans, however, would be despatched on nominated trains, as laid down in the timetables.

As each ordinary or tranship wagon in the goods shed was filled, the deck staff notified the capstanman, who then pulled the wagon out of the shed. Each of the sorting sidings outside the shed was, as far as possible, allocated to a particular service, but as the sidings were short, several might be needed for the longer trains. The capstanman then moved the wagon onto the correct siding for its train, and moved another empty wagon into the shed for loading. As the wagons were placed on the sidings the shunters coupled them up, and remarshalled them as necessary ready for departure.

As departure time approached and the work on the deck neared completion, the shipping office staff removed the invoices from their pigeon holes and sorted them into wagon number order. The invoices belonging to each wagon were put into a yellow envelope, marked with destination and wagon number, the envelopes then being placed in satchels. In the case of a few trains which ran direct from Curzon Street to a single destination, all the envelopes for that train were sorted out and placed together in a canvas bag. It was then the duty of one of the office lads, known as a 'tacker-on', to take the satchel of envelopes and put them onto the wagons. The envelopes were generally put under the spring clips mounted on the wagon solebars, which retained the wagon destination labels. However, not all wagons had them (usually through damage, or the breakage of the spring clip), so the lad took with him a hammer and pocket full of tacks, and where necessary, he tacked the envelope on to the side of the wagon — hence the title 'tacker-on'.

One of the last jobs before departure was to provide a brake van. These were, wherever possible, put on the train while it was still in the shed sidings. The shunters sent the van down an empty road to the capstanman, who crossed it over via the turntables to the correct road, and put it on the back of the train. Loaded wagons for trains which departed from Curzon Street also arrived on trip workings from other yards, such as Lawley Street, whilst wagons from Curzon Street which were to join other trains were tripped forward to the appropriate place, such as Lawley Street, Stechford, or Bescot.

The main goods trains left between about 10 p.m. and 2 a.m., and were

One of the LNW parcels trolleys on the main shed deck on 25th September 1928. The packing cases at the rear of the truck appear to have contained seed potatoes, while despite the time that had elapsed since the grouping, the sack on top of the load was marked 'Midland Railway'. The railway companies undertook a considerable trade in the hire of sacks. The view was taken looking north towards Curzon Street with the shed sidings on the right.
National Railway Museum

✠

1.15 a.m. (M), Curzon Street to Mold Junction.
From Curzon Street
Engine
Cannock Branch Goods traffic
Widnes, Garston, and Runcorn
Stafford exchange
Warrington exchange (including Wigan, St. Helens, and late Bolton wagons)
Crewe Shed
Crewe exchange
Birkenhead
Chester and exchange
Mold Junction
Brake van
At Bescot
Detach Cannock Branch Goods traffic to connect with the 4.50 a.m., Bescot to Hednesford.
Detach Warrington and exchange (including Wigan, St. Helens, and late Bolton wagons). To connect with 3.25 a.m., Bescot to Warrington.
Attach classified traffic in marshalled order.
At Bushbury
Detach Stafford exchange, Widnes, Garston, and Runcorn.
Attach classified traffic in marshalled order.
At Crewe
Detach Crewe Shed and exchange and Birkenhead
Calls at Tattenhall Road and Waverton, when required, to attach or detach Live stock, and at Beeston Castle on Thursdays to attach Live stock.

2.50 a.m. (M), Curzon Street to Copley Hill
From Curzon Street
Engine
Manchester
Warrington and exchange (including Wigan, St. Helens, and late Bolton wagons)
Crewe exchange
Ditton exchange
Adswood exchange and L.N.E. (N.E. Section)
Brake van
At Bescot
Attach classified traffic in marshalled order.

To leave Bushbury
Engine
Huddersfield
Copley Hill
Adswood exchange
London Road
Brake van
At Adswood
Detach Adswood exchange and London Road.
Attach Huddersfield.
Limited to 49 wagons and Brake van from Bushbury.

✠

7.35 p.m. (S), Curzon Street to Liverpool.
From Curzon Street, Bescot, and Bushbury
Engine
South and Central Wales important traffic
Scotch and Fleetwood Fish empties
Warrington, Wigan, and St. Helens (important traffic only)
Widnes
Ditton exchange
Liverpool
Brake van
At Stafford
Detach South and Central Wales traffic.
At Crewe
Detach Scotch and Fleetwood Fish empties, and also Warrington, Wigan, and St. Helens traffic.
At Ditton
Detach Widnes and Ditton exchange.
To be limited to 59 wagons and Brake van (S).

✠

8.5 p.m. (S), Curzon Street to Camden.
From Birmingham
Camden (fitted)
Camden Shed
Coventry Shed (Goods)
Cambridge
Camden exchange
Broad Street
Brake van
From Stechford
Engine
Camden (fitted)
Camden Shed
Coventry Shed (Goods)
Camden exchange
Broad Street
Brake van
At Coventry
Detach Coventry Shed (Goods).
Attach
Camden Shed
Broad Street
Camden exchange
To be limited to 49 wagons and brake van from Coventry.

✠

10.5 p.m. (S), Curzon Street to Manchester.
From Curzon Street
Engine
Fitted vehicles
Manchester
Manchester Docks
Division "B" Stations, via Philips Park
Bolton
Manchester
Brake van
Stafford
Wellington
Northwich
Birkenhead
N.S. Section

[Continued

Salop exchange
Central Wales
South Wales
Brake van
From Bescot and Bushbury
Engine
Manchester
Manchester Docks
Division "B" Stations, via Philips Park
Bolton
Manchester
Brake van
At Longsight
Detach
Manchester Docks
Division "B," via Philips Park
Bolton
To be limited to 49 wagons and Brake van.

10.55 p.m. (S), Curzon Street to Peterboro'.
From Curzon Street
Engine
Market Harboro'
X———
Coventry Shed (Goods)
Nuneaton exchange traffic (including Loughboro', Atherstone, Ashby, and Nuneaton Line Road Van)
Bletchley exchange
Watford exchange
Willesden
Peterboro' exchange
Brake van
At Stechford
Detach Bletchley exchange and Willesden exchange, to connect at Stechford with the 9.55 p.m. (S), Wolverhampton to Sudbury train. Attach Market Harboro', Coventry, and Peterboro' Line traffic in marshalled order.

At Coventry
Attach at **X**
Market Harboro', Bletchley Willesden, and Peterboro' wagons in marshalled order; also traffic for Oxford next to the Engine, to go forward from Rugby by 9.55 p.m., Wolverhampton to Willesden.
Goods traffic only for Peterboro' and Market Harboro' to be attached to this train—unimportant traffic to be kept back for the 12.55 a.m. (M), Curzon Street to Rugby service.

✠ (S)

11.10 p.m. (S), 10.20 p.m. (SO), Curzon Street to Carlisle.

From Curzon Street
Engine
Liverpool (four fitted vehicles next to Engine)
N.S. Section (from Mid. Division only)
Preston (four fully fitted vehicles)
Holyhead
Birkenhead (from Mid. Division only)
Carnforth exchange
Lancaster
Tebay exchange
Glasgow (Buchanan St.), Cal.
N.B. Section
G. & S. W. Section
Carlisle
Other Caledonian traffic
Brake van

At Bescot
Detach
Liverpool
Holyhead
Birkenhead
Attach
Preston exchange
Carlisle
Glasgow (Buchanan St.)
N.B.
G. & S. W. Section
Caledonian Section (including G. N. of S.)
In marshalled order.

From Bushbury and Crewe
Engine
Four fitted vehicles
Preston exchange (not exceeding 10 wagons)
Lancaster
N.B. Section
G. & S. W. Section
Carlisle (including M. & C. N.E., and Mid.)
Caledonian Section
Brake van
At Preston
Detach Preston exchange.
Attach Tebay exchange.
At Oxenholme
Detach Ham traffic only.
At Tebay
Detach Tebay exchange
Limited to 59 wagons and Brake van, Bushbury to Preston, and 49 vehicles and Brake van from Preston.
NOTE.—Conveys Live stock from South for Carnforth, Tebay, and Penrith, when required.

Marshalling details for the principal long-distance goods trains from Curzon Street in the autumn of 1925. For each train the traffics are listed in the order in which they were to be attached to the train, starting from the engine. It was important that the trains were made up in the right order to facilitate handling at intermediate yards and the destination instructions for attaching and detaching traffic at intermediate yards are also given. The cross symbol indicated the 'Maltese Cross' trains.

The only time that Curzon Street went quiet was between Saturday afternoon and about 5.0 a.m. on Monday morning. This photograph and the one at the top of the opposite page were taken on Sunday, 25th September 1938, from the New Canal Street end of the main shed. This was the Cattle Sidings end of the shed, siding 4 was on the right, and sidings 7 and 8 on the left. The sign hanging from the roof near the nearest end of siding 4 read 'Road Van Peterborough', the one to its right 'Northampton', and further right again, but hardly visible, was 'Banbury', while behind them was 'Blisworth'. Another sign said 'Beware Foodstuffs'. Other destinations signs covered Stoke, Stone, Great Bridge, Albion, Spon Lane and Oldbury. The top of the spiral staircase up to the shipping office can just be seen on the left, immediately to the right of the office building. The deck had been practically cleared of goods – it was the aim to try and have the place emptied and as much as possible delivered before the shift finished on Saturday. However, everyone was always anxious to get off as soon as possible at the end of work on Saturdays, as evidenced by the sack trucks, the electric trolley, and other items abandoned on the deck where they were last used! This pair of pictures gives an appreciation of the size of the main shed. The light iron roof was copied from the original L & B roof which remained in the centre of the shed and was quite a contrast to the wooden roofs of the other warehouses which were inherited from the Grand Junction Railway.

Collection N. Howell

scheduled to arrive at their destination in good time to be unloaded, and for the goods to be delivered during that following morning — in many cases before the customer had started his day's work.

The old excursion station, situated between the main line to New Street and the goods shed, was used as a fish landing after closure to passengers. Very little was done to adapt the old station for this purpose, and older Curzon Street staff recall the station seats, platform lamps and the waiting rooms still intact in the 1930s, largely untouched from the day the last excursion left. Most nights, one or two fish trains arrived between about 2 a.m. and 4 a.m., and a night gang was booked on to unload them. The fish was loaded onto carts, and this was generally the first traffic to leave Curzon Street each morning. The fish came principally from Hull, with further traffic from Grimsby, Fleetwood, Yarmouth and

The third of the 1930s official photographs of the main merchandise deck shows the open area at the New Canal Street end of the deck beyond the buffer stops. The area was crowded with trolleys moving goods from one place to another while other men were busy loading more trolleys. A scene of ordered chaos. The picture demonstrates something of the huge variety of shapes, sizes and weights of consignments that had to be handled and accommodated. Each trolley had a number plate at the driver's end, and several of the letter-coded batteries can be seen. The cartage yard and cart loading bays can be seen through the columns on the right. The roof in the foreground, with its decorative diagonal boarded finish, was probably the original London & Birmingham station roof. *National Railway Museum*

This and the photograph at the bottom of the opposite page were taken on 2nd February 1932 and show the Curzon Street fish landing. The main lines to New Street were at a higher level behind the wall on the left in the external view with the main goods shed to the right. Despite the prominent 'Mitchells & Butlers Bonded Stores' enamel signs on the roof ends, the bonded store was under the building to the right. The signs were placed on the fish landing roof because this was clearly visible to passengers on trains going into or out of New Street. The siding under the roof on the far right in the external view was used for unloading meat trains. The fish landing sidings were also used for loading and unloading goods not suited to the main shed and for general goods traffic at busy times when no other space was available. The fish landing started life as the Excursion station. No opening date has yet been found but it seems to have been built in the 1870s. The left-hand island platform had to be shortened when the line to New Street was widened in 1896. In the interior view the screened-off area at the buffer stops contained the old passenger waiting rooms and booking office. It was used as a mess-room by the cartage and yard staff. *National Railway Museum*

Aberdeen, though in season, this was supplemented by mackerel from Ireland, via Holyhead. In later years, traffic from Fleetwood tended to predominate. The fish dock sidings at the end of the excursion line, had room for fifty wagons.

In pre-Second World War days, the wagons of fish were normally carried on the fast freight trains and were transferred into the fish landing as soon as they arrived at Curzon Street. Some fish vans were also carried on parcels trains, or even at the tail of some passenger trains. These were detached at New Street, and either placed in the fish docks there for unloading or tripped round to Curzon Street. After the war, as a result of the concentration of the fish trade on a smaller number of large ports, separate fish trains were run to cover most of the traffic; these terminated at New Street, and any wagons destined for Curzon Street were sorted out and tripped round. Generally, Curzon Street dealt with the

A view looking towards the fish landing (former Excursion station) from a point almost opposite Proof House Junction signal cabin. The cabin's up inner homes and down starting signals gantry on the main lines to New Street is prominent on the left. The siding on the left was siding No. 1 or Excursion line and led to the fish landing (see photograph opposite). The open-sided shed on the right spanned sidings 2 and 3. This photograph was taken in about 1939/40, and since the other photographs on these pages were taken, Mitchells and Butlers had replaced their advertising signs, and tarpaulins had been hung from the roof over the open side and ends of the sidings 2 and 3 shed, either to afford some additional weather protection for the men working there or as blackout protection. *L. W. Perkins*

Curzon Street from the Lawley Street end on 29th July 1949. Curzon Street coal wharf was behind the houses and shops on the left. The Birmingham Canal bridge can be seen at the top of the rise just beyond the lorry. The large structure on the far side of the canal was the hydraulic pumping station with a large water tank on its roof. The pumping station had lost its chimney since the photograph on page 96 was taken. Beyond can be seen Franklin's screen wall to the Grand Junction station, with the roof of the goods shed and the offices behind.
Cty. D. Chapman

AOV 40

fish which was carted to the markets by the railway company.

Siding No. 2 was used as a meat landing, and trainloads of meat were unloaded here for the markets; this traffic was again generally carted to the market in the early hours of the morning. In pre-Second World War days, a large amount of beef came in from Argentina via Birkenhead, or via Canada Dock, Liverpool. This siding was also used for dealing with some wagon load traffic, and had the advantage that loads could be transferred directly to and from road vehicles, thereby avoiding double handling. As there was no regular daytime traffic, the fish and meat sidings were useful for dealing with special loads and overflow from the main shed.

The western half of the old Grand Junction station (nearest New Canal Street) served as a fruit shed, and was used for the unloading and storing of fruit and vegetables destined for the markets and wholesalers in the city. On the deck in this area could be found cases of apples, bags of nuts, boxes of lemons, barrels of grapes, cases of figs, and so on. The old passenger waiting rooms in this building remained, having been converted into offices, mess rooms and storerooms. Scraps of fading furnishing remained here and there as an indication of their former

Continued on page 101

Top: A view looking along Curzon Street, this time looking towards Lawley Street, with the end of Howe Street in the left foreground, and Franklin's screen wall or frontage to the Grand Junction station opposite. It was still little changed from the days when it was used for passenger trains. The darker areas of the wall, such as the copings, cornices and plinth, were generally those built of stone whilst the lighter areas were generally brick with a stucco facing. The tall building and chimney at the far end of the frontage were part of the LNW's hydraulic pumping station which provided the power for the capstans and lifts within the goods station area. Howe Street was named after Earl Howe who owned most of the land in this area before the railway came. The Railway Hotel on the corner of Howe Street was built not long after the passenger station opened. *Middle:* A view from the former GJ station platform across the courtyard to one of the gateways in Franklin's screen wall. A couple of the houses on the far side of Curzon Street are visible through the gates. *Right:* A close-up detail of one of Franklin's four main doorways into the Grand Junction station.

Birmingham Libraries; LMS Magazine; D. P. Rowland

The interior of one of the old Grand Junction waiting rooms which formed part of the metal warehouse. The view shows part of the quarter of a million or so pounds worth of metal that was usually to be found in this warehouse, including a heap of castings in the foreground. The neatly stacked copper ingots were warehoused at Curzon Street until required by one of the many copper working factories around the city.
LMS Magazine

A detail view of the old passenger accommodation near the west end of the old passenger platforms. Part of the courtyard, seen in the picture opposite, is visible on the right. This pictures was taken in 1932.
Public Record Office

The interior of the fruit wharf at Curzon Street, looking towards the buffer stops. This was originally one of the passenger platforms in the original Grand Junction station. The end wall was the back of Franklin's Curzon Street frontage or screen wall and consequently stood at an acute angle to the platform. In passenger days, the platform was much narrower and there were two tracks inside the shed: a siding road against the wall and the platform line to its right. The buildings on the right behind the columns were part of the original station waiting rooms and offices. Despite the shabby condition into which the building had been allowed to fall, it must have looked quite smart in passenger days when it was all new and looked after. As was common practice at the time, the roof was predominantly of wood, in contrast with the L&B roof which had an iron structure. Note the lath and plaster finish to the underside of the roof. The wide goods platform was used for the storage of fruit awaiting delivery to the markets or wholesalers around the city. The rectangular crates in the foreground contained oranges, whilst the wooden tubs and barrels probably contained apples, pears or tomatoes. The men were probably a deck gang of four, the checker being the man

This picture, taken on Sunday, 25th September 1938, shows tubs of apples, cases of oranges and other fruit stacked on the deck in the fruit wharf, ready for delivery to the fruit and vegetable wholesale markets when they opened first thing on Monday morning.
Collection N. Howell

This view of the fruit wharf was taken on 17th September 1938 and shows the hydraulically-powered heavy steel crane on the deck.
F. E. Box/National Railway Museum

The entrance to the fruit wharf in 1966 with the grain warehouse on the right and the wording 'London Midland (& Scottish Railway)' still apparent on the grain warehouse wall.
Collection M. Christensen

The interior of the fruit shed in 1969 looking towards the main line. Note the turntable and the grooves worn in the loose capstan pulleys or dummies. The new parcels concentration depot building can be seen on the right.
B. Matthews

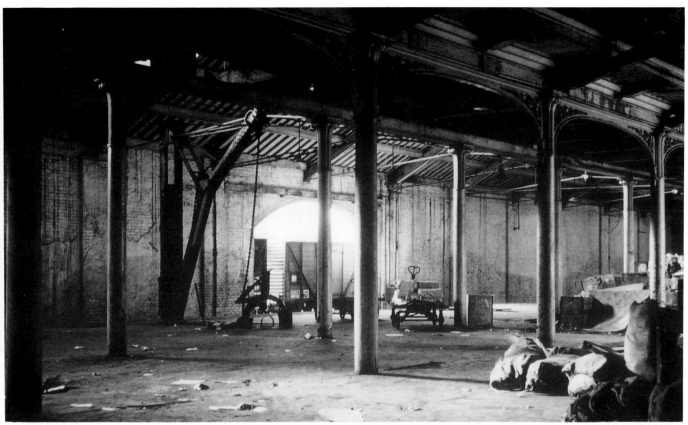

The fruit shed in 1968. The ornate columns in the foreground originally fronted onto an open yard behind Franklin's wall. There was only a small flat overhanging canopy forward of the columns. The wooden edging and support of this stub canopy can be seen in the top right of the picture. When the station was converted to goods use, part of the yard area was roofed over in the cheapest possible way by simply inserting new beams under the stub canopy. *J. Strange*

use, while as late as 1914, the old Grand Junction station bell, by then somewhat battered and with its spring heavily rusted, still hung on the wall as it had done since the place was built. A short distance away was the case of the old station clock, works and face long since gone, an empty and forlorn reminder of past glories. By 1930, the bell had been moved, as a curio, into the main New Canal Street offices.

The other half of the GJ station became a grain and metal warehouse; the grain was stored on the upper floor, and the metal on the ground floor. In addition to the grain, flour (in bags) was stored here, too. The upper floor was served by three hydraulic hoists and an electric lift, and there were chutes to send bags of flour, grain and the like down onto the waiting carts. The fruit and metal warehouse sidings had space for 162 wagons.

This photograph was taken in the grain warehouse in 1968 and shows the timber roof, plain cast-iron columns and the gas lighting still in use. *J. Strange*

It was the practice for the railway company to act as warehousemen for many commodities, storing them for a small charge until they were required, since many customers did not have storage space of their own. In the case of retail goods, the railway acted as distributor for the manufacturer or dealer, delivering as the shopkeeper or factory needed further supplies. For example, one of the carters was employed full-time on the task of delivering flour around the city — a single bakery might require a hundred bags of flour delivering in a week. Sugar was also delivered in large quantities. Until they ceased trading in 1948, Fellows, Morton & Clayton, the canal carriers, had contracts for the warehousing and delivery of sugar in the city. A regular cartage job was to take bulk loads of sugar in 2cwt bags, which had arrived by rail, round to their warehouse in Fazeley Street. After 1948, sugar was delivered direct in the same way as the flour.

In the metal warehouse and copper shed, large quantities of metal were

A view across the Top Yard in about 1938. To obtain a level site for the goods yard, the London & Birmingham had made a deep excavation into the hillside. This photograph was taken from the window of a dairy in Nova Scotia Street. This was formerly Holder's Brewery (or Midland Brewery, see pages 74 & 90 of Volume 2), being converted into dairy premises for Wathes, Cattell and Gurden Ltd (known for short as Wacaden) c.1932. The dairy was a tall building and stood on the hillside above the Top Yard. The windows of the upper storeys therefore gave a bird's-eye view of the yard. The level crossing across Curzon Street was just off the picture at the top left. The roofs of the main goods shed feature on the top left with the goods offices (former hotel) on the right. The buildings on the right of the Top Yard were the fruit, vegetable, cement and steel warehouses built by the LMS in 1930/2. The paper warehouses and stables were off the picture to the left. *A. H. Baker*

stored, awaiting delivery when needed by one of the many metal manufacturers around Birmingham. Much of this consisted of the more expensive manufacturing metals such as copper, zinc and spelter. Items which could be found there included ships' plates, brass and copper engine tubes, boilers, telephone wire, wagon wheel bosses, lamps, copper ingots, bales of copper scrap, cases of tin plate and barrels of brass filings. The value of metal stored here in 1914 exceeded a quarter-of-a-million pounds — and that was at pre-Great War prices!

On the east side of the Birmingham Canal was Curzon Street coal wharf, which dealt almost exclusively with coal traffic, and was largely self-contained. It had siding capacity for 162 wagons. Entry to the sidings was controlled by Curzon Street No. 2 signal cabin, and they could be shunted independently from the rest of the yard. This was one of the city's main coal yards, and a large number of coal merchants were based there.

On the opposite side of Curzon Street to the main yard was the 'top yard' — this was the original London & Birmingham goods yard. Top yard had two principal functions: as a potato yard, and as accommodation for the cartage horses and the carts. Originally, in the absence of any proper facilities in the town, the railway yard acted as an unofficial wholesale vegetable market, though after the Smithfield wholesale vegetable market opened in 1884, much of the market work was transferred there, but the yard remained busy dealing with the incoming traffic of vegetables. There was, for instance, a whole shed set aside for the storage of onions. New potatoes from Jersey arrived in May each year, and in LNW days some of these were imported via Holyhead.

After the turn of the century, banana traffic developed rapidly, and became particularly significant from about the 1920s. Some of the top yard accommodation was given over to sheds for the ripening of bananas. The banana traffic required careful handling as spiders and small snakes, some of which were poisonous, were sometimes hidden in the bunches of bananas when they were picked, and remained there throughout the journey to Britain. From time to time, these would fall out into the shed when the wagons were unloaded; the men had to be careful not to get bitten by any that were still alive, and would try to kill them before they escaped.

After the Second World War, the top yard was usually referred to as the 'banana yard', instead of the old description of 'potato yard'. The bananas originally came by ship to Manchester Docks, and were unloaded into railway wagons

CURZON STREET COAL WHARF – USERS

1880 Coal Merchants	1890 Coal Merchants	1900 Coal Merchants	1910 Coal Merchants	1920 Coal Merchants	1930 Coal Merchants	1940 Coal Merchants	1950 Coal Merchants	1960 Coal Merchants
William Burgum	William Burgum	John P. Lawley	John P. Lawley	George Mason	Alex Comley Ltd.	Fox & Terry	Fox & Terry	J. W. Gadsden & Co. Ltd.
J. Gothard & Co.	Charles F. Hunt	Frederick W. Henri	Mrs. Mary M. Henri	Mrs. Mary M. Henri	Mrs. Mary M. Henri	Mrs. Mary M. Henri	Mrs. Mary M. Henri	Mrs. Mary M. Henri
George F. Walker	Lawrence Miller	Lawrence Miller	Lawrence Miller	Lawrence Miller	Lawrence Miller Ltd.	Lawrence Miller Ltd.	Lawrence Miller Ltd.	Wilson Carter & Pearson Ltd.
Thomas Haydon	Thomas Haydon	Thomas Haydon	Richard W. Brown	William Morgan	William Morgan	William Morgan	Charles F. Duffill	Charles F. Duffill
Joseph Mills	Joseph Mills & Son	J. Mills & Sons	J. Mills & Sons	J. Mills & Sons	J. Mills & Sons	J. Mills & Sons	J. Mills & Sons	J. Mills & Sons
John H. Jephson	Henry Dumolo	Henry Dumolo	H. Dumolo Ltd.	H. Dumolo Ltd.	H. Dumolo Ltd.	H. Dumolo Ltd.	H. Dumolo Ltd.	H. Dumolo Ltd.
Edwin Twist	Edwin Silk	Edwin Silk	Edwin Silk	Edwin Silk	Edwin Silk	Edwin Silk	Edwin Silk & Son	Edwin Silk & Son
Colliery Proprietors		John H. Walter	Lewis Bleakman	Lewis Bleakman		Lewis Bleakman		
Cannock Chase Colliery Co.		Caswell & Bowden	Phesent Hedierne	Phesent Hedierne	Phesent Hedierne			
Earl of Shrewsbury		Robert W. Hayward	William Sadler		Kimberley Beddoes & Co. Ltd.	Kimberley Beddoes & Co. Ltd.		
Cannock & Rugeley Colliery Co.					George Haynes	(Proprietors Fox & Terry)		
Great Wyrley Colliery Co.								
East Cannock Colliery Co.								

there. In 1911, the LNW installed special plant and new sidings for discharging and handling bananas at its Garston Docks, together with warehouse accommodation, the work being authorised in November 1910. Additional insulated wagons were also constructed to handle the traffic. Elders and Fyffes, the banana importers, transferred their ships to Garston in 1912. When the traffic started, Elders had about twelve steamers, which maintained one arrival a week on average from the West Indies, though by 1926, the fleet had grown to twenty-eight vessels.

A large part of the shed accommodation was set aside for the storage of large rolls of newsprint for the Birmingham newspapers (the *Birmingham Gazette* and *Birmingham Mail*). The rolls were delivered by rail, and craned into the storage shed. As the newspapers used the supplies held on their premises, more rolls were sent round to the printing works by the railway drays or lorries. To cope with increasing demand, the storage accommodation was reconstructed in 1930, as described later.

The top yard was served by three sidings out of the main yard, which crossed Curzon Street on the level at a very oblique angle. A gateman was employed continuously at the crossing to regulate rail traffic across it, and to protect road traffic; he occupied a small hut by the gates on the top yard side of the crossing. As with most large goods yards, Curzon Street was enclosed entirely by high walls and, because of the angle of the crossing, four large gates were required to close off the space in the walls where the tracks passed through. The gaps to be filled amounted to some 88ft on each side, with the result that each gate weighed about a ton, and ran on rollers.

Engines were not permitted to cross the road, and indeed, were not allowed to cross the wagon turntables adjacent to the front of the main goods shed. Other means had therefore to be used to transfer wagons across the road, and all normal movements were made by rope and capstan. The procedure for working traffic into the top yard was as follows: the

The Top Yard from the Curzon Street level crossing gates in 1968, showing the weighbridge on the left and three powered capstans in the centre, with coils of rope laying by them. The Mobil Oil store shed on the right was built on part of the site of the paper warehouse. The wall behind the producer's banana ripening rooms at the far end was on Grosvenor Street and gives an idea of the depth to which the ground was cut away when the railway was built. ***J. Strange***

A close-up of a couple of the turntables. ***J. Strange***

pilot engine propelled the wagons to be taken into the top yard as near to the crossing as it could, stopping with the engine short of the turntables, and the leading wagon clear of the gate. When the capstanman in the top yard was ready to take the wagons, the gateman stopped the road traffic, using a red flag. The yard gates were rolled back, and the top yard hooker-on took a rope across the road and hooked it to the first wagon. The capstanman then towed the wagons across the road and into the yard. Once the wagons were clear of the road, the road traffic was allowed to resume, and the gates were closed again.

Inside the top yard, all wagon movements were carried out by capstan and rope, hence the number of turntables; shunting by capstan was quicker with turntables than it would be with points. Empty wagons to be returned to the main station were dealt with in a similar way — a capstan on the main yard side of the road now being used to tow the wagons across the road. Once in the main yard, the wagons were moved forward by capstan far enough for the shunting engine to collect them without crossing any of the turntables. The yard had a capacity of 37 wagons under the paper warehouse, and 59 in the sidings adjacent to the stables.

Banbury Street Wharf, on the south side of the main lines, dealt with all the cattle traffic. Live cattle and sheep were unloaded at the cattle pens, and driven either to the Corporation cattle market in Montague Street via the access road to Montague Street (known as Paddy's Bank), or to the abattoir in Bradford Street via Fazeley Street and New Canal Street. The yard was provided with gates at the Grand Junction end; these were

Above: The east end of the Top Yard, looking from Curzon Street. The three-storey building on the right was the LNW horse department provender store and fodder preparation lofts which dated from 1874. There were stables on the ground floor with entrances on the other side of the building. The building facing the camera at the end of the yard was the two-storey infirmary stable block which was built in about 1880. The low building between was built at the same time and housed further stables. *Left:* Turntables and warehouses in the Top Yard. *J. Strange*

The top end of Banbury Street goods yard on 3rd February 1932. The picture illustrates how the containers being introduced and heavily advertised by the LMS could be easily unloaded from a railway wagon and transferred direct to a road vehicle by a mobile crane, without the need to unpack and repack the contents, as would be necessary if a conventional goods wagon was used. Containers were especially attractive to households needing to move as it gave them some reassurance that their possessions would not be lost or damaged in transfer between road and rail vehicles. Note the advertising of the LMS household removal service on the container. A rather antiquated rail wagon mounted hand crane was being used to unload the container. It is doubtful if modern health and safety legislation would regard the method of securing the crane in place – by several half bricks wedged under the wheels – as adequate! One of the goods yard gates is visible in the background and the overhead lines bridge can just be made out behind the container and crane. *National Railway Museum*

supposed to be closed across the sidings before any cattle were unloaded from the inward cattle trains. Occasionally, a cow would escape while the wagons were being unloaded, and the gates were there to prevent the animal getting out onto the main line. Nonetheless, some escaped, and at least one beast got all the way to Saltley engine shed before it was cornered! While the chase was going on, all the main line traffic had to be stopped, and there could be a fair delay to trains until all was safe again. Once the animal was cornered, the drovers came to retrieve it and drive it back to join its erstwhile companions.

There was a gantry crane at Banbury Street, and the yard was used for unloading and loading large and heavy objects. In the 1930s, the LMS developed containers as a means of competing with the door-to-door attraction of road traffic, thereby eliminating the laborious task of loading and unloading railway wagons. These container wagons were generally sent to Banbury Street so that the crane, which was capable of lifting twenty tons, could be used to lift them on and off the railway wagons and lorries. A six-ton mobile crane was also based there to facilitate the container (and other) lifting work. At busy periods, Banbury Street dealt with traffic that could not be accommodated in Curzon Street, and was also used for coal traffic, as well as for loads which suited direct transhipment from railway wagons to road vehicles (and vice versa). It had siding capacity for 158 wagons.

Clearly, the task of carting the huge volumes of goods dealt with at Curzon Street required considerable resources and organisation. Before the Great War, some 600 horses were stabled at Curzon Street, and these fell into three groups: the Curzon Street cartage horses; the New Street parcels horses; and the horses temporarily based at Curzon Street for breaking-in and training, or for treatment in the hospital. By 1933, the total figure had fallen to a little over 300. Even at the end of the Second World War, when lorries had made significant inroads into the work, there were still about 70 horses kept there for cartage work. It was not until the mid-1950s that horses were finally displaced.

The stables were responsible for providing all the horses needed at both Curzon Street and New Street (except for the one shunting horse that was stabled near No. 1 signal cabin at New Street). The Curzon Street horses were generally heavy animals, suited to the plodding cartage work, though the requirement for New Street was different: a number of light vans were based there for the delivery of passenger train parcels, with the need for fast deliveries, so lighter and faster horses were used.

The majority of the stables were sited along the east side of the top yard. In addition, there were some small stable blocks in the yard of the old Grand Junction passenger station, on the south side of Curzon Street (which probably dated back to the 1850s). Because of its sheer size, Curzon Street became the base

for the LNW's district horse superintendent. A full-time veterinary surgeon was based in the depot to look after the needs of the animals, and there was a two-storey sick-bay area (horse hospital) to accommodate sick horses that required special attention. Horses were sent to the hospital from all over the LNW (later LMS) system.

Part of the stable accommodation constructed in the top yard in 1874 consisted of a large three-storey building with stables on the ground floor. The upper two storeys were laid out for the preparation and storage of feed for the horses, and it was here that the provender for the large number of horses employed over the entire LNW system was prepared, cut up and packed into sacks, and dispatched as required to every corner of the LNW empire. In 1920, the LNW had 5,895 horses to feed, compared with 3,800 in 1895.

The stable area also contained shops for the preparation and fitting of the large numbers of horseshoes required to keep the horses' feet in good condition and fit for work. Other shops, presided over by a foreman saddler, repaired and prepared harness. A large number of men were needed in the stables to look after the horses. One of the stable blocks contained a house for the stable foreman (originally built as the yard detective's house); this was a curious building which looked tiny from the front, with hardly any windows. The door was set at an angle in the corner of the yard with a small clock above it, whilst inside there was a small entrance lobby with a kitchen and living room beyond, and a couple of bedrooms upstairs.

At the back of the top yard, behind the potato warehouse, was a survival from the very beginnings of Curzon Street: the old London & Birmingham Railway station master's house. Over the years, the distinction between the GJ and

Interior of the top floor of the infirmary stable block at the back of the Top Yard. These pictures were taken some 30 years after the last horses had left.

The main building in New Canal Street on 17th September 1938 a hundred years to the day since the first through passenger train arrived here from London. Curzon Street's heavy haulage lorry features in the background further along the street. The car (registration No. BNK 973) parked outside the offices was also owned by the LMS. The end wall of the new paper warehouse and potato sheds which were built in 1930, shows on the other side of Curzon Street.

F. E. Box/National Railway Museum

L & B portions of Curzon Street have become blurred, and some accounts describe it as the Grand Junction station master's house. It was not used as a residence for very long, and the building was converted into a workshop for the inspection and repair of wagon sheets. Wagon sheets (or tarpaulins) were very extensively used for merchandise traffic prior to the 1930s, since most pre-grouping railway companies possessed on average about 4 times as many open merchandise wagons as covered vans. Much of the merchandise was therefore loaded into open wagons, and the load was protected during transit by sheeting over the wagons. Apart from the lower capital cost of open wagons, they had the advantage of greater versatility and, most usefully, heavy items could be craned directly into them; a fair proportion of the merchandise traffic consisted of heavy objects, or large and heavy packing cases, drums, barrels and boxes.

The wagon sheet workshop contained special equipment for inspecting and test-

The main doorway in Hardwick's frontage building. The plaque on the right-hand side of the doorway was put up in 1947 to commemorate the hundredth anniversary of the meeting held in the hotel on 27th January 1847 which led to the formation of the Institution of Mechanical Engineers. The meeting was said to have taken place in the right-hand rear room of the Hardwick building.

B. Matthews

ng the waterproofing of sheets. Externally, the building remained almost unchanged from its London & Birmingham days — it simply became dirtier and shabbier as the years progressed, in the face of the general neglect that characterised the approach to the maintenance of almost all industrial buildings.

The old London & Birmingham hotel building on the New Canal Street frontage was used as office accommodation. The Curzon Street goods agent had the ground floor for his clerical staff. Near the main entrance was the goods agent's private office with an outer office ('the front office') adjacent, for his personal staff. Housed in the large and opulent former dining and coffee room of the 1840 hotel extension was the forwarding office, where clerks dealt with the plethora of paperwork which the huge volume of goods traffic created each and every day; much of it was in small consignments, each of which required its own paperwork. Another important task was to send out the customer's bills and ensure that they were paid — not always a straightforward task. Other clerks spent their time dealing with claims for damaged, lost, delayed or short-delivered goods, and as by no means all claims proved to be genuine, the careful documentation and checking-off of consignments at every stage of their progress through the company's hands was most necessary. There were always those who wanted to save money by not paying for goods or cartage fees, claiming instead that an item was never delivered, or even claiming against the company for alleged loss. In addition, the clerks performed the usual accountancy functions associated with a large business.

Upstairs were the offices of the district goods manager. In LNW days, he had responsibility for the southern half of the company's central district, which extended from Rugby to Stafford (excluding the Trent Valley) and included the whole of the busy West Midlands area. A large number of clerical staff were employed here to organise and control the work of the district, identifying and developing new traffics, and ensuring that resources were deployed where most needed. Planning of new goods services were also undertaken. When the LMS was formed in 1923, the district goods manager took on responsibility for the ex-Midland lines within the boundaries of his area, the revised limits of which now covered Birmingham, Coventry, Leamington, Stockingford and Redditch. In 1933, 4,000 people were employed in the area. This reorganisation placed the big

The only decorative feature inside Hardwick's building was the entrance hall, with its clear space up to the roof, and its columns and railed staircase and balconies. This picture shows a detail of one of the first-floor columns and the balconies in 1938. Above the first floor, high vertical boarding was fixed against the inside of the handrails, preventing a view down into the hallway. Coat hooks were fitted all along the staircase and landing side of the boarding, which provided cloakroom accommodation for the staff. A section of the boarding can be seen at the top of the photograph.
Collection N. Howell

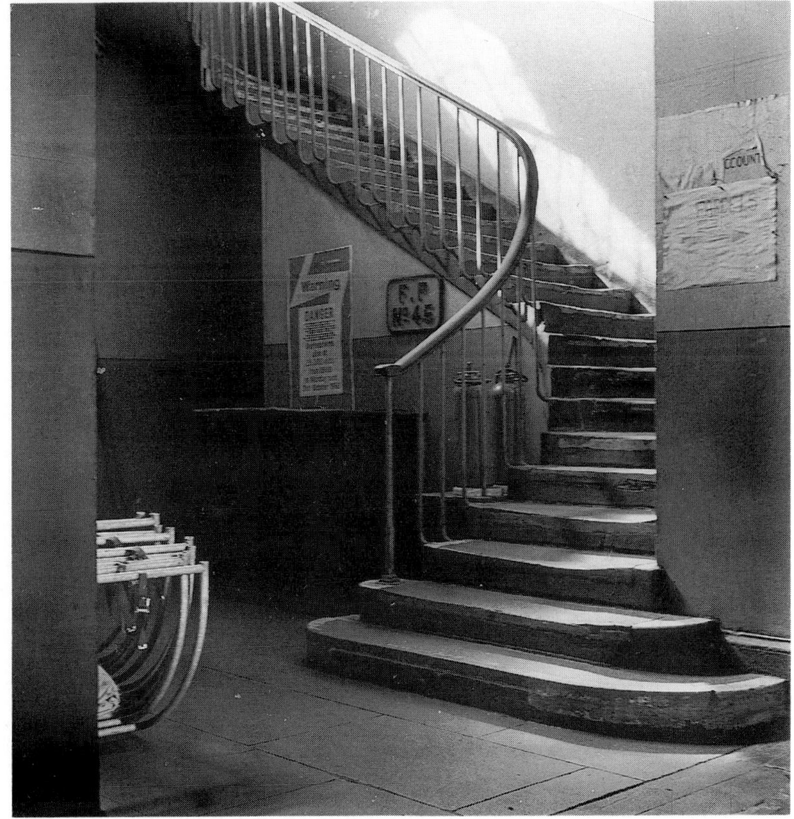

The foot of the main staircase from between the columns on the ground floor. The passageway in the far corner led to the cellar steps. *B. Matthews*

Birmingham depots of Curzon Street, Lawley Street, Central, Aston and Monument Lane under the same control, allowing the slow process of rationalization to begin, and thus eliminating wasteful duplication between them.

In the basement of the hotel extension there was a staff canteen where hot meals, tea and coffee could be purchased at reasonable prices. During the 1930s, a two-course hot meal could be purchased for about a shilling. The canteen was originally divided into two sections — one for the male clerks, one for the females — and was first set up and operated by a company called the Curzon Street Station Dining and Supply Stores Ltd, of which the office staff were shareholders. The company was reconstituted in 1917 as a result of the difficulties of trading in wartime conditions; in the following 9½ years, it carried out business totalling over £52,000, providing the twin benefits of low-priced meals, and a profit for the shareholders. The remainder of the basement, and much of the top floor of the building, was given over to the storage and filing of documents.

When the original London & Birmingham passenger station was built, the existing ground was at a lower level than that intended for the railway, and advantage was taken of this fact to incorporate a cellar under the station train shed. This was used initially as a goods warehouse, and a low-level entrance was provided on the south side (at the engine shed end) with an access road to Banbury Street. Further cellar space was provided when the shed was extended. With the expansion of the goods facilities, which occurred after the closure to passengers,

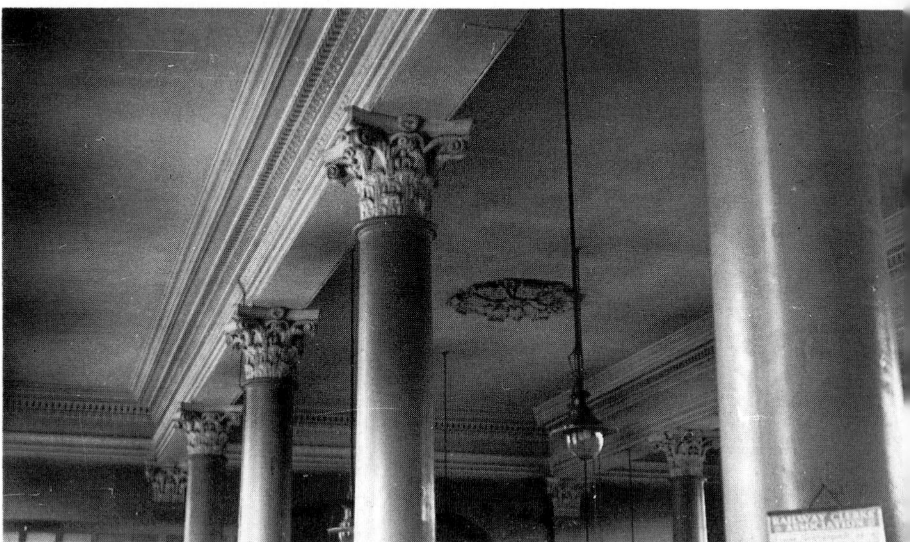

Two views of Curzon Street's goods forwarding office on the ground floor of the main building (the old hotel dining room). They were taken on Sunday, 25th September 1938, when the desks had been cleared of work for the weekend. Since the 1913 photograph on page 85 of Volume 2 was taken, ceiling-hung gas lighting had been installed, and some partitioned enclosures had been added at the far end of the room.

Collection N. Howell

Another view of the forwarding office, this time from the left-hand aisle, after the installation of electric light. Other than that, the interior had changed hardly at all since the other photographs were taken. *National Railway Museum*

the cellar (which had the great advantage of very limited points of access) was converted into a bonded store. It was then used for the storage of wines and spirits (largely in barrels), the bond having a floor area of 5,538 square yards.

The bonded store had its own staff of men, and for obvious reasons, entry was restricted to those whose work legitimately took them there. The stock, too, was carefully controlled, and booked in and out; this was not only because the wines and spirits were of high value (and hence prone to theft), but because the Customs & Excise kept the work under close control. Wines and spirits in the bond had not at that stage had Government excise duty paid on them — the duty only became payable when the wines and spirits left the warehouse. The goods were thus held under special control against a promise by the owner to pay the duty when they were removed, hence the term 'bonded store'. The duty amounted to a considerable sum of money, and the 'Revenue' supervised operations carefully to ensure that the full amounts were paid. Indeed, they made regular inspections of the bond, and tested the contents of each barrel to ensure it was still full and was still of the correct strength. A regular form of theft from the bond was to remove a small quantity of spirit from a barrel, and then fill the space with water — this could be detected by the reduced strength of the contents at the next test.

The bond provided another useful source of both traffic and income for Curzon Street, and because of the confined space, the air in the store had a noticeable alcoholic aroma to it, and those not used to alcohol could feel quite light-headed after a session working in there!

Curzon Street was an early user of motor lorries for collection and delivery work. The LNW had intended to increase this fleet rapidly from 1914 onwards, but the programme had to be cancelled when war was declared. After the Great War, the long years of depression and shortages of money made progress slow, but by 1929, vehicles were arriving at the rate of one a month, and by 1933 the motor fleet had grown to fifty vehicles. In some cases, the lorries themselves were old (in several instances ex-army vehicles) and most had open cabs with no protection from the weather. They had crash gear boxes, and had to be started by means of a crank handle, which could be dangerous. The handle gave a vicious kick when the engine fired, and if the operator was not prepared, he could end up with some nasty bruises, if not a broken arm. In the winter, the radiators had to be filled with hot water if there was to be any hope of getting the engine started! The driver and his mate needed every piece of clothing they could find in order to keep warm and dry.

The motor drivers considered themselves superior to the rest of the cartage staff. Most expected that, when they booked on for duty, their mate would have ensured that the lorry was loaded and was ready, with engine running and delivery sheet to hand so that they could start out straight away; all they wanted to know was where the first drop was to be. It was the practice, through to the beginning of the 1960s, to base a heavy haulage unit in the Curzon Street fleet for handling special loads. The unit was not confined to the Curzon Street area, and roamed far and wide over the country performing heavy haulage tasks.

During 1930, the biggest changes of the interwar years at Curzon Street occurred, with the demolition of the old potato warehouse and the adjoining buildings in the top yard. In their place, a huge, steel two-storey warehouse was built in the centre of the yard. The upper floor was used as a paper warehouse for the storage of the newsprint needed for Birmingham's newspapers, and with a floor area of some 10,000 square yards, could house up to 4,000 tons of paper (amounting to about 30,000 miles if unrolled!) Each reel of paper weighed about half-a-ton, and was unloaded from the railway wagons on the ground floor of the shed using a crane equipped with a special grab, designed to avoid damaging the edges of the paper. The reels were lifted by an electric hoist to first floor level for storage, travelling hoists being provided in the warehouse to move the reels around and stack them.

Further new, single-storey warehouses were built alongside the paper warehouse (in the south-eastern corner of the yard, adjacent to Curzon Street and Grosvenor Street) to store fruit and vegetables, potatoes, cement and steel. The wagons bringing in those commodities could also be unloaded under the paper warehouse, which allowed the work to be carried out in the dry. The construction work was completed at the beginning of 1932.

At an early stage in this rebuilding work, the sheeting department (housed partly in the old station master's house) was closed, on 15th May 1930, allowing all the buildings (except the station master's house) to be demolished. On the same day, the sheeting foreman, Peter Williams, who had been in charge of the Curzon Street establishment since 1899, retired; he had started his railway service back in 1884 at the LNW sheeting department in St. Helens. Henceforward, the sheeting requirements were dealt with from the former Midland sheet stores at Trent. The station master's house survived the rebuilding, and continued in use as a small warehouse for the storage of merchandise and stationery.

As the numbers of horses decreased, some of the stable accommodation was converted for other uses. First to be modified were the small stables in the old Grand Junction station yard, which became the home of some of the first motor lorries. Stable blocks in the top yard were converted to make additional lorry and cart accommodation, while one block was converted into banana ripening rooms.

Interior of the huge new paper warehouse built at Curzon Street in 1930. Curzon Street was used to hold the stocks of paper for the Birmingham papers *Birmingham Post, Mail, Gazette* and *Despatch*. As the printers used the small stock kept at their works, further rolls were sent out from Curzon Street to order. When this photograph was taken in 1932, the stock amounted to some 7,000 rolls. The total weight was some 3,000 tons and, since each roll contained some 4¼ miles of paper, the stock, if unrolled, would stretch some 30,000 miles! After the warehouse was destroyed, the paper was kept in the grain warehouse.
LMS Magazine

The paper warehouse in the centre of the Top Yard was destroyed in an air raid. After the war the site was cleared and utilised for road vehicle parking. This view, from the dairy premises, was taken soon after the war, and shows a number of motor tractor units lined up in the parking bays, the majority of which were of the Scammell three-wheel articulated type. The 'Mechanical Horse' was largely developed by the railways and the special couplings between the motor units and trailers were designed by railway employees. Vehicles of this type dominated much of the railway delivery and collection work in the first few years after the war. Note the heavy haulage unit in the middle row, dwarfing the other vehicles. *A. H. Baker*

A special cargo being unloaded in Banbury Street yard in 1930. The Banbury Street mobile crane is shown unloading two glass-lined metal tanks, each weighing 4½ tons from a rail trolley onto a road trolley. The tanks were 10ft 1in in diameter and had come from London under the out-of-gauge load arrangements. A police escort was required for the delivery lorry.
LMS Magazine

The Second World War brought labour shortages as men joined the armed forces, and for the first time, women began to appear in the goods yard and on the deck, working alongside those men who remained. By the end of 1941, the LMS was experiencing considerable difficulties in handling the goods traffic at a number of major centres, including Birmingham. This led to a backlog of wagons awaiting unloading and goods awaiting despatch, with consequent congestion in the yards and on the main lines; in turn, this led to shortages of wagons and further delays. Appeals were made to the railway staff, and a number of the company's clerical staff volunteered to give up some of their evenings and Sundays to help with the goods station work. They received payment for the hours worked.

By April 1942 the work was again falling behind, and insufficient volunteers were coming forward from among the railway staff. Appeals were therefore made in the local papers for anyone prepared to work for two hours or more in the evenings between 6 p.m. and 9 p.m., and on Sundays. During a typical week at the Birmingham LMS goods depots, 141 volunteers worked on Sunday and 132 people on weekdays, giving an equivalent of 62 men working a 48-hour week. Further appeals were made in April 1943, when the rates of pay were quoted as 1s 6¼d per hour for men, and 1s 4¼d per hour for women for their first 13 weeks, then 1s 5¼d. This time the scheme was extended to New Street, with female volunteers being drafted there to assist with the parcels work. By the time that men began to reappear from the forces in 1946, the depot was staffed almost entirely by old men — many of whom were past retirement age, and had stayed on — and by women and a few young lads.

During the 1940 Blitz there was intense bombing of the city, and in August of that year an oil bomb and an incendiary fell on the roof of the main office block. As was so often the case, the water used to put the fire out probably did more damage to the interior of the offices than the fire. Consequently, the district goods manager's staff were transferred to Lawley Street, bringing to an end a continuous association with Curzon Street which had lasted for eighty years. The move to Lawley Street was short-lived. Just four weeks later, the office buildings there (which were situated at the corner of Lawley Street and Viaduct Street) were destroyed in another air raid, and the district goods manager moved to Central Goods. Some of the staff, including the centralised accounts, moved to Sutton Park station, where they remained until the end of the war. After the end of hostilities, the main buildings at Curzon Street were made habitable again, and the goods manager's centralised accounts office was moved back into them.

The top yard received a bomb hit, destroying the recently-built paper warehouse. Fortunately, the adjacent stable blocks survived with only minor damage, but a number of men risked their lives through the night calming the horses and leading them away to safety. The site was simply cleared, and some of the work continued in the open. From this time onwards, the paper was stored in the metal and grain warehouse in the main yard, and the potatoes were dealt with in the fruit shed. The remainder of the yard largely escaped direct hits, although a number of incendiaries fell on the depot and caused minor damage and small fires. At first the men dealt with the incendiaries themselves, but later the Germans started fitting delayed-action explosives in them. After this, they were firmly left alone! The carriage and wagon examiners' hut near the Overhead Lines bridge was destroyed in one raid, while on another occasion a bomb fell right through the deck of the Midland side main line bridge over Fazeley Street, and landed in the street below.

Although the bombing had its effect, the greatest cause of disruption at Curzon Street were the air raid warnings. When enemy planes were around, the yard lights had to be turned off, and this effectively brought shunting and much of the other work to a standstill. Air raid warnings came both when there were raids in Birmingham itself, and when there were raids on other places which involved the planes passing over or near Birmingham. Thus, several nights work were lost while the bombers passed over on their way, as it turned out, to Birkenhead. The delays caused by the warnings could result in the preparation of outward trains not being completed until the morning. Similarly, the inward trains could arrive at any time during the day as a result of delays in loading at their originating station (especially from London) and en-route. While there was risk of raids, all the messenger and telephone lads were taken off the night shifts and replaced by men.

The troubles at Lawley Street had started some time before the war. The main goods shed, which incorporated a two-storey warehouse above (and was said to be the second largest on the LMS), was completely destroyed in a spectacular fire on 26th May 1937. All the goods in transit inside the shed and stored in the warehouse were lost, although through some brave and speedy work by the shunters, a large number of the railway wagons in and around the shed were moved away to safety. The damage was estimated at £1 million.

Following the fire, as much as possible of the goods shed work was moved to other Birmingham depots (notably

Central, and to a lesser extent, Curzon Street). Some work could not be moved, however, and this had to continue in some temporary accommodation, or failing that, in the open. The loss of the shed came in the middle of a long-term examination by the LMS of its goods handling methods and depot facilities. No immediate decision was therefore made about the future of Lawley Street, and the staff were left to get on with the work as best they could.

As well as the destruction caused by the 1940 air raids at Curzon Street and Lawley Street, further damage occurred in the yard at Lawley Street. At Central, the goods shed and warehouse were almost entirely destroyed by bombing, and some very hasty temporary repairs and rebuilding had to be undertaken to allow the shed work to continue.

With the loss of so much of the merchandise handling facilities in Birmingham, something had to be done urgently. The LMS Board therefore authorised a comprehensive scheme to rebuild and modernise Lawley Street. The work was to consist of four main parts: a large new goods shed to deal with the merchandise (miscellaneous) traffic, a new general warehouse, a new warehouse for the storage of non-ferrous metals, and a new office block. In wartime conditions only essential works were permitted by the Government, and of the works authorised, only the goods shed fell into this category. The LMS produced evidence to justify wartime construction on the grounds of delays to essential traffic and consequent congestion on the main lines resulting from traffic waiting to be dealt with. Even so, it was 1944 before the first parts of the shed were sufficiently complete to allow partial occupation. It was officially opened on 29th October 1945.

The new shed was laid out in accordance with the latest practices of efficient operation, and was equipped with the best available electrical and mechanical aids, such as conveyors. It was capable of dealing with 11 million packages a year. The contrast between the efficiency of Lawley Street and older depots such as Curzon Street, where equipment and methods had hardly changed in 30 years, was obvious. The aim was to concentrate as much of the merchandise traffic at Lawley Street as possible, although the extent to which this occurred was limited by a number of factors: the capacity of the depots; the management structure of the railway (which still for many purposes operated the former LNW and Midland lines as separate companies, 20 years and more after the grouping); and the lack of good connections between the former LNW and Midland lines, which made it difficult to get trains from the LNW lines (particularly from the south) to Lawley Street. Gradually, however, a large proportion of the merchandise traffic was transferred to Lawley Street. Central was developed as a centre for parcels traffic (that traffic which travelled by parcels and passenger trains, rather than by goods trains). Curzon Street's role as a general merchandise depot slowly declined.

John and Edwin Wright's Ropes manufacturing works lay alongside the Midland down Gloucester line at Exchange Sidings, although the railway was at a much higher level than the works. Wright's normal practice was to send its products to Banbury Street or Lawley Street for loading into railway wagons. Wright's, however, specialised in undertaking special orders such as the supply of very long ropes, which often required special transport arrangements. An order for an exceptionally long rope demanded positive action and arrangements were hurriedly made with the Midland Railway to have a private siding constructed adjacent to the works near Exchange Sidings signal cabin. Just a few days after the siding was completed, the rope was ready to be loaded. This photograph, taken on 15th March 1922, shows loading in progress. The Midland had provided two bogie wagons (diagram 340) specially adapted with a steel and sleeper pen arrangement to carry the coiled rope. The single length of plaited strand wire rope was 36,300ft long and weighed a total of 65 tons. The rope was being drawn straight out of the works via the drum winch and then onto the wagons by means of the shear-legs and pulley. To fit all this rope on the wagons involved about 180 loops round the combined length of the two vehicles. Unfortunately, it is not recorded who wanted a rope nearly 7 miles long! The siding was retained for the occasional similar special load. Exchange Sidings signal cabin can be seen behind the wagons, as can part of the bridge carrying the LNW main line over the Midland lines from Derby to New Street. The fence separated the siding from the down Gloucester line. *National Railway Museum*

CHAPTER SIX
LIFE AND WORK AT CURZON STREET

RAILWAY work was traditionally a male preserve, and until the Great War, it was generally believed that the majority of the work could only be done by men. A few ladies did penetrate the more genteel surroundings of the district goods manager's office, but they were kept well away from the outside staff and goods yard; even in the offices, they were confined to certain areas. Originally, the practice was that the ladies left the company's employment as soon as they got married. Within the offices, they were kept under the watchful eye of a matron, part of whose job it was to keep them away from the men (and more particularly, the men away from them). Male staff were only allowed in the ladies' offices for specific purposes in connection with the company's business, and could be sure that the matron's watchful eye would be on them the whole time! Some of the ladies stayed a long time; Miss A.B. Harrison served as matron of the accounts department from 1905 until she retired on 30th September 1931.

MR. T H. SHIPLEY

MR. J. G. HUMPHREYS.

J. G. Humphreys was the Central District Goods Manager from 1898 until retirement early in 1914. T. H. Shipley became Assistant Goods Manager at Curzon Street in Humphreys' time, eventually succeeding E. Wharton as Goods Manger in 1920. He retired in 1930. C. R. J. Woodward was the Curzon Street Goods Agent from 1909 to 1925, and referred to as 'Dolly' by the staff.

MR. C. R. J. WOODWARD.

Female staff first appeared in significant numbers during the years just prior to the Great War when, much to the surprise of some of the men, it was found that they were very good at operating typewriters, something which had hitherto been a male-only preserve. The labour shortages of the Great War, with so many men away in the army, forced the railway to employ far more women, and by the end of the war they were firmly established in many areas of office work; indeed, by the mid 1930s, there were more women than men employed in the goods manager's offices. The strict separation of the sexes in their work continued until the Second World War, and it was only then that women were employed in the goods yard itself, working in the goods sheds, battery room, on the deck, and driving the electric trolleys.

For the office staff, there were always problems to be sorted out with the customer accounts, and the accounts office staff had to be forever vigilant. As an example of the problems encountered, in the late 1920s, one of the firms which sent and received a large volume of goods through Curzon Street appointed a new chief buyer. This fellow, anxious to save his firm money, hit on the notion of claiming a quantity discount (as he no doubt did with every other supplier); he therefore deducted ten percent from each bill, and refused to pay the balance. The railway was not prepared to accept the lower payment, and the staff tried everything they could think of to get the rest of the money, but letters, further bills and personal calls were all to no avail. The man was adamant — he would not pay. Finally, a very simple solution was found: the unpaid amount was added to the total of the next month's account. Sure enough, the man paid the full bill, less ten percent, and that ten percent was carried forward to the next bill, and so on. Now everyone was happy; the railway got its money, and the buyer thought he had achieved a discount. The following year, it was learnt that he had received a handsome rise in salary in recognition of the large amount of money he had 'saved' his employer!

Since a large part of the work was tedious and dull, some of the staff would occasionally seek a little light relief by playing on the trust of newly-employed lads straight from school. One such trick was for one of the clerks to tell the lad confidentially that one of the other clerks kept a water otter hidden in the offices. The tale would be backed up by others, and the lad was eventually induced to ask the gentleman concerned if he could see the animal. This would, after some persuasion, lead to a promise to be shown it 'next time'. In due course, the expectant lad was ceremonially led down into the basement storeroom where the clerk would produce a kettle and turn triumphantly to the lad, and say 'there is my water hotter!' It would then take the poor lad weeks to live the story down. Occasionally, one of the office staff would enliven his colleagues' routine (or frighten them, as the case may be) by bringing in one of the fearsome-looking spiders that had been found in among the bananas that had arrived in the top yard. This might be a live one in a glass jar, or he might leave a dead one around somewhere.

Following the Victorian business ethic, the senior staff tended to develop an aura of remoteness and superiority which made many of the staff somewhat afraid of them, a situation reinforced by the

Photographs of the rear of the goods offices (former hotel building) are quite rare. This one was taken from Curzon Street in 1965 and shows Hardwick's building on the left and the 1840 extension right, with the goods yard wall in the foreground. *T. J. Edgington*

In acknowledgement of the 100th anniversary of the first train from London to Birmingham, these two photographs of the Curzon Street District Goods Manager's Office staff were taken in September 1938. By this date the ladies of the Accounts Department (Abstracts) considerably outnumbered the men. A few years later the difference became even more acute as many men went off to the war. The small number of young men present in the men's photograph was probably a product of the long years of depression when the railways had taken on relatively few new employees. *Cty. Mrs. W. Brunton*

social distance between top and bottom. Both the goods manager and agent had their own personal horse and trap with driver (replaced at a very early date by chauffeur-driven cars). The same respect and fear was accorded to the agent's front office, and most people avoided going anywhere near it. Underneath the facade, things were not quite what they seemed. A junior clerk, sent by his chief to fetch a poster, entered the inner sanctum in trepidation and diffidently approached the first man he came to, and asked: 'I have been sent to fetch a poster about not spitting on the floors and walls'. The man looked up, turned and shouted across to a colleague on the other side of the room: 'Hey, have you got any of those posters that says you *can* spit on the ceiling?' Illusion shattered: the front office staff were human, just like everyone else.

Nicknames were a common feature. C.R.J. Woodward, the goods agent, was for some reason referred to as 'Dolly', but in respect of his rank and in fear of dismissal, only when everyone was sure he was nowhere around! One of the yard staff (of ample figure) was inevitably called 'Tubby' by all his mates. When he was made up to foreman, he decided his nickname did not go with his new elevated status, and sought an interview with Mr Woodward with a view to getting the practice stopped. Woodward listened patiently to the grievance and then said: 'Well, I'm the goods agent and they still call me Dolly, so I can't see what you have to complain about.' The tale caused a minor sensation in the offices and yard, since everyone had thought that Woodward did not know about the nickname.

Until about the time of the Second World War, the offices were gas lit (as was the whole of the yard area, and the various goods sheds). The lamps had been converted from the old open jet burners to the much brighter incandescent gas mantles about 1910 — all but one old burner on the stairs that is, which was not normally used. A prank often carried out late at night, when the last work in the offices was finished and the last few office staff were on their way out, was for someone to turn this burner on and blow hard into it. The resultant air lock instantly put every light in the place out, leaving people stranded in a pitch dark building — a trick perpetuated by generations of schoolboys with the bunsen burners in school chemistry laboratories.

A perennial problem in depots the size of Curzon Street, and especially those employing so many men, was pilfering. This was another reason for the careful control by paperwork of the packages through the various stages of their journeys. As an example, in June 1903, two of the workmen were prosecuted for pilfering chocolate — no doubt en-route from a certain establishment in Bournville.

Until the 1950s, horses were a very important part of life at Curzon Street, and they engendered mixed feelings among the men. Generally, the feelings were of affection, but this was not always so. Curzon Street's horses were a very mixed bag, varying from some of the finest show-horses to some miserable creatures that looked as if they might have escaped from the knacker's yard. Temperaments varied, too, from the best to the vicious and awkward. There were a fair number of problem horses, no doubt as a result of something that had happened to them in the past, and some of these were prone to kicking and biting; they could inflict nasty injuries if the men were not careful.

The older stable blocks in the top yard were conventional single-storey structures opening on to a stable yard, whilst some of the later blocks had stable accommodation on the upper floor. Each stable was divided into bays, which were themselves divided by wooden partitions. Each bay housed several horses which were kept loose, but separated by loose ropes and boards. In the case of difficult

CURZON STREET GOODS STATION
L& NW & LMS District Goods Managers

Frederick Pierce Broughton	1860-1863
John Mason	1864-1870
William John Nichols	1871-1897
J. G. Humphries	1898-1913
L. Speakman	1914
E. Wharton	1915-1919
Thomas Henry Shipley	1920-1930
J. B. Scattergood	1931-1940
S. Roberts	1941-1943
L. C. Brittlewell	1944-1945
W. W. Hall	1946
L. C. Brittlewell	1947-1948

Goods Agents at Curzon Street

C. R. J. Woodward	1909-1924
F. O. Moore	1925-1942
C. W. Jones	1943-1948

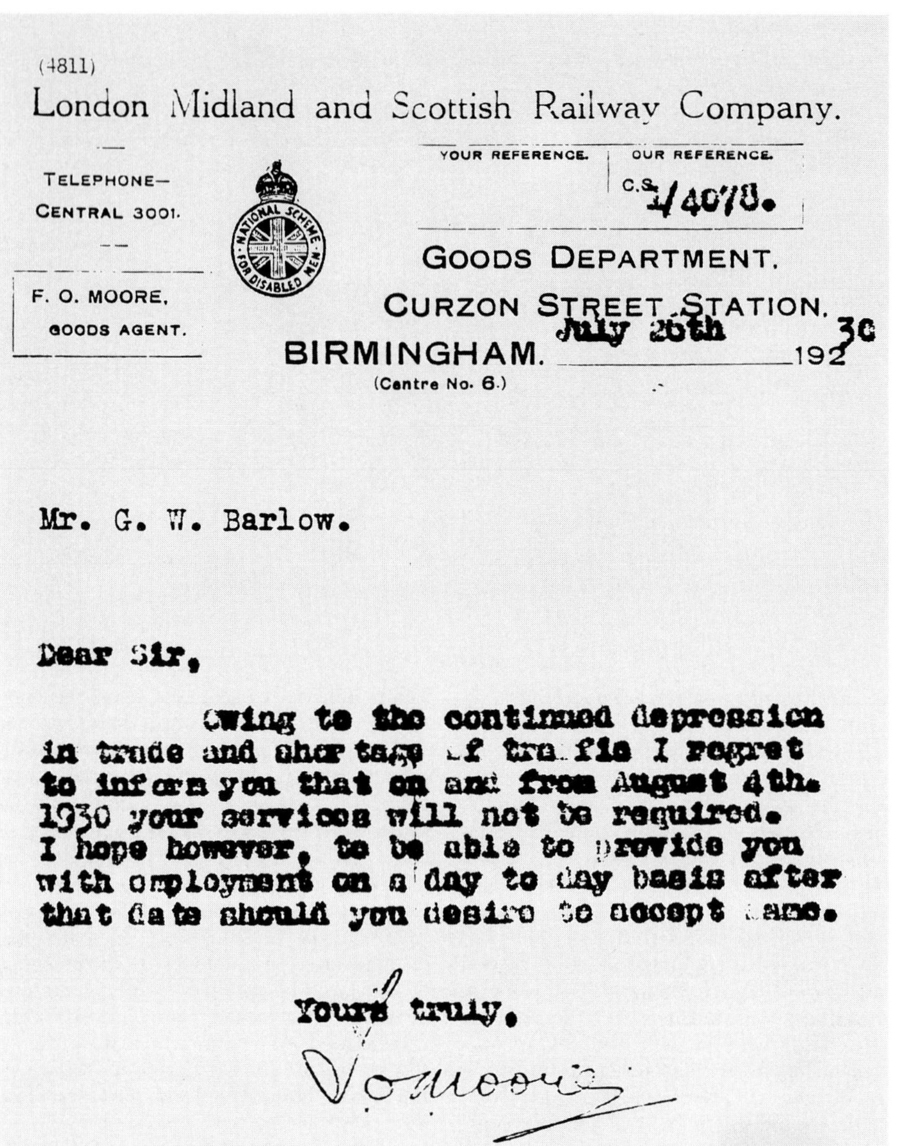

(4811)

London Midland and Scottish Railway Company.

TELEPHONE—
CENTRAL 3001.

F. O. MOORE,
GOODS AGENT.

YOUR REFERENCE. | OUR REFERENCE.
C.S. 1/4078.

GOODS DEPARTMENT.
CURZON STREET STATION.
BIRMINGHAM. July 25th 1930
(Centre No. 6.)

Mr. G. W. Barlow.

Dear Sir,

Owing to the continued depression in trade and shortage of traffic I regret to inform you that on and from August 4th. 1930 your services will not be required. I hope however, to be able to provide you with employment on a day to day basis after that date should you desire to accept same.

Yours truly,

The unfortunate fate of many of the lads employed at Curzon Street in the 1930s when they became of age and entitled to men's wages.

or sick horses, the men had to be careful about going into the bays to attend to the horse because they could easily be kicked or bitten. In the case of a particularly violent horse, one means of protection was for the man to take a length of timber with him — if need be, he could then quickly move into a corner and wedge the timber between the partitions in order to stop the horse reaching him.

The carters tended to work with the same horse so that a working relationship could be built up; those animals were usually the best and most reliable. The carter was responsible for preparing his own horse and harnessing it, and also for looking after his harness, keeping it properly waxed (to keep the leather soft) and the brasses polished. Usually, the men tried to arrive at the stables early so as to give themselves a bit more time to spend with the horse, feeding it titbits and giving it an extra grooming. In many cases, the wives and children got to know the regular horse too, and it could become almost part of family life. One carter who had a particularly close relationship with his horse would occasionally, in a slack moment, have a game of hide-and-seek with the animal in the yard — he would dodge between the pillars, the horse thoroughly enjoying the game of coming round looking for him.

When the cart was to be away from the depot for any length of time, the driver would take a bucket for some water and a nosebag of feed for the horse, to ensure that it would be adequately provided for while out on the road. In the winter, it was usually necessary for the driver to obtain lamps from the stores in order to light the cart after nightfall. These were usually oil lamps, and had to be returned to the stores for safe keeping, trimming and filling. Three lamps were required: two white lights for the front and one red to hang on the back of the cart.

On the flat, a good horse could pull up to about four tons of load plus the cart, which weighed about another ton. The load that could be pulled up hills was considerably less, and there are plenty of hills in Birmingham. In addition, there were problems in starting heavy loads; it was easy to get stuck with a heavy load if it was necessary to stop on a slight rise, either for a delivery or at a road junction. While many of the horses knew what they could manage (and would become difficult if made to take much more), it was important that the driver knew the city and the roads he would have to use — there was no point in taking a big load if this would lead to getting stuck later.

Generally, if a cart got stuck there was no alternative but to ask for assistance, and this would be provided in the form of chain horses. These were additional horses with chains or ropes that could be hooked in front of the regular horse, so that the combined effort of the two horses would get the load up the hill. The chain horse was walked out from the stables, usually by a relief driver. In the heavily-used streets around the depot where there were often problems on the hills (such as Lawley Street and the approach roads to Banbury Street goods yard) it was customary, when difficulties were expected, to station chain horses at suitable points, ready to assist any carts that needed help; in these cases the problem was quickly overcome. When he was further from the depot, the driver had to telephone for assistance and wait, and as the delay could be considerable, the men therefore did their best to avoid getting stuck.

A driver who knew his town well could overcome most problems by taking routes that avoided the steepest hills. Where a hill had to be surmounted, the driver would adopt a roundabout course (something akin to that taken by a sailing vessel heading into the wind), using the adjoining streets to 'tack' backwards and forwards across the hill so as to climb it in easy stages.

Descending hills was a problem too, and great care was required to prevent the cart from pushing the horse, as many of the vehicles were not fitted with brakes. The only form of restraint on these was the slipper brake, a curved steel shoe chained near one of the rear wheels. At the top of the hill, the wheel was run on top of the slipper, and the cart would then descend the hill with the wheel sliding over the road surface on its slipper. If necessary, the brake chain, which was also fastened near the rear wheels, could also be used to lock the wheel so that it would not turn.

In the case of particularly heavy loads, special large trolleys were sent out to do the collection or delivery, together with sufficient horses to pull the loaded vehicles. Some of the biggest loads might require as many as 18 horses to get them to the yard. An example of such loads were coils of wire rope from Latch & Bachelor in Hay Mills, and from Wrights in Garrison Street.

The driver had to take care to ensure that his horse did not slip, since this could result in it falling. The old-fashioned cobbles generally provided a better grip than tarmac because of their slight ridge and furrow texture, but the biggest problem was tram rails. A horse putting his foot on a tram rail while pulling hard, climbing hills or turning could easily slip and fall, as the steel horse shoes slid easily on the steel rails. Indeed, the driver had to choose his position on the road carefully at all times to keep clear of slippery surfaces. If a horse did fall, the driver could usually get it up again, providing it was not injured. The animal would be released from the shafts, and sacks would be placed under its feet to help it grip. It was then a question of calming the animal and coaxing it gently, taking plenty of time, until it was able to get up. Where the horse could not get up or had been injured, it was necessary to summon assistance. Normally, people were only too willing to help if a horse was involved, and a fallen or injured horse would always attract a lot of sympathy and petting from passers-by and shop girls, who would fill in the time while the assistance was on its way by feeding it little titbits. The driver was rarely offered anything!

Assistance would be sent out in the form of men and additional horses, as appropriate, or if necessary the horse ambulance and vet would be sent. Injured horses were either led back to the yard, or loaded into the ambulance and taken back that way. A fresh horse would take over the cart and complete the round.

From time to time, a horse would cast one of its shoes, usually through getting it stuck in something (such as a tram rail). It was then necessary to call for a new horse and driver to be sent out to take over the cart whilst the original horse was carefully walked back to the yard, taking care not to injure the foot, which was usually tied in a sack to protect it. Very occasionally, a driver in desperate need of some overtime money might induce his horse to lose a shoe!

A further problem encountered with horses was the runaway, usually caused by something frightening the horse, or the animal just taking it into its head to go off. Very occasionally, a horse might even decide it was time to go home, and set off back to the yard! If the driver was on the cart he had to do his best to stop the horse, and while he was doing this to guide it, as best as he could, clear of other traffic and pedestrians. If the horse had just decided to go off, the main problem was that it would continue on its unauthorised journey oblivious of road junctions and stop lines! When the driver had to leave the cart to make a delivery, the correct procedure was to detach one of the horse's tug-chains and put the brake chain around one of the back wheels. However, if the man was in a hurry, or it was only a 'quick' delivery, he would often omit to do this in order to save time. Occasionally, he would then come back to find the horse and cart gone, and it was then a question of giving chase, hoping the runaway would stop before too much damage was done. Once stopped, the driver would make sure the horse and cart were all right, and if they were, he would usually have to retrace their steps to retrieve all the packages that had been shaken off the cart during its flight. If there was damage or injury, assistance had to be summoned.

In one incident, a driver was making a delivery of frozen New Zealand lamb at the meat markets in Bradford Street one day. The driver had put the horse's nose bag on, and had detached the nearside tug-chain. A pig's carcass being transported on a pulley caught the horse's eye and frightened it, and off it went with the driver in hot pursuit. Since the one tug-chain was off, the cart pulled the horse round, but before the driver could catch up the whole ensemble crashed into a ladies toilet, smashing the cart's shafts. Fortunately, the horse was not injured, and the driver was able to walk him back to the station after ensuring the remainder of the load had been taken off the cart. Had the tug-chain not been off, the whole lot would have probably ended up inside the coffee shop on the opposite side of the road! A fresh horse and a new pair of shafts had to be sent out to fetch the cart in.

Frost, ice and snow were a problem for the horses, mainly because of the difficulty in keeping their feet. In snow, studs could be fitted to help the horse's feet grip, and about five steel studs would be hammered into each shoe (there were holes in the shoes to take these, and they were gripped by the ridges in the shoe). The studded shoes gave a good grip in the snow, but this did not cover all eventualities. In the bad winter of 1947/8, all collections and deliveries were suspended for several days during the worst of the weather, due to the bad road conditions. It took six horses to move the provender carts around the yard, let alone anything else. During that winter, many of the cartage men were redeployed on snow-clearing duties on the railway in order to help in keeping essential rail traffic on the move.

Working conditions for the men were rough, too. There were very few covered carts, and even these had open driving positions; the men therefore spent practically the whole day out in the open, and in all weathers. In the wet, the men's clothes would gradually become soaked, making them very heavy, and eventually the water would get right through. The wet did not only come from the rain: as the horse walked along, water was splashed from its hooves onto the driver, making things even more unpleasant. If the men lived locally they would try, when it was raining, to call at home during the day to change into some dry clothes. Then there was the cold. The men would do anything to keep warm, wearing as many layers of clothing as they could get on — or could afford. A common practice was to tie layers of newspaper round the legs and body beneath the clothes, to provide more insulation, whilst old sacks were often tied round the shoulders and placed across the knees to keep some of the rain off and the cold out. After the two wars, the old army boots and uniforms came in very handy! The horses did, however, have one particular advantage — many could find their way back to the depot in the thickest fog much better than the drivers could.

Horses were used within the goods yard for moving empty and loaded carts around, and to and from the loading platforms. This work was undertaken by a vansetter and was generally known as 'backing-up', since a large part of the work involved taking carts and 'backing them up' against the deck for loading or unloading, or into corners of the yard to await their next job. At least one man and horse would be on this duty all day, and as each cart was loaded up, the backer-up would hitch his horse to it, take it away, and park it at a convenient spot in the yard. He then scouted around for another empty dray, brought that up, and backed it against the deck in place of the loaded one.

In the afternoons, when the loaded carts came in, the draymen would back their carts up to the deck for unloading if there was space; if not, they would park the cart in the yard, and the backer-up would later put it up to the deck when a space became available. It was on this work that most of the cartage staff first learnt to handle horses and harness them. Some horses did not like going backwards, and were very troublesome when they had to do it. In addition, it was a hard job for the horse to push a loaded cart back against the dock. The experienced men learned many tricks to get the horses to back-up their load — generally, a difficult horse could be made to back up if a bag was put over its head so that it could not see.

One of the regular backing-up horses, Horace by name, discovered that if men walking to or from the mess-room, shops or canteen carried paper bags, it usually meant that they contained some food. Given the slightest chance, Horace would break free of his driver and be off across the yard at a gallop in an attempt to snatch a supposed tasty snack off some unsuspecting railwayman.

Curzon Street was particularly well-equipped to deal with sick animals. When sick horses could not be properly looked after at their home depot, they would be moved to Curzon Street. If the illness or injury was bad, the horse would be brought in the horse ambulance, otherwise someone was sent out to walk the horse across (for example from Monument Lane, Soho or Aston). This sometimes required care, since sick horses were prone to kicking and biting. As so many horses were kept so close together, illnesses would sometimes spread through the stables and strike down many of the horses at once (most usually the horse equivalent of the winter flu epidemic). Occasionally, this resulted in the virtual suspension of collections and deliveries by horse, and in such circumstances, some of the drivers were redeployed into the stables to help look after the animals.

New horses were generally taken 'on approval', and were tried out at Curzon Street for a while to gauge their suitability for the work. They were only paid for if they were satisfactory, otherwise they were returned to the vendor. Many of these horses required breaking-in to the cartage work before their suitability could be fully assessed, and a common way of getting the horse used to working with the carts was for one of the stable men and a driver to hitch it to an empty cart, load on an adequate supply of feed and water, and set off for a journey to Stonebridge and back. The horse's tendency to race off would be subdued by the simple expedient of leaving the cart brake on. A few journeys like this and most horses would be broken-in, and had developed the steady and reliable plod that was required for the work. Those horses that would not adapt were returned. There could be other reasons for not accepting an animal — one horse, after a perfectly normal trial run, was groomed and returned to its stable, but when the men returned for it, the creature was dead!

Once a year, on May Day, a horse parade was held in Birmingham, with specially decorated horses and carts, and in which Curzon Street took part. Prizes were awarded for the best turned-out animals, and the men whose horses were

Stableman Jones with Curzon Street bay horse 'Colonel', the 1932 Horse Show prizewinner.
LMS Magazine

Once the railways made it possible to bring large quantities of fresh fish into Birmingham, the resultant increase in the fish trade quickly swamped the somewhat rudimentary facilities available for selling it. Eventually, the Town Council was forced to admit that the lack of a proper fish market was restricting trade and leading to high prices. In 1861 it purchased a plot of land on the corner of High Street and Bell Street for the provision of a new wholesale fish market. However, such was their anxiety to improve the supply of reasonably priced fish that it was 1869 before the new fish market was opened. Needless to say, once it opened, trade increased by leaps and bounds and the space in the market was soon used up. It was to be 1884 before the much-needed extension to the fish market was opened. By the 1930s, space was short again and the fish trade had spread across Bell Street into a series of lock-ups and stalls under and around the Retail Market Hall. This photograph was taken on 29th March 1938. It shows fish from Hull being sold by auction at Griffith's stall which was sited outside the Market Hall to the right of the main steps from Worcester Street (opposite the end of Queen's Drive). Mr. Griffith is the man in the trilby hat. G. R. Griffith & Son were still to be found trading from the basement of the shell of the gutted Market Hall in the 1950s. They were then advertising themselves as Egg Merchants and Poulterers.
Collection C. C. Green

Moat Lane, busy with market traffic in 1936. The fruit and vegetable market building features on the left and traders' premises had evidently overflowed into the buildings on the right-hand side of the street. It was congestion like this in the streets around the markets, which could delay vehicles for long periods, that brought about the Curzon Street carters' anxiety to get their loads into the market at the earliest possible moment. The premises on the far right were occupied by James Barragwanath & Co. with Francis Nicholls Ltd (with the firm's own lorry outside) next door.
Birmingham Gazette, cty. C. C. Green

entered spent many extra hours in the stables giving their charges special attention and grooming as the judging day approached.

The cartage work was hard, the hours were long, and the pay was not exactly generous, either. The earliest start in the mornings was for those who worked on the fish traffic, which required booking on at the depot soon after 4 a.m. in order to get the horse ready, and have the fish at the fish market when it opened at 5 a.m. While the driver was preparing his horse, the unloading gang were busy offloading the train and packing the fish boxes onto the drays ready for the drivers to take out. As with all the cartage work, the aim was that the carts should be loaded up and parked ready for the driver to take out as soon as he arrived in the yard with his horse. As a rule, the drivers would aim to have the loaded carts waiting outside the fish market by the time the gates opened at 5 a.m.

The fish drivers were followed closely by the fruit and vegetable market drivers. These markets also opened at 5 a.m. and in both cases the market traders were keen to have their produce delivered as early as possible, as prices (and hence profits) were generally higher at the beginning of trading, and fell gradually as the day progressed — this was simply because most purchasers wanted to buy the fresh goods promptly, and get them to their own premises as soon as possible. Some traders gave the drivers small tips for good service (such as early deliveries), so there was an incentive for the driver to make his delivery as early as possible. There was another reason for the driver to be early — if he got there first, it was often possible to get straight into the market, make the delivery, and be off on the next job. A later arrival would probably get caught in a queue of vehicles, and hence lose a lot of time. As a general rule, drivers tended to deliver to the same traders each day, thus building up a relationship where each would look after the other's interests.

Occasionally — though it was quite a rare event — the fish (or one of the other trains) would be late arriving, with the result that the carts would not be ready for the drivers to take out. If there was nothing else to do, the drivers would adjourn to the messroom, or go across the road to one of the coffee shops which were to be found in the streets around the depot, to wait in the warm and dry until their loads were ready.

The general delivery drivers started work at about 7 a.m., by which time the unloading of the inward merchandise traffic would be well advanced, and the first batches of carts would have already been loaded. The round could begin as soon as the cart was ready (with its delivery sheet), the horse had been hitched, and the factories and shops to be served were open. Each round consisted of a set area,

The railway companies maintained offices wherever there was sufficient prospect of traffic. These performed two functions: first to give a convenient point of contact with customers where problems and complaints could be quickly sorted out, thus ensuring that the customer felt he was getting a personal service, and second as a base from which to canvas for traffic. This photograph shows the LMS office in Birmingham's Smithfield wholesale fruit and vegetable market on 13th September 1927. The office was situated at one end of the balcony which ran along the side of the 'new' portion of the building. This had a lower roof than the old section which was to the right (the stairs up to the balcony can be seen between the columns). On the extreme right, part of one of the ornate iron main entrance gates is visible. The papers hung outside the LMS office no doubt contained details of LMS excursions and other LMS services. The tall narrow barrel-shaped cases or half barrels on Henry Simkin's stall below probably contained green Spanish Almeria grapes. The bunches of grapes were packed in cork dust to prevent damage in transit. The tall circular wicker baskets appear to have contained cabbages or cauliflowers and the shorter ones apples. At this time the majority of the goods came packed in straw.
National Railway Museum

The interior of the Smithfield market c.1938, with produce stacked everywhere and the roadways jammed with a mixture of lorries (mostly belonging to traders) and horse-drawn drays. This picture again illustrates very clearly why the Curzon Street carters were so keen to get their loads to the market as quickly as possible. As well as the problems in the streets outside, once the place became busy, a cart could be stuck inside the market for long periods waiting for room to get to their unloading point, or, once unloaded, an opportunity to get out again. The picture makes an interesting comparison with that on page 95 of Volume 2 which shows how the market looked nearly 30 years earlier. *Collection C. C. Green*

and the rounds were all numbered for reference. A typical round might involve about 15 to 20 drops, depending on the size of each delivery. Few people would accept deliveries unless the driver took the goods to the warehouse, store or stockroom, and stacked them there; the driver had therefore to be fit and strong, since sugar and flour (for instance) came in 2 cwt sacks, and he was expected to lift and carry them single-handed. Even if a sack truck could be used, the bags still had to be manhandled on and off. And some places had stairs — bakeries in particular tended to store the flour in upstairs store rooms, which had the advantage of being warm and dry because of the ovens beneath.

Again, it was common for regular customers to pay small tips to drivers in cash or kind (a penny or two, or perhaps a penny packet of tea), in order to ensure that they would get good service. Very occasionally, relations with shopkeepers were not all they might be, though the delivery men could 'get their own back' if they felt hard done by. Heavy footsteps or a slight change of direction as they carried the heavy sacks across the shop floor could ensure that the shop's carefully-arranged, stacked displays of tins or packets would come crashing to the floor, while the man was able to claim innocence or the need to avoid a customer.

Few shop staff were strong enough to lift the two-hundredweight flour and sugar sacks, so the shops relied very much on the men putting them in the right place (usually standing on one end). The top of the sacks had a cotton strand seal which could easily be pulled out to open the sack. The shop staff then weighed the contents into small quantities, as required, and packed this into blue paper bags for sale in the shop. When it was empty, the shop was left with a good, intact sack which could be sold or used for another purpose. If there had been a disagreement with the shopkeeper, the carter might 'accidentally' leave the sacks upside down, which usually meant that the shop staff had to cut the bag at the bottom, causing inconvenience and ruining the bag.

In any group of men, there are always a few who have a more gentlemanly demeanour than the norm. These 'gentlemen' drivers usually seemed to gravitate onto the rounds that covered the more classy areas, such as Edgbaston and Harborne. Somehow, these men usually ended up with the smartest and most freshly-painted carts, and the best-looking horses!

One problem with cartage work was that any persistent smells from the loads would get into the clothes of the driver and stay with him. The powerful and persistent odour of fish is well-known, and it was not hard to recognise the men who regularly worked with that traffic. However, there was another regular traffic at Curzon Street which was, if anything, worse than the fish. By 1870, the Birmingham & Midland Counties Butchers' Hide, Skin, Fat & Wool Company had established premises at the far end of New Canal Street. The company dealt primarily with the non-edible parts of the animals slaughtered for meat in the nearby slaughterhouses. Whilst meat went to the meat market, the hide and skins were prepared at the hide and skin company's premises, and many were subsequently dispatched by rail to tanneries and other users all over the country. There was thus a regular collection to be made by the carters to bring the hides into the goods depot. The men who did the work were well advised to wear only their oldest clothes when undertaking this job, and there were usually no volunteers to carry out the task unless overtime was being offered! An added unpleasantness was that some of the skins could be crawling in maggots, especially during the summer months. The hide company changed its name in the 1880s to the much simpler Butchers' Hide, Skin, Fat and Wool Co. Ltd., and continued to send regular consignments of hides by rail until the early 1960s.

Inside the main yard entrance to Curzon Street from New Canal Street, on the right, was a range of small buildings. These housed the chief foreman's office, the pay office, time office, carmen's office, toilets, and finally, inside the end of the fish landing (the old excursion station), was the yard and cartage men's messroom. Here, the men could rest between duties, brew the inevitable railway tea, dry their clothes (there was a drying room in later years at the end of the messroom) and eat their meals. Most men brought their food from home, wrapped in newspaper. For some, even the tea started in newspaper — a mix of tea, sugar and three spoonfuls of condensed milk was wrapped in it. Once the water was boiling, the mix was scraped out of the paper and into the cup, and was said to always produce a good cup of tea.

For many years there was a general store opposite the yard gates. It sold practically everything in the food line, including penny packets of tea, pickles, single slices of corned beef, and so on. Many of the men would pop over there during their lunch break to buy some additional bits and pieces to supplement their meal. The shop was run by Italians, and in the 1930s the area around Curzon Street had a high population of them, being effectively the Italian quarter of the city. It was quite a common sight in the early morning during the summer to see the men preparing Italian ice cream carts in the streets prior to setting off into the city for a day's trading (see page 99, Volume 2). Throughout the rest of the year there were barrel organs, some complete with monkeys, being tuned-up ready for a day's stint in the city.

Back in the messroom, card games were inevitably a common feature during meal- breaks. Sometimes, the last rounds were only completed after a surreptitious dash across the yard and back to clock in for the rest of the shift! Few of the men used the clerks' canteen under the main building — apart from the general tendency of the clerical and manual staff not to mix, the usual reason given by the drivers for not using it was that they could not afford the prices. As with most such general messrooms, the atmosphere could get quite thick inside, with the majority of the men smoking, kettles boiling, and others cooking things on the stoves. On wet days the situation could be much worse, with the smells coming off the wet clothes; this was particularly so if some of the men from the fish or hide rounds were in!

Not all the difficulties of the messroom were unavoidable. From time to time someone would play a prank, either just for fun, or because they disliked (or were feuding with) someone in the room. One trick was to quietly deposit a handful of sprouts on the top of one of the hot stoves, standing there to shield them from view until they were burning nicely. The perpetrator would then make a hasty retreat, leaving behind a growing and pungent smell of burning sprouts, often leading to a wholesale evacuation of the premises! A more subtle trick was to bank up the stoves with coke as far as possible with the dampers open. Gradually, the fire would build up until the stoves were glowing red hot. If done properly, the heat inside the messroom eventually became unbearable, again forcing the occupants out. Where the stove could not be reached (such as those in the weighbridge and gate offices), the same effect could be achieved by climbing onto the roof with a bucket of coke and pouring it down the chimney. Usually the occupants would not realise anything was amiss until it was too late, and the stove and stove pipe were glowing!

Friday was payday for the yard staff, and because of the large number of men employed in the yard, a means had to be found of ensuring that people did not claim someone else's wages. The system adopted — pay tokens (see page 85, Volume 2) — was common throughout Victorian industry, and was used at practically all of the engine sheds, large stations, yards and works on the railway. This arrangement continued, almost unchanged, until the early 1960s. At the appropriate hour, the man went to his time office, where he was handed (and signed for) a metal disc called a pay token (the time office clerks would recognise the majority of their men). The man then took the token to the pay office (where the inevitable queue formed as paying-out time approached) and handed it to the clerk, receiving in exchange his pay tin (pay packet in later years) containing the week's wages. The tokens acted as a receipt, and were returned to the racks as a record of who had been paid. Afterwards, they were kept in a safe until required the following week.

Hidden away in a corner of the top yard was the sticking shed; there, big cast-iron pots of fish or animal glue constantly simmered away on the stove. A rather greasy-looking man spent his time in the pungent atmosphere, gluing the used invoices and consignment notes into large tarpaulin-backed books, which were then stored away for future reference. This man's appearance was said to reflect his job very closely! The use of old pieces of tarpaulin as covers for the invoice books was approved by the LNW Goods Conference in June 1910 as a means of reducing the cost of storing the documents.

For a lad leaving school at the age of 14, and wishing to start a career on the railway, one approach was to go to Curzon Street as an apprentice clerk in the offices, or as a messenger boy, telephone attendant or caller-up in the yard. More lads commenced work in the despatch and cartage offices, whilst others found employment as van boys with the parcels delivery carmen, or as mates to the carters.

A lad working in the despatch office spent some of his time taking invoices around the coal merchants' offices in the city, or informing them that their coal wagons had arrived in Curzon Street wharf. A deck runner attached to the cartage office was responsible for collecting bundles of invoices from the checkers as they loaded each delivery cart. These were taken to the despatch office in the main building where a duplicated delivery sheet was made out, detailing delivery instructions and listing the instances where the drivers were required to collect cash on delivery. Those sheets were taken to the cartage office, where the foreman made up the final delivery notes ready for the carters.

A couple of lads were attached to the shipping office (above the main goods shed deck) as messenger boys. At the peak of loading the outward traffic, two messenger boys would be fully occupied; taking half the shed each, they would collect the completed consignment notes from the checkers, and take them up to the shipping office. Some checkers released their notes straight away, while others liked to keep theirs until they had completed a whole batch, which of course delayed the clerks in starting their work. In between these busy periods, they would help the clerks or run errands.

As departure time for the trains approached, one of the lads took on the role of tacker-on, and went round the yard putting the invoices on the wagons. The job was not always straightforward, as for much of the year, a lot of this work had to be carried out in darkness; at night, the lad therefore had to carry a hand lamp in addition to hammer and tacks, and one or more satchels full of envelopes — quite a lot to have to lug about. The lamp was needed to see the wagon numbers — the gas lamps in the yard were not very powerful at the best of times, and certainly did not provide sufficient light to do the work. Added to this, the paintwork on some wagons was so bad that the markings could not be read at all, and the number had to be found from the wagon plate on the sole-bar.

The tacker-on then had the job of finding the wagons — which could be anywhere — and putting the appropriate envelopes on them. This could be a time-consuming task, and often dangerous, with shunting going on all round. Where a whole train was going to one destination, the canvas bags of invoices were generally placed on the brake van for the guard to look after and deliver on arrival.

Sometimes, the trains would begin to pull out before the job was finished, and it was then a question of trying to get as many envelopes or bags as possible on to the vehicles as they passed. In the case of sheeted or open wagons the package could be thrown on top, in the hope it would stay there and be found at the other end. For the rest, the lad had to try to throw them onto the verandah of the brake van as it passed, and hope the guard would find them. Needless to say, some fell off and were lost, or chewed up by the train wheels, whilst other packets would occasionally end up on the wrong wagon because the numbers were so difficult to read in the poor light.

At the end of the work there would inevitably be a number of invoices left over, either because the wagon could not be found, or because the invoices had not been ready in time. Towards the end of the shift, at about 2 a.m., two of the messengers would walk up to New Street station with the remaining invoices, and hand them in for forwarding by the first available passenger trains.

The yard master's office was in the small brick building adjacent to Curzon Street No. 1 signal cabin, and accommodated a chief clerk and a time office for the yard staff and guards. Yet more lads were based here, serving as telephone attendants, messengers and assistants to the clerks. Curzon Street was the signing-on point for a large number of guards, and one of the lads' functions was to act as 'caller-up' for those men; any guard who lived within a certain distance of the depot was entitled, if he was required to book on for work between about 1 a.m. and 6 a.m. to be called up. A guard wanting such a call would enter his name, address and 'knock-up' time in a book during the previous day. One of the clerks would then work out a schedule for the lad, allowing time for him to get from one address to another. Not everyone who asked for a call got one if their home was a long way away, or the address did not fit in with other calls required about the same time. For this work, the lad was given a bicycle with carbide lamps. It was not always a pleasant job as many of the guards lived in rather disreputable districts, and the lads never knew what or who they would find; one night, a lad had his bike commandeered by a policeman who was trying to chase a burglar. As the years went by, there was an increasing trend for people to live further away from work; eventually, 'callers-up' were dispensed with at Curzon Street as it was found that the majority of the guards lived too far from the depot.

The lads in the yard master's office also dealt with the yard men's and guards' time-sheets. When the guards came into the office to book off, a lad telephoned the guards' controller at New Street to ascertain if there was any more work for them, and the time they were required to come on duty the following day. They also kept the guards' rosters up to date. During the war, these duties were taken over by class 4 clerks, one on each shift.

The main duty of the van boys who worked with the parcels carmen and carters was to help them with delivery and collection work, hence speeding up deliveries and enabling more work to be done during the shift. Where necessary, they would also look after the load while the driver was away making deliveries, in order to prevent thefts.

As the lads gained experience, many would try to obtain promotion and move on to other permanent jobs on the railway, and a considerable number were successful. However, during the 1930s, many were not so lucky, as employment was hard to find and the railway took on very few staff — it had great difficulty in finding work for the men it already had. Thus, when the lads reached the age of 20 and became entitled to men's (instead of lads') wages, the majority were dismissed, and their places taken by younger lads. Those that still wanted to stay, or could find nothing else, were given the option of casual work; this involved reporting to the yard foreman early each morning to see if there was any work that day. Some of those who persisted might eventually have been lucky enough to be taken on permanently, but the rest would have had to look for work elsewhere.

In addition to its own rostered freight duties, the Curzon Street guards' depot acted as a relief to New Street. Curzon Street men could therefore be called upon to relieve regular guards at New Street on passenger and parcels trains, and would frequently work special passenger services. All these duties were arranged through the guards' controller at New Street.

Because of the limited space available around the wagons when they were in the shed, and to save time, it was customary to remove any wagon sheets and open the wagon doors before they were placed in the shed. In the reverse direction, the doors would usually be closed and secured, and sheets put on those wagons that needed them, after the vehicles had been taken out of the shed. This practice required men to work in the sidings among the shunting, and occasionally accidents occurred. In the late evening of 5th July 1900, a loader and two goods porters were engaged in sheeting-up four wagons forming part of a group of ten standing in No. 13 siding; these were to form part of the 11.4 p.m. express goods from Curzon Street to Camden. At 10.50, with the sheets in place (though not secured), the three men commenced tying the strings. Ten minutes later, before the work could be completed, the process of making the train up ready for departure began. The ten wagons were drawn out of No. 13 siding and set back onto some more vehicles in No. 15 siding. One of the porters, Henry Lacy (aged 21), informed the loader that he had not finished tying the strings, and was told to go back and finish the job. To do this he had to get between the wagons, and whilst in that position, at 11.4 p.m., the train started. Lacy was able to cling onto the side of a wagon with his hands, though his feet were hanging just above ground level. He hung on like this for about half-a-mile until his feet caught on something, causing him to lose his hold and fall to the ground somewhere near Exchange Sidings signal cabin. Fortunately, he fell clear of the rails, and remarkably sustained only cuts and some injuries to his right arm.

The original cause of the accident lay in the rush to get the train made up, resulting in the wagons being moved before they were ready. This was compounded by Lacy's lack of experience, and by the loader, who was in charge of the work, failing to ensure his safety. Just how easy it was to make a mistake in these circumstances is illustrated by the statement of the shunter in this case. He said that he had walked down the side of the wagons in No. 13 road to check them before moving them to No. 15 road. There, he had walked along the train before signalling to the guard that it was complete and ready to leave. On neither occasion did he see any of the men who were working on the sheets.

The practice of preparing wagons in the yard was the cause of an injury to the fingers of a hooker-on in March 1922. The man, Joseph Trueman, was riding on a turntable with a wagon destined for the goods shed so that he would be ready to drop the stop key into its slot at the moment the turntable came into line with it. At the same moment, the wagon shifted forward on the turntable and the door, which had been dropped open ready for the load to be dealt with in the shed, caught and crushed his fingers against the stop key. The wagon was supposed to have been scotched with a rope, but due to the wet weather, this had slipped.

Curzon Street had its social side, too. There was a social club, which included a number of sporting activities in its programme, and a dining club. For some years prior to the Great War there was an active rifle club, and the company provided them with space for a rifle range, for practice. Miss E. Follows (of the district goods manager's staff) became a crack shot, and in 1927 won the *Daily Mirror* Ladies Championship Silver Cup and medal with a score of 198 out of 200, at the National Rifle Championships at Bisley. Curzon Street also boasted an excellent male voice choir. Under its conductor, Dr. Alfred J. Silver, it won the LNW male voice choir trophy in 1911 and 1912, and after the Great War won it on four more occasions under the conductorship of Ernest Maw, from the accounts department.

Around the turn of the century, there was a general movement throughout the railway industry towards the formation of benevolent and hospital funds, to help those who were off work through illness, or needing hospital treatment. Those staff who became members paid a small weekly contribution (a penny a week was common in the 1920s), and the money accumulated was used to provide assistance to members while in hospital or off sick. Curzon Street had a number of these funds: there was a Clerical Benevolent Society, a Hospital Fund, a Goods and Cartage Hospital Fund, and a Cartage Benevolent Fund. The Clerical Benevolent Society had been formed in 1903, and by 1924 had raised over £2,000, with some £1,500 paid out in financial assistance to members, and almost £500 in contributions to local hospitals. In 1925, the LMS Hospital Fund was created for the salaried staff. This fund was assisted financially by the company, and so offered better prospects than the Curzon Street Clerks Fund, which was wound up in 1927. The funds for the wages staff continued.

The early summer months were punctuated by a series of annual outings for different sections of the depot staff. There were, for example, separate outings for the agent's clerical staff, the goods manager's staff, the staff office, the accounts staff, and various groups from the goods yard. It was generally accepted that either the goods manager or the goods agent would accompany each outing, so the two men had a busy time during the season. There was little respite for those gentlemen in the winter, as one or the other had to attend the dinners and annual meetings of all the station's clubs, funds and other organisations. Not only that, but the district goods manager usually found he became honorary president of most of them!

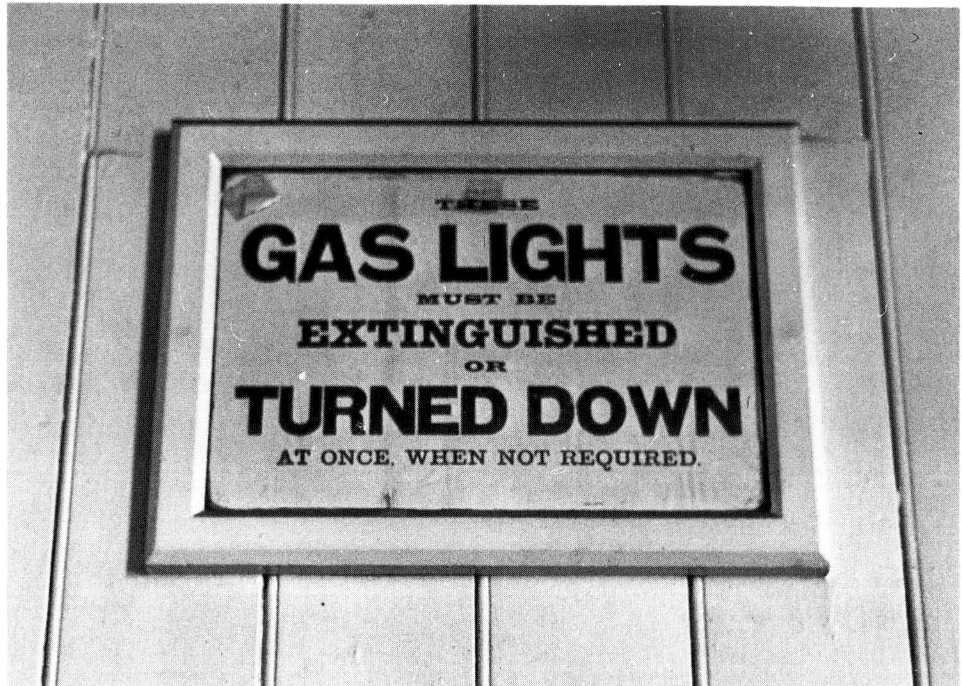

Great efforts were made by the railway companies to instill in their staff the need for the strictest economy in all aspects of the work. This included saving fuel wherever possible. Notices like this appeared all over places like Curzon Street. This one was on one of the office walls and remained in place until closure. Some of the gas light notices were even to be found still intact in areas that had been converted to electric lighting long ago! *B. Matthews*

SUPPLEMENTARY INFORMATION TO VOLUMES 1 & 2

Since these volumes were published, some snippets of additional information have come to light which amplify the original text, and I would also like to point out a few errors.

VOLUME 1

Map inside front cover: Add to key, E = Lawley Street. The Bordesley Junction shown is, of course, the canal junction, and the full name of the Saltley Canal is the 'Birmingham & Warwick Junction Canal'.

Page 13: First line of photo caption, delete 'on the previous page' and insert 'on page 10'.

Page 15: Line 7 to lower photo caption, for 'right' read 'left'.

Page 28: Upper picture. F. W. Radcliff and Co's Anchor Ironworks opened in 1894, making rolled wrought iron, and later dealing with the re-rolling of steel. It never dealt with brass or copper. Ratcliffs (Great Bridge) Ltd. was a separate firm and this did make brass and copper strip. The works there closed in 1990.

Page 29: The works is Prince's Electric Generating Station, Nechells, Birmingham, and the boats were on the Birmingham & Warwick Junction Canal. This works was replaced by the new Nechells Power Station, constructed on an adjacent site. This in turn closed a few years ago and the majority of the site has now been cleared for redevelopment.

Page 34: The location is Ashwood Basin, Kingswinford, on the Staffordshire and Worcestershire Canal, an interchange point between the Pensnett Railway and the canal. The majority of the traffic here was coal from the Pensnett Railway. This was discharged from wagons on the high-level tracks into the boats. Some traffic, mainly supplies for the collieries and ironworks served by the railway, travelled in the opposite direction and there were low-level tracks alongside the basin for loading it into railway wagons.

Page 39: Third column, line 43. 'J. J. Braham' should read 'J. J. Bramah'.

Page 53: Caption to engraving, line 9, for 'right' read 'left'.

Page 71: The Grammar School moved to temporary premises in Bristol Road, Edgbaston in January 1936 and demolition of the New Street building began shortly afterwards.

Page 76: Caption to photo, first column, line 11, for 'Livelock' read 'Livock'.

Page 80/81: The locomotive tender on the right was a Midland Kirtley design.

VOLUME 2

Map inside front cover: Add to key, E = Lawley Street.

Page 4: Second column, line 5, for '100 years' read '10 years'.

Page 7: Drawing of Vauxhall Viaduct, caption note should read '. . . for New Street to pass clear on lines into Curzon Street'.

Page 8: The date of installation of J & W Wright's Rope Works siding should read 'March 1922'.

Page 9: Second column, line 28, for 'Duddeston' read 'Duddeston Road'.

Page 12/13: The area of the Inkleys and Green's Court is just off the top centre of the 1864 plan as printed.

Page 14: Caption, line 6, for 'room' read 'floor'.

Page 26: First line of lower caption, for 'flat truck' read 'open carriage truck'.

Page 29: Second column. There were no regular Manchester and Liverpool to the west trains until 1st October 1910, when a Manchester to Bournemouth service was introduced (see also page 48).

Page 31: Caption to photo. The picture was taken from the top of the steps down from the booking office/concourse area.

Page 39: Lower picture. 'Right hand' refers to the lamp as seen in the photograph. Strictly speaking, left and right for lamps apply to the driver's left and right, facing in the direction of travel. In later years at least, station pilots normally showed four lamps, one on each corner, front and back.

Page 48: Delete the caption and insert: LNW 'Claughton' class 4–6–0 No. 2204 *Sir Herbert Walker KCB* at the south end of Platform 4 with the daily Manchester to Bournemouth train at midday on 2nd January 1922. This train, composed of Midland stock, was one of the very few to cross over from the LNW to Midland sides in New Street. It normally used Platform 4 and crossed over to the Midland side at the north end of the station. In later years the train became known as the 'Pines Express'.

Page 49: The train headed by No. 514 was possibly not for Harborne as Harborne line trains were usually worked by tank engines. The 'Precursor' on the right was a 4–4–0.

Page 51: The boy on the right was Cyril Baker.

Pages 52/53: The Midland train was composed of a mixture of Clayton and Bain designs of carriages and the variations of roof profile were typical of many Midland trains at this period. The second vehicle from the engine was a covered carriage truck with its own distinctive roof profile.

Page 54: Top picture. The term '2P' was an LMS designation and was not introduced until late 1927.

Page 54: Bottom picture. For '2–4–0' read '4–4–0'.

Page 55: Line 32. In later years ticket collection was always done at Stechford.

Page 61: Line 29. For 'J. W. Livelock' read 'J. W. Livock'.

Page 98: Top picture, 6th line of caption. For 'The fronts of Nos. 4 to 5' read 'The fronts of Nos. 4 to 8'.

Page 99: On the right of the picture is one of Birmingham's first pillar boxes. Three of these 'fluted giant' boxes (with vertical letter slit) were made by Smith and Hawkes of Broad Street in 1856. Two were erected in Birmingham (the other was believed to have been at New Street station, the first pillar letter-box location in Birmingham) while the third was sent to London. With an overall height of 8ft, these boxes dominated their surroundings. Needless to say, they were so expensive that no more were made. The New Street example was probably removed during the 1880s rebuilding and the one illustrated here disappeared about 1900.

Page 101: Add credit to invoices, 'R. Shill Collection'.

Page 108: Insert train times in 1913 column.

Trains from Curzon Street:

8.30
–
11.15
10.35
–
1.00
8.50
11.55
9.25
9.05

Trains to Curzon Street:

8.50
–
9.30
12.30
2.00
8.15
11.35
–